Reconstructing the Past

Parsimony, Evolution, and Inference

Elliott Sober

A Bradford Book
The MIT Press
Cambridge, Massachusetts
London, England

This book was set in Palatino by Asco Trade Typesetting Ltd, Hong Kong, and printed and bound in the United States of America

Library of Congress Cataloging-in-Publication Data

Sober, Elliott.
  Reconstructing the past.

  "A Bradford book."
  Bibliography: p.
  Includes index.
  1. Evolution—Philosophy. 2. Biology—Philosophy. I. Title.
QH371.S63   1988   574/0.1   88-9324

ISBN 978-0-262-19273-6 (hc.:alk. paper) ISBN 978-0-262-69144-4 (pb.:alk. paper)

for Norma

Contents

Preface

... concepts which have proved useful for ordering things easily assume so great an authority over us, that we forget their terrestrial origin and accept them as unalterable facts. They then become labeled as "conceptual necessities," "a priori situations," etc. The road of scientific progress is frequently blocked for long periods by such errors. It is therefore not just an idle game to exercise our ability to analyse familiar concepts, and to demonstrate the conditions on which their justification and usefulness depend, and the way in which these developed, little by little, from the data of experience. In this way they are deprived of their excessive authority.
Albert Einstein

The philosophy of biology, as the name suggests, lies at the intersection of two sets of concerns. It is there that issues specific to biological inquiry make contact with broader questions in the philosophy of science. Much of biology, and much of philosophy as well, takes place outside of this intersection. When unencumbered by conceptual confusion and methodological difficulty, biology can take the form of a Kuhnian "normal science," in which well-understood techniques are brought to bear on well-defined problems. When cast at a very general level, questions in philosophy can be addressed without the need to focus on any particular scientific theory or problem. The separate sciences may afford examples of explanation or confirmation, for instance, but the examples are often thought to exhibit general patterns that are not subject matter specific.

Until recently, this separation of Kuhnian normal science from perfectly general philosophical inquiry has been taken to describe most of what goes on in both science and its philosophy. But it has become increasingly evident that this picture is seriously incomplete. In addition to normal science, there is science at the frontiers, where techniques are developed but not immediately understood and where problems are new enough that their proper formulation is more a goal than a given. In addition to traditional philosophical problems focusing on science in general, there are the philosophical questions that grow out of the specifics of particular scientific theories and problems. This sort of philosophical question is of longest standing in the philosophy of physics; more recently, it has made itself felt in philosophy of psychology and philosophy of biology.

This book is located at the intersection of evolutionary theory and the philosophy of science. It concerns a biological problem that has occasioned a great deal of conceptual and methodological discussion within evolutionary theory itself. At the same time, it involves a set of philosophical problems about confirmation and theory evaluation that, having traditionally been approached at a level of great generality, would benefit from making contact with the details of specific scientific controversies. The problem of phylogenetic inference brings biological and philosophical questions together, so that it is sometimes difficult to say whether a given issue is of one sort rather than the other.

Evolutionists have vigorously debated the proper methods that should be used in reconstructing how species are related to each other. If the organisms we now observe are a consequence of descent with modification, then the resulting tree of life will be such that some species are closely related while others are related more distantly. We do not observe this branching process directly; it is not by direct inspection that we know that human beings and chimps are more closely related to each other than either is to snakes. Rather, evolutionists seek to recover the relationships engendered by this branching process by examining its end product. We observe species and their characteristics; we begin with these similarities and differences and hope to use them as evidence supporting some hypotheses of relationship and disconfirming others.

During the last twenty years or so, biologists have developed several different methods for inferring relatedness from facts of similarity and difference. These methods often disagree with each other. As a result, biologists hoping to address problems of phylogeny have been forced to address the prior issue of methodology.

Questions of method are often raised in science, and often they are routinely dispatched. But this has not happened in the present case. For some twenty years the debate has continued, with no resulting consensus. Why has this methodological problem proved so recalcitrant? One central reason is that it recapitulates a very difficult problem that has for some time bedeviled philosophical thinking about theory choice in science. One of the methods of phylogenetic inference that has been widely employed is called *parsimony*. As will be explained in chapter 1, this method holds that a set of observations best supports that phylogenetic hypothesis that requires the fewest parallelisms and convergences. The question naturally arises as to what the use of this method assumes about the evolutionary process; does preferring parsimonious hypotheses presuppose that evolution proceeds parsimoniously?

In this way, a contemporary biological problem has made contact with a long-standing issue in the philosophy of science. Philosophers have often asserted that simplicity is one of the criteria that scientists use in evaluating competing explanations. But how could this policy be legitimate, unless science is likewise entitled to assume that nature is simple?

The reader will already see one central agenda of this book. We shall have a detailed look at the biological debate, with an eye to connecting it with philosophical discussions of parsimony and simplicity. Chapter 1 sets the biological problem; chapter 2 describes the way philosophers have typically discussed the general methodological issue.

We shall see that a proper understanding of parsimony cannot isolate that concept from broader questions of hypothesis testing and theory evaluation. Parsimony may be a virtue; but to understand why it is, we must see its connection with other methodological constraints. It is an unsatisfactory mixture of hand waving and numerology to insist without argument that less is better than more. Ockham may have been right, but we need to see just how and why.

In chapter 2, I trace the provenance of our current philosophical understanding of the idea of simplicity. This will involve a detailed look at Hume's ideas about induction. Hume's claim that induction presupposes that nature is uniform is an ancestor of the modern idea that scientific inference relies on a simplicity criterion. I shall argue that an appreciation of what is right and wrong in Hume's skepticism about induction helps bring into focus the status of parsimony and simplicity as methodological criteria.

This approach is broadened and deepened in chapter 3, where I switch from inductive inference to the problem of inferring causes from observing their effects. If two events are correlated, this may be due to their sharing a common cause, or the correlation may be a coincidence, if the two events are the result of quite separate causes. Hans Reichenbach defended and Wesley Salmon elaborated a principle governing such inference problems. The principle of the common cause, as they called it, operationalizes a very Ockhamite idea: postulating a single (common) cause is often more plausible than postulatng two (separate) causes. In this third chapter, I develop two rationales for this principle. We shall see that each rationale provides assumptions that suffice to justify the principle, but, perhaps what is more important, we shall see that the principle cannot claim a universal validity.

So the results of chapters 2 and 3 are meant to induce a healthy skepticism about some familiar global methodological pronouncements. Are explanations that postulate fewer entities or processes to be preferred over ones that postulate more? Not always. Are common cause explanations always preferable to ones that invoke separate causes? Again, not always. Besides encouraging this sort of circumspection, these two chapters are meant to begin the task of developing tools that will allow us to say when a given inference principle makes sense and when it does not.

In chapters 4 and 5, we shift back to the details of the biological controversy. Biologists subscribing to the approach now called cladism have devoted considerable effort to disarming criticisms of parsimony and providing that notion with a powerful justification. In chapter 4, I explore the strengths and limitations of the nonstatistical arguments they have constructed. In chapter 5, I take up the statistical arguments that have been developed both for and against cladistic parsimony.

The verdicts in these two chapters are largely negative. Attempts to justify parsimony have not been successful, but neither have attempts to show that it is fatally flawed. The methodological problem of phylogenetic inference is still a very open one, although some progress has been made.

Chapter 4 largely concerns the effort by cladists to use Karl Popper's ideas on falsifiability and simplicity. My approach in this chapter is not to criticize Popper; nor is it to argue that cladists have misunderstood him. Rather, I shall argue that hypothetico-deductivism—the idea that hypotheses are tested by deducing observational predictions from them (in conjunction with auxiliary assumptions)—is not the logical form taken by the problem of phylogenetic inference. The chapter concludes with some untrendy, but hopefully sober, words on the theory/observation distinction.

Chapter 5, as I said, wades into the details of the statistical arguments. But there is material of broader philosophical interest to be found here as well. For example, I address the question of whether a reasonable method of inference must converge on the truth in the limit. Besides bearing on the phylogenetic inference problem, this issue also pertains to reliability theories of justification and to epistemological problems posed by Descartes' evil demon. At the same time, this chapter explores the problem of nuisance parameters in likelihood inference, carrying further an important theme first introduced in chapter 3.

The net result to this point is a general framework for thinking about the use of parsimony arguments in science and a detailed critique of discussions of parsimony (both for and against it) in the biological literature. In the last chapter, I attempt something more positive on the biological problem. By exploring a simple model of an evolutionary branching process, I try to contribute to an understanding of the circumstances in which parsimony makes sense as a tool of phylogenetic inference.

I am only too aware that the audience for this book is quite heterogeneous. This book brings together biology, philosophy, and some statistical ideas. A reader from any one of these disciplines will probably not be conversant with the ideas drawn from the other two. I have tried to build almost all the ideas I need from the ground up (one of the few exceptions is the assumption of a few simple facts about probability). I therefore must ask your indulgence when you come upon an idea that is right up your alley, and your patient attention when an idea is new.

Given the way academic disciplines have become compartmentalized, it is inconvenient that philosophers must look to biology and statistics to tell them something about methodological ideas they have long thought of as their special subject matter. It is likewise inconvenient that biological systematists should find themselves facing a recalcitrant methodological problem that requires foundational ideas from philosophy and statistics for its elucidation. But academic divisions are, to some significant degree, accidents of history; there is no guarantee that the problems that actually arise in inquiry can always be resolved by methods internal to a single approach. It is my belief that progress on the problem of phylogenetic inference requires the crossing of disciplinary boundaries. I hope that biologists will learn something about parsimony from this book and that philosophers will as well. No doubt, what the one group learns will be very different from what the other does.

Willi Hennig, the founding father of cladism, emphasized that theory and observation bear on each other by a process of "reciprocal illumination." The working hypothesis of this book is that the diverse collection of ideas brought together here forms a unity because of the way they throw light on each other. So in justifying the inconvenient demands this sort of project sometimes places on the reader, I can only say that it was the logic of the problem that drove me to it. The patient and open-minded reader, I can only hope, will concur.

Acknowledgments

All the people whom I must thank contributed to this book either by discussing with me the philosophical and scientific issues that bear on the problem of phylogenetic inference or by providing me with their comments on earlier drafts. Some even did both.

In terms of their ongoing involvement with this project, I first must acknowledge frequent and detailed discussions with Ellery Eells and Carter Denniston. I am extremely grateful to them for their generous help over the long haul. For their careful and useful suggestions for improving the book, I must single out Martin Barrett, Nancy Cartwright, Joel Cracraft, A. W. F. Edwards, Berent Enc, Steve Farris, Joe Felsenstein, Malcolm Forster, Ted Garland, Ian Hacking, David Hull, John Kirsch, Philip Kitcher, Arnold Kluge, Carey Krajewski, Ernst Mayr, Alexander Rosenberg, Mark Springer, Dennis Stampe, and Ed Wiley.

Philosophy of Science has granted permission to reprint material from "Likelihood and Convergence" (Sober [1988]). This is gratefully acknowledged.

Last, I would like to thank the National Science Foundation, the National Endowment for the Humanities, and the Graduate School of the University of Wisconsin, Madison, for financial assistance.

January 1988

Reconstructing the Past

Chapter 1

The Biological Problem of Phylogenetic Inference

In this chapter, I introduce the basic structure of the biological problem of phylogenetic inference. In section 1.1, I argue a general, and preliminary, point: the knowability of the past depends on whether the physical processes linking past to present are information preserving or information destroying; this cannot be settled *a priori*, but depends on the specific processes at work and on the data available to the scientist. In section 1.2, I discuss the distinction that systematic biologists draw between phylogenetic pattern and evolutionary process; hypotheses about the former describe the genealogical relationship of species as well as their similarities and differences. Hypotheses about the latter seek to explain these two aspects of pattern by saying why new lineages appear and why new characters evolve. In section 1.3, the technical vocabulary of monophyletic group, synapomorphy, and symplesiomorphy is introduced. I also explain the difference between using overall similarity and cladistic parsimony to infer genealogical relationships. In section 1.4, I show how homoplasy and character incongruence complicate the task of phylogenetic inference.

1.1. When Is History Knowable?

Philosophers have often viewed the question of the past's knowability as an occasion for treating more general issues about the possibility of knowledge. For example, Bertrand Russell [1948] elaborated this question by asking how we know that the world was not created five minutes ago, replete with misleading memory traces and a misleading fossil record. Although his question was ostensibly about history, it might just as well have been about empirical knowledge in general. The very same issues arise if we substitute Descartes' questions for Russell's. How do I know that I am not dreaming? How do I know that my senses are not systematically deceived by an evil demon?

Philosophers have struggled long and hard with these fundamental questions about the reliability of the testimony of the senses. Scientists, on the other hand, generally accept at the outset that their senses are capable of providing evidence about the world outside the mind. This does not mean they think the senses are infallible or that nature is not sometimes misleading. But careful, cross-checked, and repeated observation is something scientists are taught to prize, presumably on the assumption that this procedure has some connection with the goal of knowing the world as it really is. It has been for philosophers to wonder why one is entitled to think that the senses possess this sort of reliability. Is there a convincing argument for saying that the senses have this property, or is the reliability of the senses an undefended and indefensible assumption of the attitude we dignify with the label "scientific"? The latter option threatens to lead to skepticism—to make science look like a house of cards.

I do not propose to enlist in the war against this form of skepticism. With most scientists, I shall assume that the testimony of the senses is to be taken seriously. My question about the knowability of the past, unlike Russell's, is far less sweeping in scope. It is not an excuse for exploring general issues about the possibility of empirical knowledge as a whole; rather, it concerns a set of epistemological difficulties that are peculiar to the historical sciences.

Skeptical puzzles of the kind described by Descartes and Russell have a common structure. Science and common sense tell us that the past produced the present via a particular causal pathway. The philosopher then describes an alternative causal explanation for our current observations and asks how we know that this construct is false and the deliverances of science and common sense are true. Note that this epistemological problem is generated by stepping *outside* of what is regarded as a well-confirmed description of the historical process. By stepping outside of science to invent an alternative explanation, Descartes and Russell hoped to throw in sharper focus their question about the rational credentials of science itself.

The philosopher's preoccupation with this epistemological problem may suggest that the knowability of nature would be vouchsafed if this sort of skeptical puzzle could be solved or dissolved. If we somehow could dismiss fantasies about evil demons and worlds that began five minutes ago, would this suffice to show that the past is, at least in principle, an open book? What we now must see is that rousing ourselves from the philosopher's epistemological nightmares is not enough; epistemological problems about the knowability of the past can be generated *within* science. The structure of a well-confirmed scientific theory can have epistemological implications for the question of whether the past can be retrieved from the traces it bequeaths to the present.

David Hume made philosophy contemplate the implications of the fact that one cannot deduce the future from the present.[1] If a deductive argu-

---

1. This observation, part of Hume's skeptical argument about the justification of induction, will be considered in detail in chapter 2.

ment is to forge this connection, further premises will be needed. The same holds if we consider nondeductive arguments from present to future. If we wish to say that the present state of a system makes one possible future more probable than another, we must appeal to premises additional to the one that merely describes the system's present state.

All this applies when we reverse the temporal direction of our inference. The past cannot be inferred from the present unless further premises are provided.[2] The obvious supplement that secures this inferential relationship is a generalization about how past and present are connected. In this way, theories of process help underwrite predictions about the future as well as retrodictions about the past.

A process theory can be thought of as a mapping from possible initial conditions onto possible subsequent ones.[3] The form this mapping takes engenders a continuum of epistemological possibilities, which reflects whether historical inference will be difficult or easy. The worst possibility, from the point of view of historical science, arises when the processes linking past to present are *information destroying*. If the present state would have obtained regardless of what the past had been like, then an observation of the present will not be able to discriminate among alternative possible pasts. However, if even slight differences in the past would have had profound effects on the shape of the present, then present observation will be a powerful tool in historical reconstruction. These two extreme possibilities are depicted in figures 1a and 1b, respectively.

The worst-case scenario (figure 1a) arises if the system under investigation *equilibrates*. Think of a bowl (a perfect hemisphere) on whose rim a ball is positioned and released. The ball will roll back and forth, eventually reaching equilibrium at the bottom. When the ball is moving down or up the bowl's side, the ball's position at any one time allows something to be said about its initial state. We know that the ball, once released, travels along "great circles," so the position of the moving ball picks out two points on the rim at which the ball might have begun. However, once the ball reaches equilibrium, nothing can be inferred about its starting position.

It is sometimes thought that historical sciences have difficulty retrieving the past because the systems under study are complex, or because theories describing those systems are incompletely developed. Although this is

---

2. A more rigorous formulation of this claim would have to be couched in terms of logical relations among statements: a statement that is *about* the present and the present alone does not allow one to infer a statement that is strictly *about* the past. I offer no account of "aboutness" to flesh out this idea. I shall note, however, that the problem of making aboutness precise is hardly unique to the problem at hand; it arises, for example, in the context of trying to formulate a rigorous and general thesis of determinism (see, e.g., Earman [1986]).
3. This characterization glosses over the fact that there are *probabilistic* theories of process, but for the moment this is a harmless simplification.

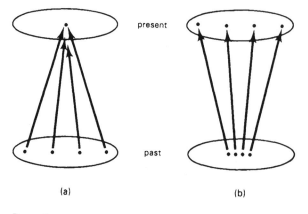

present

past

(a)   (b)

Figure 1.
Whether observing the present state of a system provides evidence about its past depends on whether the process linking past to present is (a) information destroying or (b) information preserving.

frequently true, matters are otherwise in the present example. It is not the complexity of the system or our inability to produce an accurate theory that makes historical inference difficult in the case of the ball. It is the nature of the physical process itself, correctly understood by a well-confirmed theory, that destroys information. The fault, dear reader, is not in ourselves, but in the bowl.

In contrast with this circumstance in which the initial state makes no difference is a physical system in which different beginnings lead to different end states. Instead of a single hemispherical bowl, imagine that the bowl contains numerous wells, so that a ball placed on the rim will roll to the bottom of the well directly below it. In this case the ball's final resting place reveals a great deal about its origins. With a single hemispherical bowl, the final resting place points indifferently to all points on the circumference; but when the bowl is divided into multiple wells, the end state delimits possible initial positions far more narrowly.

The single hemispherical bowl may serve as a metaphor for any historical process that tends toward a global stable equilibrium. If a physical system will end with a particular characteristic, no matter what the characteristic was with which it began, then the initial state will not be retrievable from the end state. This will be true of balls in bowls, of populations of organisms, of stars—of anything.

The bowl divided into many wells represents any historical process in which there are multiple local equilibrium points. The range of possible initial conditions may be segmented into groups; within each group, there is an equilibrium toward which the system will progress. But different sets of such initial conditions tend toward different end states. With a physical process of this kind, the past will be more retrievable from the present. Indeed, the more local equilibria there are (*ceteris paribus*), the more accurately the past will be preserved in the present. In the limit, each possible initial condition will correspond to a unique final state; here the physical process will be perfectly information preserving.

The distinction drawn here between information-preserving and information-destroying processes could be complicated in two ways. First, the notion of observational error could be introduced. Suppose we cannot tell with perfect precision what the final state of a system is. In this case, we can discriminate between two hypotheses about the past if their implications about the present are grossly different; however, if their predictions differ only slightly, imprecise observation may lead the hypotheses to blur together into indistinguishability.

The other complication, not unrelated to the first, allows that the processes linking past to present should be probabilistic, not deterministic. With each possible initial state, we now associate different possible future states, each with its own probability of coming true. Two possible pasts will be more or less distinguishable, depending on whether they confer different or similar probabilities on the observed present state of the system.[4]

The point I wish to stress, however, can be seen quite clearly without bringing these complications into play. It is an empirical matter whether the physical processes linking past to present are information destroying or information preserving. Indeed, we must fragment the single and seemingly simple question of the past's knowability into a multiplicity: We must not ask whether the past is knowable, but whether this or that specific aspect of the past is knowable.

Because of this, it would be folly to try to produce an *a priori* argument that shows that evolutionary history must always be recoverable. Whether this is true depends on contingent properties of the evolutionary process. The folly would be greater still to try to mount some general philosophical argument to the effect that the past as a whole must be knowable. The history of stars, of living things, and of human languages, to mention just three examples, will be retrievable only if empirical facts specific to the processes governing each are favorable. This is no global question for the armchair philosopher to answer by pondering evil demons or other epistemological fantasies. Rather, the pertinent questions are local in scope, which the astronomer, the evolutionist, and the linguist can each address by considering the discriminatory power of available data and process theories.

---

4. The idea of *likelihood*, which will be introduced in chapter 3, allows this idea to be made more precise.

1.2. Pattern and Process

The problem of *genealogical inference* is peculiar to historical sciences. A central example is the task of *phylogenetic* inference: how can we tell, for example, whether human beings are more closely related to chimps than they are to gorillas? However, it is not just species that have genealogies. Single organisms have family trees. Languages evolve and are related to each other by varying degrees of propinquity of descent. Ancient texts, copied by scribes whose copies are then copied, also are related genealogically. Indeed, social, political, economic, and artistic traditions exhibit descent with modification, so they can exemplify ancestor/descendant relationships as well.[5]

When we say of a set of objects, which begot which, we specify their genealogy. Begetting is a special sort of causal relationship. One object begets another, not in virtue of causing it to have some property or other, but in virtue of causing it to exist. When the reproductive relationship also involves resemblance of parents and offspring, these two ideas are easily confused. Parents bring their children into existence; they also transmit many of their characteristics to them. But reproduction does not conceptually require heritability. Though evolution by natural selection requires heritability of characteristics, the bare idea of a genealogy does not. Even when traits are transmitted with grossly imperfect fidelity, parent/offspring relationships may still exist. Indeed, saying that there is zero heritability or imperfect fidelity of transmission already presupposes that there is a determinate genealogy in which the fidelity of the mechanism of inheritance can be assessed.

In this book I shall concentrate on genealogical relationships that take the form of a *tree*. As we pass from base to tips, we find branching, but no merging. An ancestor may give rise to many immediately following descendants. But a given descendant has just one immediately preceding ancestor. Put differently, there is a unique ancestor/descendant chain leading from the base to any point on the tips. In a treelike genealogy, if *a* and *b* are ancestors of a given object, then *a* is an ancestor of *b*, or *b* is an ancestor of *a*.

Species that do not hybridize or otherwise pass genetic material among themselves have this treelike genealogy. The same can be said of uniparental organisms. However, there are many kinds of objects that have genealogies in which branches merge as well as split. Their genealogies are said to be *reticulate*. Both hybridizing species and biparental organisms

---

5. Platnick and Cameron [1977] cite some affinities between the tasks of reconstructing the genealogies of species, of languages, and of texts. See also Hoenigswald [1960] for discussion of the linguistic issues.

have genealogies of this sort. The cultural objects mentioned above, like languages and political institutions, often have more than one immediate ancestor as well.

The distinction between trees and reticulate networks is sometimes clearer in theory than it is in practice. Consider the phenomenon of *secondary borrowing* in the genealogy of languages. Modern French has borrowed some words from English, but English is not an ancestor of Modern French. Though French has been influenced by a variety of sources, its preeminent debt to Latin allows us to designate Latin, not English, as an ancestor. Both English and Latin have contributed to modern French. Presumably, our reluctance to count both as ancestors is due to the fact that the former has made a paltry contribution, compared to the latter. If the two contributions had been more equal, we might count both as ancestors.

In the case of phylogenetic relationships, secondary borrowing can take the form of gene flow that affects a species after it has come into existence. The reproductive isolation of separate species is often imperfect. It also is possible for a virus to reconstitute the genetic material in a host's cells. If the genetic profile of a species is largely shaped by its ancestral relation to a single parent species, and is only modestly affected by Johnny-come-lately secondary borrowing, it is natural to maintain that the genealogy is treelike rather than reticulate.

Undoubtedly, there are subtle line-drawing problems here, ones that would have to be explored if a full understanding of the begetting relationship were required. However, my focus in what follows will be on treelike genealogies; the issues I shall address are ones in which the meaning of the parent/offspring relationship is assumed to be well enough understood.

Systematics is the branch of evolutionary biology that aims to recover the genealogical relationships underlying organic diversity. It also happens to be the part of evolutionary biology that constructs classifications of living things. Biologists have argued passionately over how these two enterprises are related. *Cladists* have held that genealogy and nothing else should influence classification; *pheneticists* have held that overall similarity, rather than propinquity of descent, should determine classification; and *evolutionary taxonomists* have maintained that classification should reflect both genealogy and adaptive similarity.[6] I note this dispute only to set it to one side. My interest will be in how genealogy can be inferred; how inferred phylogeny should influence classification I shall not discuss.

It is worth emphasizing this simple separation of problems, because the names of the systematic schools do double duty (Felsenstein [1984]). Cla-

6. Sell Hull [1970], Eldredge and Cracraft [1980], Wiley [1981], and Ridley [1986] for discussion.

distics, besides embodying a view about classification, also deploys its own distinctive method of phylogenetic inference. Pheneticism, likewise, can denote a principle about inferring genealogical relationships as well as a thesis about how to classify. And evolutionary taxonomists, though they disagree with cladists about the construction of classifications, often agree with them when it comes to inferring genealogies.

In seeking to reconstruct the genealogy of species, systematists deploy an important distinction between *pattern* and *process*. Claims about ancestor/ descendant relationships among species—of phylogenetic relationship— are claims about pattern. They may take the form of saying that one species is an ancestor of another. Or, what is more important, they may involve comparative judgments about propinquity of descent, such as saying that human beings and chimps are more closely related to each other than either is to gorillas.[7]

When systematists speak of process, they have in mind the different possible causal explanations that might underlie the changes that occur in a genealogy. That human beings are descended from apes is a fact about life's pattern. *Why* this speciation event occurred is a problem of process. That human beings possess novel characteristics not exemplified by their nearest living relatives is a fact about pattern. *Why* these evolutionary novelties arose is a question of process.

The careful reader may already suspect a difficulty in this biological distinction. How can the proposition than human beings are descended from apes be a fact of pattern, not process, since my statement implies that there is a process of descent with modification linking human beings with an ancestral species?

This objection shows that the distinction between pattern and process must be stated more carefully. A systematist addressing the question of human beings, chimps, and gorillas will typically assume at the outset that all three trace back, sooner or later, to a common ancestor. This "process assumption," if one wishes to call it that, is not at issue when one considers the three species just mentioned. Rather, the biologist focuses on this question: Given that there is a genealogical relationship here, what is it?

Of course, one might demand to know why the assumption that there is a genealogical relationship of some sort is legitimate in the first place. In

7. Because this work is about phylogenetic inference, not classification, nothing will be said about the current controversy concerning so-called "pattern" cladism. As I understand it, pattern cladists believe that taxa can be grouped on the basis of their characteristics, where the groupings need not be interpreted as indicating phylogenetic relationship. Whether this is coherent is quite separate from the issue of how genealogy may be inferred from similarities and differences. See Ridley [1986] for references to the primary literature.

answer, systematists might assemble evidence that primate species are more closely related to each other than any is to, say, horses. But here again they will assume that horses and primates eventually trace back to a common ancestor. So perhaps the minimal assumption at work in problems of phylogenetic inference is that the organisms that systematists study all trace back to a single origination event.

One might wish to step back from this standard assumption and ask why it is ever proper to assume that some taxa are related to others. That this question has most recently been pressed by creationists may lead some scientists to dismiss it with contempt. Indeed, the misuse of facts and the spurious arguments of "Creation Science" do merit stern criticism (vigorously provided by Kitcher [1982]). But the question itself is a perfectly fine one, to which Darwin [1859] gave a sustained answer. By this I mean that much of the *Origin of Species* is a defense of the hypothesis of evolution—of descent with modification. This should be clearly distinguished from Darwin's other great thesis—the quite separate claim that natural selection is the principal cause of life's diversity.[8]

In a more modern context, we can ask what reason there is to think that all life traces back to a single origination. Two kinds of answers are often given, the first based on the characteristics found in present organisms, the second citing an assumption about the evolutionary process.

An example of the first kind of argument is afforded by the genetic code. The 64 nucleotide triplets (codons) found in an organism's messenger RNA each code for one of twenty amino acids. Current evidence indicates that, with minor exceptions, this genetic coding of amino acids by nucleotide triplets is universal among all contemporary life forms (see, for example, the data in Lane, Marbaix, and Gurdon [1971]). Evolutionists take this as evidence that all present-day organisms trace back to a common ancestor, from whom they inherited this genetic code. The reason is that this shared code is to be expected if all life is related, but would be rather surprising if genetic codes arose independently in separate lineages (Crick [1968]; Dobzhansky et al. [1977, pp. 27–28]).[9]

The pattern of this kind of inference—from an observed similarity to a hypothesis of common ancestry—is something that we shall scrutinize with great care in much of the rest of this book. Notice, for now, that the inference presupposes that alternative encodings of amino acids are pos-

8. For discussion of Darwin's argument for the hypothesis of descent with modification, see Ghiselin [1969], Ruse [1979], and Kitcher [1985].
9. Of course, the observed similarity would not be surprising if god constructed each separate species with the idea that they should share the same genetic code. The universality of the code is evidence for single origination as opposed to multiple originations, where the latter is *naturalistically* construed.

sible; without this assumption, the universality of the code would be predicted by the hypothesis of multiple originations just as much as it is by the hypothesis of common ancestry (Crick [1968]). I mention this argument here as an example of the kind of observation that leads evolutionists to hold that all present-day terrestrial organisms are related.

Besides arguments based on observed similarity, the hypothesis of relatedness is supported by an assumption about how the evolutionary process worked at its beginnings. It is plausible to think that the sequence of events that can lead from inorganic materials eventually to the emergence of organisms started numerous times and fizzled before anything in the way of an organism was produced. But once the process moved some distance down this sequence of events and genuine organisms made their appearance, those living forms destroyed the conditions necessary for any subsequent start-ups from inorganic materials to get very far. This set of transformations would arise, for example, if living things eat the macromolecules that are the potential ancestors of living things[10]

According to this picture of prebiotic evolution, there were numerous start-ups of the process of life's evolving from nonlife, both before and after the one that resulted in the living world we now observe. There is no assumption among evolutionists that all organic *molecules* trace back to a single *molecule* that was the ancestor of all of them and of all current life as well. Rather, the more modest hypothesis is that all present *organisms* trace back to a single *organism* ancestor. In this way, a process assumption about prebiotic evolution leads to a conclusion that harmonizes with inferences based on the observed similarity of current life forms.

This brief discussion is meant to indicate that the question of why one should think that observed species are related genealogically is entirely legitimate; my remarks are not intended as a full answer to this reasonable question. Rather, my point is that this question is quite different from the ones a practicing systematist usually poses. Other part of evolutionary theory address the general question of life's origination. Systematics assumes that all current and fossil organisms are related and attempts to identify the structure of these relationships. This is why the idea of descent with modification is not treated by biologists intent on phylogenetic reconstruction as a process assumption. Or if they grant that it is a process assumption, they will view it as the most minimal and innocuous of ones.

Perhaps the best way to separate pattern and process is to think of hypotheses as ordered in terms of their *logical strength*. By logical strength and weakness, I do not mean relative degrees of plausibility and evidential

---

10. See Shapiro [1986] for a readable review of current theorizing about the origins of life.

support. Rather, I mean that if one proposition logically implies another (but not conversely), then the first is logically stronger than the second. Logically stronger hypotheses "say more" than ones that are more circumspect (weaker). So the hypothesis that human beings, chimps, and gorillas are related is a very weak claim compared to a more detailed description of how they are related. And still more ambitious (and risky) is a hypothesis that not only says what the genealogical relationships are but also sets forth an explanation for why the postulated speciation events occurred.

I have said that the subject of this book is genealogical inference. The major problem we shall study concerns the relationship of pattern and process. If one wishes to reconstruct phylogenetic pattern, how much does one need to know about the evolutionary process? One can examine human beings, chimps, and gorillas and record their characteristics. Some characteristics will be found in all three species, while others will have more limited distributions. From these data, drawn from the present, one wishes to reach a conclusion about the past. The data by themselves do not allow one to deduce what the genealogical relationships are. What else do we need to know to make this historical inference?

A principle of "less is more" governs this problem. This less we need to know about the evolutionary process to make an inference about pattern, the more confidence we can have in our conclusions. From the point of view of an evolutionary theory that wishes to uncover phylogenetic relationships, the best outcome would be that minimal process assumptions suffice to identify pattern. If, on the other hand, a detailed understanding were required of why evolution proceeded in the way it did, then an inference about pattern would have to await a detailed understanding of process. This could be gloomy news indeed; it is not unusual for process to be at least as poorly understood as pattern. If we do not know the phylogenetic relationships that obtain within a set of species, then we also may be quite ignorant of the specific evolutionary processes that were at work.

The following diagram illustrates the epistemological problem of pattern and process:

Data of Character Distributions	+	Process Assumptions	→	Phylogenetic Pattern

The data in and of themselves do not permit us to conclude that one genealogy is true and all alternatives are false. Rather, we hope that minimal and plausible assumptions about process will allow us to use the data to discriminate among competing phylogenetic hypotheses. Just how minimal such assumptions can be and still do the work we expect of them—of forging an evidential connection between characters and genealogy—is the central problem in the foundations of phylogenetic inference.[11]

The arrow in the above diagram is worth pondering. If our process theory were purely deterministic, we might hope to *deduce* phylogenetic patterns from characters plus process assumptions. An example of this situation outside biology is afforded by Newtonian physics, which is "backward deterministic." If I specify the position and momentum of the particles in a closed Newtonian system, I can deduce not just the *future* of those particles (as Laplace stressed) but their *past* as well.[12] However, if process theories are probabilistic in character, no such deduction will be possible.

This latter alternative is undoubtedly the right one for phylogenetic inference, since a stochastic element plays an essential role in evolution. The magnitude of the importance of chance is now hotly debated in evolutionary theory, but that it is nonzero is entirely uncontroversial.[13] Because of this, the arrow in the above diagram cannot mean deductive implication. What we can hope is that plausible process assumptions allow us to use character distributions to reach conclusions about the relative *degrees of confirmation and disconfirmation* of competing phylogenetic hypotheses. We do not deduce the truth of a genealogy from character distributions and process theory; rather, we infer that one genealogy is better supported than another.

This way of posing the problem of phylogenetic inference—in terms of the relationship of pattern and process—is not entirely true to the history of how that subject has developed during the last twenty years. Systematists usually did not begin by elaborating process theories and then see how genealogical relationships could be inferred from them. Rather, biologists invented a variety of *methods* for using the characteristics of species to infer phylogenetic relationships. Only after those methods had been developed and applied did biologists begin to ask why they make sense. Systematics is now divided into several schools; each deploys arguments

11. There is a more attenuated usage of "pattern," favored by advocates of "pattern cladism," according to which pattern involves just the similarity and differences of organisms, without regard to their genealogical relationships. In this usage, the idea of "inferring" pattern from data is a misnomer; rather, a pattern hypothesis in this sense merely summarizes the data without venturing beyond them. In the usage to be followed here, however, hypotheses of *phylogenetic pattern* attempt to specify the genealogical relationship of species, whereas hypotheses about the *evolutionary process* propose explanations for the relationships and characters found in the tree of life.

12. This is a somewhat crude representation of the idea that Newtonian theory is backward deterministic. For refinements and qualifications, see Earman [1986].

13. See Sober [1984c, chapter 4] for discussion of how the concept of chance figures in evolutionary theory.

for why its methods are right and competing methods are wrong. In systematics, it is not process theories that have been developed so much as methods for analyzing data.[14]

Substituting methods for process assumptions in the previous diagram, we obtain the following one:

$$\begin{array}{ccc} \text{Data of Character} & & \text{Method of} & & \text{Phylogenetic} \\ \text{Distributions} & + & \text{Inference} & \rightarrow & \text{Pattern} \end{array}$$

The problem is that the competing methods at times disagree over which phylogenetic hypothesis is best supported by a given data set. What needs to be sorted out is which methods make sense and why.

A process hypothesis may bridge the gap between data and genealogy. So too do the various methods of inference that have been invented by systematic biologists. There must be a deep connection here: methods must correspond to assumptions about evolutionary processes. The best method, if there is just one, will make the most plausible assumptions about process; where our knowledge of process is meagre, the plausibility of assumptions will depend crucially on how logically weak they are. In short, the way to resolve this methodological debate in systematics is to identify clearly the process presuppositions of the main competing methods.

1.3. Objects and Properties

A first guess about how character data bear on genealogy might be this: *Similarity* is evidence of propinquity of descent. If two species are found to be more similar to each other than either is to a third, then this evidence points to the conclusion that the first two are more closely related to each other than either is to the third. For example, King and Wilson [1975] examined a variety of genetic and biochemical data and found that human beings and chimps are about 99% similar. If each of these species is much less similar to lemurs, for example, would that not provide serious evidence that human beings and chimps are more closely related to each other than either is to lemurs?

This first guess—that similarity is the appropriate indicator of common ancestry—is the intuitive idea behind one of the main positions we shall need to scrutinize. *Pheneticism* was developed as a two-pronged thesis—

---

14. If we look at systematics before the mid-1960s, we find considerable inexplicitness about methods and process models as well. The systematic schools that emerged in the 1960s moved away from what they saw as imprecise appeals to "intuition" by explicitly formulating methods of inference; the issue of what such methods presuppose about process emerged later.

one concerning taxonomy, the other about phylogenetic reconstruction (Sokal and Sneath [1963]; Sneath and Sokal [1973]). First came the classifactory idea—that taxa should be grouped into a Linnaean hierarchy of species, genera, families, etc., on the basis of their *overall similarity*. Evolutionary assumptions were explicitly ruled inappropriate and evolutionary interpretations gratuitous. Taxonomy was to proceed without recourse to theories of process; the goal was to construct an "all-purpose classification," not a classification whose special task was the representation of phylogenetic relationships.

Although pheneticism began by abjuring the pertinence of evolutionary assumptions or the importance of evolutionary interpretation to the taxonomic enterprise, a number of its advocates argued that groupings based on overall similarity could be interpreted as having an evolutionary significance (Colless [1970]; Sneath and Sokal [1973]). This is the pheneticism we shall consider; it is the thesis that overall similarity is the appropriate device for inferring phylogenetic relationships.

In competition with the idea of overall similarity are various formulations of the notion of *special similarity*.[15] It is not just any sort of similarity that confirms genealogical relatedness, so this idea goes, but only similarities of certain sorts. The main, but not the only, development of this idea now being used in systematics is *cladistic parsimony*, stemming from the work of Willi Hennig [1965, 1966].[16]

How are we to tell whether overall similarity or some form of special similarity is the best measure of propinquity of descent? Indeed, why should any form of similarity count as evidence? What entitles us to dismiss the idea that more closely related species are apt to be more *dis*similar? I raise this question not because anyone seriously believes that dissimilarity is evidence for propinquity of descent. The point is that we must uncover the basis of this conviction. What is it about the evolutionary process that makes *dis*similarity a silly measure of phylogenetic relatedness?

Our goal is to examine various methods of genealogical inference and uncover the process assumptions they make. We shall begin by seeing how simple process assumptions can themselves dictate a choice of method. This will provide the opportunity to explain some needed technical vocabulary and to set the stage for the difficult epistemological problems we eventually shall confront. So I will proceed by telling an epistemological fairy tale. *If* evolutionary processes had the properties I now shall stipulate, cladistic parsimony, rather than overall similarity, would be the method of choice.

15. I owe this terminology to Farris [1979].
16. The idea of using parsimony in phylogenetic inference was also discussed by Edwards and Cavalli-Sforza [1963, 1964] and by Camin and Sokal [1965]. Their development of the idea, as well as Hennig's will be considered in chapter 4.

My story about evolutionary processes will be a fairy tale, because we know that it is untrue. Does this mean that cladistic methodology rests on an illusion? Not at all. My fairy tale describes a *sufficient* condition for cladistic parsimony to be correct. Nowhere will it be suggested that these false process assumptions are *necessary* for parsimony to make sense. The question about necessity will occupy our attention later. Our eventual goal will be to confront the issue of what process assumptions a method must make. Establishing sufficient conditions for a method to make sense does not address this problem.

However, before this process assumption can be stated, we must obtain a clearer view of the tree structure in which character evolution takes place. We first must grasp precisely what genealogical hypotheses assert; only then shall we be able to see how a process assumption can bring observed similarities to bear on them.

Let us imagine a branching process of the sort illustrated in figure 2. We begin with a single ancestral species, Zero. After a certain length of time, it gives birth to two daughter species, One and Two. Then, after the same length of time, these produce species Three, Four, Five, and Six. And so on, so that 2^n new species make their appearance in the nth generation of this process. The resulting branching structure is a bifurcating phylogenetic tree, with Zero at the root and numerous species in the interior and at the tips (these last are sometimes called "terminal taxa"). The circles represent species and the arrows joining them represent the "begetting" relation.

This branching structure is an idealization, in that it excludes a number of realistic possibilities. Notice that the tree bifurcates every generation. It would be more realistic to allow for variation in the number of daughters a parent species can produce and for variation in the amount of time it takes for speciation to occur. Furthermore, I have assumed that the resulting genealogy is treelike rather than reticulate. As noted in the previous section, this excludes the possibility of species being formed by hybridization.

The basic question of phylogenetic inference can be represented as a sampling problem. We draw a number of species from this phylogenetic tree and try to infer how they are related. We observe some characteristics of the sampled taxa; we observe various facts concerning their morphology, behavior, physiology, genetics, and biochemistry.[17] These

---

17. Other sources of evidence (for example, the biogeographical distribution of the taxa considered) cannot be excluded as irrelevant. But we focus here on a narrower problem: How do the "intrinsic" characters of species provide evidence about phylogenetic relationships?

It is also worth emphasizing that the introduction of molecular and biochemical data does not magically solve the problem of phylogenetic inference. This is not to deny that they provide useful (and often voluminous) evidence. But genealogy is not self-evident in

character data are then interpreted by some method of phylogenetic inference—overall similarity or cladistic parsimony, for example—and a phylogenetic hypothesis is singled out as the one that is best supported by the data. Our task, then, is to understand what evolutionists mean by an hypothesis of relationship and to grasp what kinds of characteristics might count as potential data.

An outsider to the work of systematists might imagine that figuring out phylogenetic relationships for a set of species is like placing people onto a family tree. For example, if Sam and Aaron are to be placed in the same family tree, we would try to determine whether Sam is Aaron's brother, uncle, father, cousin, or son (or none of the above). The phylogenetic tree shown in figure 2 shows pairs of species that have these various relationships to each other.

However, the enterprise of inferring phylogenetic relationships, at least according to cladistic theory, does not aim at anything so specific. Rather, what matters is identifying *monophyletic groups*. A group is said to be monophyletic precisely when it is made of a species, all of that species' descendants, and nothing else. What I shall call the "cut method" is a useful way of understanding this property of a group. Draw a "cut" across a given branch in figure 2. The species immediately above that cut and all its descendents constitute a monophyletic group. Notice that monophyletic groups obey the following principle: If a species is in a given monophyletic group, so are all its descendants.[18]

Evolutionists rarely hope to identify *all* the members of a monophyletic group. Typically, their goal is to discover which species are in monophyletic groups to which other species do not belong. If we contrasted the species depicted in figure 2 with some species X (an outgroup) that is not a descendant of Zero, we could say that the species in the figure belong to a monophyletic group that does not contain X. To say this, it is not neces-

---

the light of molecular similarities any more than it is in the light of morphological ones (Wiley [1981, p. 339]). The problem of justifying a method of inference that links data and hypotheses remains to be addressed.

18. This definition of monophyly is narrower than others that have been proposed. Simpson [1961, p. 124], for example, allows that a group of taxa failing the cut test may constitute a monophyletic group, if they are similar in certain ways (Mayr [1969] concurs). Mayr, following Ashlock [1971, 1972], uses the term "holophyly" to coincide with what cladists mean by "monophyly." The question of how monophyly should be understood takes on more than terminological importance if one agrees that all taxonomic groups should be monophyletic. But this, notice, is a thesis about classification, not about phylogenetic inference. Since my interest here is solely in the problem of phylogenetic inference, I chose that definition of monophyly that is most convenient for the problem at hand. The cladistic definition of monophyly given above, stated solely in terms of features of the branching process, is the more convenient choice.

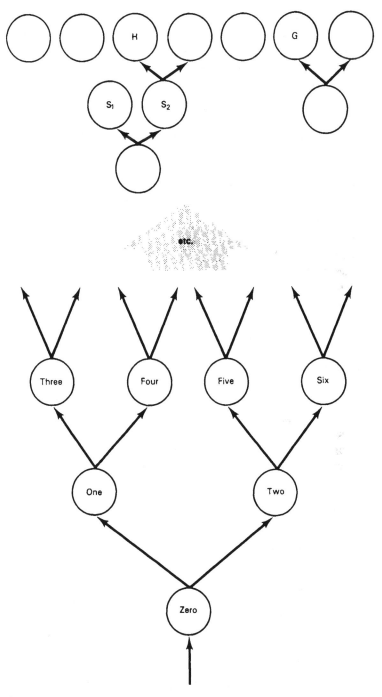

Figure 2.
A bifurcating branching process in which each species produces two descendants after a
fixed length of time.

sary that figure 2 be *complete*; it need not list each and every descendant of species Zero. Rather, all that is required is that the species depicted are each of them Zero or one of Zero's descendents, whereas X is not.

Figure 2 also represents numerous, more limited, monophyletic groups. For example, species Three and Four belong to a group that does not include Five. And species Six and Two form a group apart from Zero. However, if Three and Four are the *immediate* descendants of One, no two of these form a monophyletic group apart from the third. The cut method defines *clades* (from the Greek for "branches").

This definition of monophyly implies that the complement of a monophyletic group is not itself a monophyletic group. Although the cut method entails that the group made of species Two and its descendants (and nothing else) is monophyletic, the rest of the tree does not comprise a monophyletic group unto itself. The reason is that the rest of the tree includes Species Zero. But if Species Zero is to be in a monophyletic group, so must *all* its descendants. The reader may want to use the cut method to verify that "leftovers" (complements) of monophyletic groups are not monophyletic.[19]

Another consequence of the definition of monophyly is that two monophyletic groups may be disjoint and one may be a subpart of the other, but they cannot overlap *partially*. If species A and B belong to a monophyletic group that fails to include C, then B and C cannot belong to a group that fails to include A. The two hypotheses—abbreviated as (AB)C and A(BC)—are incompatible (a point that will have considerable importance in section 1.4). Again, the cut method is useful for seeing why this is so.

Taking monophyletic groups as the "natural objects" of phylogenetic reconstruction has some striking implications about the relevance of more traditional taxonomic categories. Many of these involve leftovers of the kind just described. Eldredge and Cracraft [1980, p. 164] present the following as a fairly standard traditional classification of the Vertebrates (Chordata):

A. Invertebrata (non-Chordata)
AA. Chordata (notochord, dorsal nerve cord, etc.)
    B. Acrania (absence of cranium, vertebrae, brain)
    BB. Craniata (= Vertebrata) (cranium, vertebrae, brain)
        C. Agnatha (absence of jaws and paired appendages)
        CC. Gnathostoma (jaws, paired appendages)

19. In this respect, cladistic ideas recapitulate Plato's remark (*Statesman* 262d) that even if *Greek* marks a natural unit, its complement, *barbarian* (= non-Greek) does not (quoted with approval in Nelson and Platnick [1981, pp. 67–68]). See also Eldredge and Cracraft's [1980, chapter 5] discussion of what they call "the *A*/not-*A* dichotomy."

    D. Pisces (nontetrapod, "aquatic" gnathostomes)
   DD. Tetrapoda (tetrapod, "terrestrial" gnathostomes)
      E. Amphibia (anamniote egg)
    EE. Amniota (amniote egg)
     F. Reptilia (absence of advanced avian or mammalian characters)
    FF. Aves
   FFF. Mammalia

They go on to assert that Invertebrata, Acrania, Pisces, Reptilia, and perhaps Amphibia are not monophyletic groups. Those who think that evolutionary ideas have not much changed the classifications biologists draw up have not attended to the details of the cladistic revolution.

Reptilia is not monophyletic, because birds and crocodiles are more closely related to each other than either is to snakes. In saying this, I do not mean that the reptiles are not *members of* a monophyletic group. Reptilian species, after all, are vertebrates, and Vertebrata is monophyletic. Rather, I mean that there is no monophyletic group whose members are *all and only* the reptiles.

When taxonomists confront a list of species, they rarely, if ever, will think that their sample is complete—that the list includes all species closely related to the ones they wish to consider. So, for example, a systematist might consider a species of bird (call it B), a species of crocodile (C), and one of the snakes (S). In saying that $B + C$ is monophyletic, we mean that they are members of a group that does not contains S. In saying that $C + S$ is not monophyletic, we mean that there is no group that contains them without containing B as well. However, if we considered a different "outgroup," this judgment would change: there *is* a monophyletic group that contains both C and S, but that fails to include human beings.[20] Judgments of monophyly are *contrastive*: two items belong to a monophyletic group only in contrast to a third one that does not.

It is essential to see that the identification of monophyletic groups does not involve saying that a given species is an ancestor of another. For example, suppose we recover a fossil that has many protohuman characteristics. This may suggest that human beings and the species this specimen comes from belong to a fairly narrow monophyletic group. But how are we to tell whether the fossil is related to *Homo sapiens* (species H in figure 2) by being its ancestor (S_2) or by being the "sister" (S_1) of its ancestor? Cladists generally regard this question as unanswerable (or, at least, as being *very* difficult) and restrict themselves to the more modest task of

---

20. In tracking this idea, it is important not to confuse the idea that C and S are members of a monophyletic group with the idea that there is a monophyletic group composed of C, S, and nothing else. The latter implies the former, but not conversely.

identifying monophyletic groups. They hold that evidence can be adduced to show that H and the fossilized specimen (which may correspond to either S_1 or S_2 in our tree) belong to a monophyletic group to which gorillas (G), for example, do not belong (Nelson [1972]).

It is sometimes thought that the main impediment to reconstructing phylogenetic relationships is "the incompleteness of the fossil record." That this does occasion problems is not in question. Nor can one deny that dating a fossil allows one to ascribe a minimum age to every monophyletic group to which the fossil belongs. But it is important to realize that fossils do not wear their genealogies on their sleeves. A fossil may have similarities to human beings in the same way that a living chimp may show such similarities. A fossil, like any newly discovered species, may provide useful data about the phylogeny of the groups to which it belongs. But the epistemological problem of reconstructing relationships from characteristics remains fundamentally the same. This point should not be obscured by loose talk about the discovery of our hominid "ancestors." What we can discover in the first instance is that these extinct species are our *relatives*, just as various extant species are.[21]

The claim I would make here is that establishing that A is an ancestor of B, rather than just that A and B are close relatives, is often difficult, not that it is out-and-out impossible. If the fossil record is reasonably complete and within species change has been gradual enough, the biologist may have some confidence that A has existed for longer than B. If one is confident, furthermore, that there is no third species C (an ancestor of both) from whom both A and B inherited their special similarities (since no fossil traces of C have been found), then the hypothesis that B is descended from A may be confirmed. Perhaps reasoning of this sort underlies the confidence we may have in saying that the polar bear evolved from the Alaskan brown bear. In another vein, consider the fact that there is often no real doubt that hybrid species (allopolyploids) are descended from—not just related to—certain pairs of other species. When species A and B come in contact, species C is found; moreover, C combines the chromosomes found in A and B. The natural hypothesis is that C is a hybrid, whose parents are A and B. So the modest point I would make about ancestor/descendant relationships is this: When a biologist claims that A is an ancestor of B, the evidence on which this is based must do more than merely support the weaker hypothesis that A and B are related. The mere fact of character similarity between A and B is not enough to provide this extra ingredient.[22]

21. See Hennig [1966, pp. 140–142], Schaeffer, Hecht, and Eldredge [1972], Nelson [1973], Farris [1976], and Eldredge and Tattersall [1982] for discussion of the problem of inferring whether one species is an ancestor and not just a relative of another.
22. I thank David Hull (personal communication) for emphasizing these points to me.

It is patent that species are ancestors in the branching structure depicted in figure 2. However, it is worth nothing that monophyletic groups of species are not ancestors of anything (Wiley [1979ab, 1981]). A monophyletic group begins with some first member and then extends all the way up to the tips of the tree. This group is an ancestor of one of the species found at the top of the tree no more than the Sober family is one of my ancestors.

This is why cladists are apt to wince when they hear it said that Mammalia is descended from Vertebrata. Each is a monophyletic group and the former is a proper part of the latter. But if parts are not descended from the wholes to which they belong, it is hard to see how the second group is an ancestor of the first. Were it not for the confusion such statements engender, we could view them as harmless ways of saying, for example, that Mammalia (a monophyletic group) is descended from a species that was a vertebrate (also a monophyletic group), but was not a mammal (nonmammals, of course, not being a monophyletic group).

This confusion and an extra one to boot are suggested by the statement that birds are descended from reptiles. Aves is thought to be monophyletic, though Reptilia is not. The statement of descent would be true if it meant only that Aves is descended from a species that had certain reptilelike characteristics. But this modest statement should not be confused with the doubly mistaken idea that Reptilia is an evolutionary unit (= monophyletic group) ancestral to the birds.

A further consequence of thinking about the connection of the ancestor/descendant relation to the concept of monophyly is that a *species* will fail to be monophyletic if it is an ancestor of any other species. Note that the cut method, applied to figure 2, implies that no interior node is itself a monophyletic group. Species *belong to* monophyletic groups, but it is false that each of them *is identical with* a monophyletic group. The cladistic demand that *all* taxa be monophyletic, therefore, does not apply at the species level or below (Rosen [1978], Ereshefsky [1988]).

The goal of phylogenetic inference, then, is to describe how the taxa at hand fall into more and less inclusive monophyletic groups. Taken at its simplest, the problem might involve just three species (A, B, and C), the question being which two of these belong to a monophyletic group that does not include the third. The alternative groupings are three: (AB)C, A(BC), and (AC)B.[23]

Such hypotheses about monophyly are standardly represented in

23. If trifurcation is taken seriously as a possible mode of speciation, then there is a further genealogical hypothesis—namely, that no two of the species form a group apart from the third. Note that the bifurcating branching process assumed in figure 2 excludes this possibility.

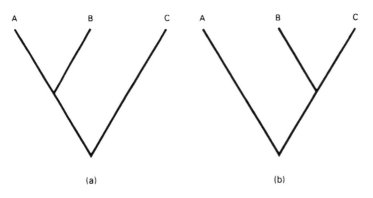

Figure 3.
Cladogram (a) expresses the hypothesis that A and B belong to a monophyletic group that does not include C, whereas cladogram (b) says that B and C belong to a group that does not include A. The two cladograms are incompatible.

branching diagrams called *cladograms*. (AB)C is depicted in figure 3a and A(BC) is shown in 3b.

Each of these two branching diagrams says only that two species belong to a monophyletic group that does not include the third. But as we have already seen, there are many specific ancestor/descendant relationships that may place A and B in a group that does not include C. For example, (AB)C is consistent with both of the following ancestor/descendant relationships: It might be true that none of these three is an ancestor of the others, but that A and B have an ancestor that is not an ancestor of C. Or it may be that A is descended from B and that B is descended from a species that is also an ancestor of C. These two alternative relationships are represented in figures 4a and 4b. Applying the cut method to each of them yields the same monophyletic grouping, (AB)C. In figures 4c–4f we see other ancestor/descendant relationships, each of which is also consistent with the (AB)C hypothesis.

Figure 4 describes six *phylogenetic trees*. In the sense of these terms that I shall use, a tree implies a cladogram, but not conversely. Cladograms assert the existence of monophyletic groups and nothing else; trees assert the existence of such groups *and* say something more about specific ancestor/descendant relationships. Notice that a cladogram displays taxa at its tips only, whereas a phylogenetic tree will have species at its tips, in its interior, and at the root.

This distinction between tree and cladogram has been quite central to the development of cladistic theory and is the standard stumbling block for those making their way into these ideas for the first time. One reason it is easy to confuse these ideas is that one of the the trees (4a) consis-

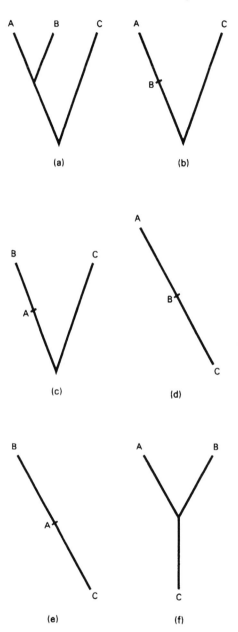

Figure 4.
Six phylogenetic trees, each conforming to the cladistic grouping (AB)C. In each case, the
cut method implies that *A* and *B* belong to a monophyletic group that does not include *C*.

tent with the cladogram shown in figure 3a looks exactly like it. I hope
the above discussion makes it clear how these ideas are separate, though
related.[24]

Figures 4b–4f *may seem* to demand that speciation is possible without a
branching event. But this, I want to claim, is not so. The idea of *phyletic
evolution* or *anagenesis*—wherein a lineage changes so much that later organisms are no longer thought of as "similar enough" to count as con-
specific with earlier ones—was defended by Darwin. But more modern
theory has usually emphasized that the geographical splitting of a species
into separate populations—either before (allopatry) or after (sympatry)
reproductive isolation mechanisms are fixed—is an important factor in
speciation (see, for example, Mayr [1963]). In addition, many evolutionists
hold that branching is not just important), but conceptually necessary.
They reject the idea that anagenesis is ever properly treated as a kind of
speciation. A lineage may change through time and still remain the same
species, just as a human being may change from birth to death and still remain numerically the same organism. On this view, speciation, by definition, requires a branching event.[25]

Figure 4 does not beg this question about the speciation process. Imagine that the three species under investigation (A, B, and C) are sampled
from the branching structure shown in figure 2. The fact that branching
events are not depicted in some of the trees shown in figure 4 does not
mean that none occurred. For example, it is consistent with figure 4d that
the historical fact of the matter was this: C split, thereby giving rise to B,
and B then split, thereby begetting A. By the same token, I have labeled
the separate nodes in figure 2 as separate species, but nothing in this representation precludes the possibility that a branch linking a species with
one of its descendants underwent numerous anagenic speciation events.
What the trees of figure 4 imply about the speciation process is really
quite minimal. Nodes represent species; connecting branches stand for the
begetting relation. Whether begetting requires splitting is left open. I

24. Attention was first drawn to the difference between trees and cladograms by Nelson
[ms]. Cracraft [1974], Platnick [1977], and Wiley [1979a,b, 1981] further developed the distinction. Nelson and Platnick [1981] departed from these earlier ideas by giving the notion
of cladogram a purely nonevolutionary meaning; for them, cladograms simply represent
certain sorts of similarities among taxa, not how those taxa fall into monophyletic groups.
Although Wiley [ms] has gone over to this newer usage, I persist in following the older
one; for me, both cladograms and trees express *evolutionary* hypotheses. The biological
usage of these terms has been too varied for my definitions to coincide with what all biologists have said; my hope, rather, is that what I have said is clear, internally consistent, and
well suited to the problem at hand. See Hull [1979] for historical reflection on the changes
that have occurred in cladistic terminology.
25. For discussion of the closely related idea that species are "individuals," see Ghiselin
[1974] and Hull [1978].

see no reason to build more than this into the concept of a phylogenetic tree (though others, of course, are free to propose different notational conventions).

The trees of figure 4 and the one shown in figure 2 also are agnostic on the question of whether species continue to exist after they have undergone splitting. Hennig [1966] took the position that a parent species ceases to exist whenever it splits to produce daughter species. Several cladists have held that there is no reason to assume that this always happens (e.g., Eldredge and Cracraft [1980], Wiley [1981]). If a worldwide species buds off a peripheral population in Madison, Wisconsin, which then evolves into a separate species, it is more plausible to hold that the parent species has survived the production of a single daughter. Hennig's principle seems most natural in the case of perfectly symmetrical splitting, but it is hard to believe that this is the general rule.[26]

Figure 2 depicts each species as appearing in a specific generation of the branching process; in subsequent generations, those species that originated earlier no longer appear in the figure. Does this mean that our representation requires Hennig's general view about the identity conditions of species? Not at all. There is an analogy here with family trees. This familiar form of representation does not presuppose that parents cease to exist when their children are born. This may be true, but the branching representation does not say that it is. Trees, in this sense, depict the temporal order in which species make their appearance, but do not say when they exit from the scene.

Enough has now been said about the goal of phylogenetic inference—determining monophyletic groupings among the taxa under investigation. We now need to understand how overall similarity and cladistic parsimony interpret the characteristics of taxa as bearing on competing hypotheses about relatedness.

Each of the species shown in figure 2 has numerous characteristics. For example, we might ask of each of them, whether it has or lacks a spinal chord, whether it has or lacks a heart of a certain sort, and so on. For simplicity, we shall assume that each character comes in just two states. Since species Zero is the ancestor of the taxa shown in figure 2, all its character states are, by definition, the *ancestral* (*plesiomorphic*) ones. These are con-

26. Philosophers will notice that this is a special case of the general problem of the identity conditions of enduring physical objects (cf., e.g., Hobbes's ship of Theseus). Perfectly symmetrical splitting is not best interpreted by treating *one* daughter rather than the other as identical with the parent (since this would be arbitrary), and identifying *both* daughters with the parent is ruled out, since transitivity of identity would then imply that the daughters are identical with each other. Since the daughters are all that remains after splitting, it follows that the parent has ceased to exist. See Splitter [1988] and Kitcher [ms] for discussion of this general point in connection with the problem of individuating species.

ventionally coded by a "0." Descendants of Zero may, of course, differ from this ancestor in one or many respects. These alternative character states[27] are termed *derived (apomorphic)* and are coded by a "1."

We now can formulate the problem of phylogenetic inference. Let us imagine that we sample three species from the tips of the tree depicted in figure 2. These species, once drawn, we shall call A, B, and C.[28] We then study each of these species to determine whether it has the ancestral or derived form for each of a given range of characters. To obtain this description of the taxa, we must know each character's *polarity*—which state is ancestral and which derived.[29] We wish to use the characters of the species to infer whether they are related as (AB)C, A(BC), or (AC)B.

The table below shows the (imagined) result of scoring the three species for each of the 51 characters we shall consider. Ignore the last character for the moment—pretend that we have before us the distribution pattern for the first fifty characters alone:

		Species		
		A	B	C
	1–45	1	0	0
Characters	46–50	1	1	0
	51	0	1	1

Focusing just on characters 1–50, we notice that B and C are by far the most similar pair. B and C are 90% similar, A and B are 10% similar, and A and C are 0% similar. So, if we let overall similarity guide us in making a phylogenetic inference, we shall take this data to best support the conclusion A(BC).

Note that this calculation of overall similarity takes account of two quite different kinds of matching. Characters 1–45 have the 100 distribution.[30] They involve *symplesiomorphies*—ancestral similarities. Characters of the second kind, which have the 110 distribution, involve *synapomorphies*—derived similarities. Since the data include 45 instances of the first kind of similarity but only 5 of the second, overall similarity reaches the conclusion that A(BC) is the true genealogical relationship.

27. The fact that the ancestral/derived distinction is relative to a level of hierarchy will be discussed in the next section.
28. I exclude the possibility of sampling from the interior of the tree just to simplify the exposition. Sampling from the tips ensures that tree (a) in figure 4 must be true if (AB)C is the correct cladistic grouping.
29. Assume for now that this is known; how it can be inferred will be discussed in section 6.5.
30. I shall follow the convention of describing character distributions in alphabetical order; a 100 distribution means that A is apomorphic (1) and B and C are plesiomorphic (0).

Cladistic parsimony takes the view that synapomorphies are evidence of phylogenetic relationship, but that symplesiomorphies are not. Given the 50 characters we are considering, cladistic parsimony would ignore 1–45 and would take 46–50 as best supporting the conclusion that the relationship is (AB)C. Cladistic parsimony, recall, is an elaboration of the idea of *special* similarity. It is not just any kind of matching that counts as evidence of common ancestry; it is derived—not ancestral—similarity that has evidential meaning.

The methods disagree about this simple example. Which is correct? That depends on the assumptions we are willing to make about character evolution. Earlier I promised an epistemological fairy tale that would provide an example in which parsimony makes sense, while overall similarity does not. Here it is: Let us suppose that each character can change at most once in the tree shown in figure 2. Since species Zero begins with all its characters in the ancestral state 0 (by definition), this stipulation means that a character may change once from 0-to-1, but can never change from 1-to-0. The once only rule also implies that the same character cannot change twice from 0-to-1.

This stipulation—that novelties originate once and are never lost[31] —implies that the synapomorphies present in characters 46–50 must correspond to a monophyletic group (AB)C. This would be true even if there were just one character with this 110 distribution. For imagine how evolution must proceed in this case. Zero begins in the plesiomorphic (0) state. Then, in some later generation, the apomorphic (1) form makes its appearance for the first time. Draw a cut there. All its descendants up to the tip of the tree must retain that novelty, and nowhere else in the tree may that novelty evolve again. This means that when we sample from the tree, the synapomorphic resemblance between A and B must indicate that A and B belong to a monophyletic group that does not include C.

What is the evidential meaning of the first 45 characters? These all involve symplesiomorphies. Since taking them as evidence of relatedness would conflict with the dictates of characters 46–50, we reject them. Notice, however, that the ancestral similarity of B and C is consistent with any possible degree of relatedness; it may be, for example, that B and C are maximally unrelated—that their most recent common ancestor is species Zero. On the other hand, our assumption about character evolution implies that species with a shared apomorphy *cannot* be maximally unrelated; they must have a common ancestor more recent than species Zero.

---

31. I introduce this as a highly contingent (and not generally plausible) assumption, not as a definition of "novelty." The idea that "real" novelties, by definition, cannot have multiple originations will be discussed in section 4.2.

A great deal will be said in succeeding chapters about the evidential meaning of synapomorphy and symplesiomorphy. My point here is just to provide a simple example that illustrates how cladistic parsimony can differ from the method of overall similarity. Overall similarity accords equal weight to synapomorphy and symplesiomorphy; cladistic parsimony views only the former as evidence of phylogenetic relationship.

The discussion thus far says nothing about whether cladistic parsimony or overall similarity is to be preferred, of course. The reason is that we have been working with the manifestly false assumption that novelties evolve once and can never be lost. If evolution obeyed this stipulation, overall similarity would be wrong and cladistic parsimony would be right. But this tells us nothing about the merits of these methods under other, more realistic, assumptions.

Since overall similarity accords equal weight to synapomorphy and symplesiomorphy, it does not need to determine which state of a character is ancestral and which derived. Cladistic parsimony, on the other hand, holds these two types of matching to fundamentally differ in their evidential significance. Because of this, the use of cladistic parsimony requires that one ascertain, for each character, which state is ancestral. The character states of species Zero are not given to us by direct observation; they are inferred. How this can be done—how one can determine the *polarity* of a character—I shall discuss in chapter 6.

1.4. *Character Incongruence and the Problem of Homoplasy*

It is easy for a philosopher to show that knowledge is possible in a world in which there are no illusions, hallucinations, misleading evidence, errors of reasoning, and so on. But whatever its idealizations and simplifications, philosophy has always grappled with the fact that the world is no epistemological paradise. The senses can malfunction. And even when they function properly, the world can generate misleading evidence and so make falsehood look more plausible than truth. The simple model of evolution just surveyed is a comparable paradise; if we know which character state is ancestral and which derived, and if we know that each character can change just once, then we cannot err in inferring monophyletic groups from synapomorphies. However, it now is necessary for the serpent to make his entrance.

We so far have considered the bearing of the first 50 characters (which, recall, show the 100 and the 110 patterns) displayed in the table of data given above. What happens if we add the fifty-first character to our data, which, recall, has a 011 distribution? The answer is that there must be some mistake. We have already seen that our assumption about character evolution—that a character may change just once—allows us to *deduce* that (AB)C is true from each of characters 46–50. However, when we take character 51 into account, this same assumption allows us to *deduce* from this new character that A(BC) is true. The problem is that (AB)C and A(BC) cannot be true together; recall that monophyletic groups cannot partially overlap.

If we were confident that characters cannot change more than once, we would have to look for a mistake in the way we scored the characters. Our observations would have to be wrong if this assumption about character evolution were correct. Perhaps the error was in thinking that character 51 involves a synapomorphy rather than a symplesiomorphy; we might, after all, have been mistaken about the *polarity* of the character—about which character state is ancestral and which derived. Other mistakes are possible too. But evolutionists will recognize that one thing that led us astray was the assumption about character evolution. As already noted, it just is not plausible to insist that evolutionary novelties can never arise more than once and can never be lost.

We now need to attend more carefully to how cladistic parsimony evaluates competing hypotheses in the light of incongruent data of the kind just described. Intuitively, the idea is that 110 favors (AB)C over A(BC), while a 011 character tells in the opposite direction. In exploring the implications of cladistic parsimony for such incongruent data, we are, of course, abandoning our fairly tale of once only changes.

Let us consider in more detail how (AB)C and A(BC) might account for the 51 characters in our example. We are assuming, recall, that these three taxa are sampled from the tip of the tree depicted in figure 2. This assumption about sampling allows us to associate a unique phylogenetic tree with each of the cladistic groupings (AB)C and A(BC). These two trees are shown in figure 5.[32] In this figure, I have labeled the branches in the two phylogenetic trees and also have written the 51 characters in the data set across the top.

Notice that a 110 character (i.e., any of characters 46–50) can be accommodated on the (AB)C tree with only a single evolutionary change occurring in the tree's interior. Species Zero begins in state 0, of course; if a single 0-to-1 change occurs on branch 4 and no other changes occur elsewhere in the tree, the 110 observation will be obtained at the tips. Other scenarios are possible, of course. Any odd number of changes on branch 4 with no changes elsewhere would suffice. And an odd number of changes on branch 4 with the other branches displaying an even number of changes would do the trick as well.

---

32. This simplifying assumption—that none of the three species is an ancestor of any of the others—is harmless, as far as the way parsimony calculations proceed. The reader is invited to recast the explanation of parsimony that follows in terms of cladograms rather than trees.

characters

| 1-45 | 46-50 | 51 |

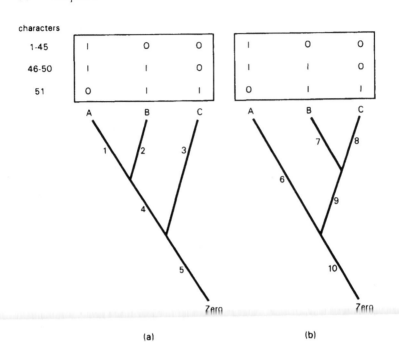

Figure 5.
Two phylogenetic trees and a data set of fifty-one characters that each tree must explain.
Tree (a) can account for characters 1–50 without requiring a homoplasy, but requires a
homoplasy to explain character 51. Tree (b) can account for characters 1–45 and 51
without requiring a homoplasy, but requires one homplasy for each of characters 46–50.
Tree (a) is therefore more parsimonious.

A 011 character (in our data set, character 51) on the (AB)C tree requires a different interpretation. At least two changes are necessary, if a
011 character is to evolve on the (AB)C tree shown in figure 5a. Two
0-to-1 changes on branches 2 and 3 would suffice. So would a 0-to-1 change
on branch 5 and a 1-to-0 change on branch 1.[33]

The mirror image situation arises when we ask the A(BC) hypothesis,
depicted in figure 5b, to account for these two kinds of characters. A 011
observation might have arisen on the A(BC) tree with a single 0-to-1
change in branch 9, although larger numbers of changes are consistent
with the tree's generating this character distribution. However, the A(BC)
tree cannot produce a 110 observation without there being at least two
changes in the tree's interior; for example, two 0-to-1 changes on

33. It is important to see that it is species Zero, not the most recent common ancestor of A,
B, and C, which is by definition plesiomorphic in all its characters. This is why (AB)C is
consistent with the apomorphies in a 011 character being homologues of each other. The
concept of homology will be discussed later in this section.

branches 6 and 7, or a 0-to-1 change on branch 10 and a 1-to-0 change on branch 8, would suffice.

We now can see why cladistic parsimony is properly so-called. This method of inference holds that the best supported phylogenetic hypothesis is the one that requires the fewest evolutionary changes. A 110 character counts in favor of (AB)C and against A(BC). The reason is that (AB)C requires only a single change, but A(BC) requires two, to account for a 110 character. Symmetrically, the 011 character counts against (AB)C and in favor of A(BC), because (AB)C requires more changes than A(BC) does to account for this sort of observation.

Note, in contrast, that both hypotheses can accommodate a 100 symplesiomorphy by postulating a single evolutionary change. In minimizing the number of evolutionary changes, it is synapomorphies, not symplesiomorphies, that play an evidential role. According to cladistic theory, a symplesiomorphy is explained equally well by any genealogical hypothesis and therefore fails to discriminate among them.

So what are we to do with the 51 characters in the data before us? Characters 1–45 can be set aside; they do not help us decide between (AB)C and A(BC). Characters 46–50 each exhibit the 110 pattern, so these characters favor (AB)C. Character 51 has a 011 distribution and therefore favors A(BC). So there are five "votes" favoring (AB)C and only a single "vote" favoring A(BC). If we assign the characters equal weight, then (AB)C is better supported, relative to all the data.[34] For the 51 characters taken together, (AB)C requires 45 + 5 + 2 = 52 evolutionary changes, whereas A(BC) requires 45 + 10 + 1 = 56.

I have described cladistic parsimony twice over. The method holds that synapomorphies, not symplesiomorphies, are evidence of genealogical relationship. It also holds that the best-supported hypothesis requires the fewest evolutionary changes. These two formulations are equivalent; they are two ways of understanding the same criterion for hypothesis evaluation. It also is customary to describe parsimony as holding that the best phylogenetic hypothesis requires the fewest *homoplasies*. This new concept requires definition.

If two species have a trait because one inherited it from the other or because they have a common ancestor that possessed it and transmitted it unchanged to them, then the trait in one species and the trait in the other are said to be *homologous*. However, if the resemblance is due to separate origination events, then the matching constitutes a *homoplasy*.[35]

34. The significance of character weighting will be discussed in section 6.6.
35. Homoplasy corresponds roughly to the more traditional term *analogy*. It subsumes both *parallelism* and *convergence*. In both cases, two descendants share a characteristic because of independent evolution. In convergence, the descendants resemble each other (in that respect) more than their ancestors did; in parallelism, they do not (Dobzhansky et al. [1977, p. 265]).

The synapomorphy found in a 110 character *might* be a homology if (AB)C is the true tree. The (AB)C tree does not require this, but leaves open the possibility that there was a single evolutionary change on branch 4. However, a 011 character must involve a homoplasy, one way or the other, if (AB)C is correct. If a 0-to-1 change had occurred on both branches 2 and 3, then the shared derived character exhibited by *B* and *C* would be homoplasious. On the other hand, if a single 0-to-1 change had occurred in branch 5 and a single 1-to-0 change in branch 1, then the synapomorphy shared by *B* and *C* would be homologous, but the ancestral character shared by species *A* and species Zero would be homoplasious. So (AB)C demands a homplasy to account for a 011 character, but does not require any to explain a 110 character.

If we shift our attention to the A(BC) tree, we reach symmetrical conclusions: this tree does not require any homoplasies to account for a 011 character, but does demand a homoplasy to explain a 110 character. Notice that neither tree requires a homoplasy to explain a symplesiomorphy (characters 1−45 in the data set).

This detailed examination of how different genealogical groupings can account for different kinds of character distributions shows that homologies and homoplasies differ in their epistemological properties. The conjunction of a tree with the data of (polarized) character distributions may imply that a particular character is homoplasious, but it never by itself implies that any character matching is a homology. It follows that synapomorphies and symplesiomorphies may be homologies, but they need not be. To speak of shared derived or ancestral characters is to indicate a *matching* between a pair of taxa, relative to the character state of some ancestor. But the details of character evolution between that ancestor and the two matching taxa are not vouchsafed by either claim of matching. Of course, if the idealized assumption we considered before that a character can change just once were correct, then both sorts of matching would be homologies. But without this assurance, it is a matter for further conjecture whether a synapomorphy or a symplesiomorphy is a homology.[36]

I noted before that the existence of incongruent characters is inconsistent with the rationale of cladistic parsimony described in the previous section. You cannot obtain characters showing the 110 and the 011 dis-

---

36. The term *synapomorphy* is frequently used in such a way that synapomorphies must be homologies. This terminological convention then leads to the distinction between "putative" synapomorphies (i.e., matching derived characters) and "real" ones (homologous derived characters). My alternative usage, wherein a synapomorphy may or may not involve a homology, is not without biological precedent and has several useful features. I attend to how biologists have used this concept in chapter 4 and to the advantages of my usage in chapters 4 and 6. Again, my goal in setting up terminology is clarity and consistency, fidelity to all the different usages presently in the field being impossible, even if it were desirable.

tribution (where "0" means ancestral and "1" derived) if novelties originate just once and are never lost. But let us consider replacing this absolute
prohibition against multiple originations and reversions with something
probabilistic. The tree in figure 2 has many branches. Let us suppose that
the probability of a change on any branch is sufficiently small that the expected number of changes in any character in the entire tree is far less than
unity. Rather than saying that independent originations and reversions are
impossible, we now maintain that they are very improbable; the expectation is that each character changes at most once.[37]

This modification has several implications. Here I shall speak fairly
loosely about what this probabilistic model says about the bearing of characters on hypotheses of descent. The opportunity for greater care will
come later, especially in chapter 5 and 6.

First, we must view synapomorphies as providing evidence for monophyletic groups, rather than as absolutely guaranteeing that they must
exist. A 110 character does not *deductively imply* that A and B form a monophyletic group apart from C; nor does a 011 character deductively imply
that B and C form a group apart from A. We cannot deduce phylogeny
from (polarized) character distributions anymore. Rather, characters are related to phylogenetic hypotheses the way a symptom is often related to a
disease. The presence of a symptom may support one disease hypothesis
better than it supports another; however, the best-supported hypothesis
may be false, even when the symptom is really present. A 110 character
favors (AB)C over A(BC), because the latter hypothesis would require
more changes, and we regard changes as very improbable events. Symmetrically, a 011 character favors A(BC) over (AB)C, because the former
requires fewer improbable events to explain the observations than the latter. Overall, we prefer that phylogenetic hypothesis that minimizes the
number of improbable events it requires. With changes assumed to be
very improbable, we are led to a sufficient condition for cladistic parsimony that does not rule out the possibility of incongruent data.[38]

Again, this rationale of parsimony is suggested as a (so far rough and
incompletely analyzed) sufficient condition, not a necessary one. Perhaps

37. Besides allowing incongruent character distributions to be possible, this probabilistic
proposal also has the virtue of avoiding action at a distance, which is apparently what it
would take for an evolutionary tree to satisfy the once only rule stated before. If a change
occurs in one part of the tree, how is this event supposed to foreclose the possibility of
changes occurring elsewhere? Physical mechanisms for propagating such causal influences
are not inconceivable, but it seems implausible to think that they will be present as a general rule.

38. Here we see a premonition of how the concept of *likelihood* can be used to assess the
plausibility of a phylogenetic hypothesis in the light of character data, given some assumptions about the evolutionary process. This will be discussed in detail in chapters 5 and 6.

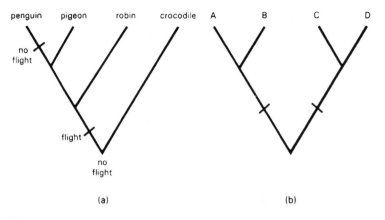

Figure 6.
(a) Flight is an apomorphy when the group considered includes penguins, pigeons, robins, and crocodiles, but the same trait is a plesiomorphy when the group is restricted to penguins, pigeons, and robins. (b) The similarity between A and B is a homology, as is the similarity between C and D, but the similarity between A and C is a homoplasy.

there are other reasons for thinking that synapomorphies and symplesiomorphies have the very different meanings that parsimony claims for them. We shall have to see. Indeed, we shall have to see whether the sufficient condition just mentioned stands up to critical scrutiny. For the moment, I hope it is clear that the implausibility of our initial process model (at most one change per character) leaves it open that another process model might take its place, one that shows why parsimony is preferable to overall similarity. And there is also the possibility that there are process models in which overall similarity makes sense as a method of inference. That too is something we shall have to consider.

The formulation of the principle of cladistic parsimony so far attained must be fine-tuned a little more. A character is not apomorphic or plesiomorphic absolutely, but only relative to a level within a branching process. If we were classifying pigeons, robins, and crocodiles, we might count the fact that the first two can fly as an apomorphy. However, if we were classifying penguins, pigeons, and robins, flight would be a plesiomorphic trait.[39] This relativity is illustrated in figure 6a.

The concepts of homology and homoplasy exhibit a comparable sort of relativity. Figure 6b shows a tree on which a character arose twice (slash marks indicate these events) and then persisted unchanged. The four ter-

39. It has been questioned whether flight was a novelty marking the origin of birds; perhaps flight was inherited from a flying reptilian ancestor. In any event, the conceptual point above about the relativity of the plesiomorphy/apomorphy distinction does not depend on this historical question.

minal species share the character in question. The matching of A and B will thereby count as a homology, as will the matching of C and D. On the other hand, that same character, as it occurs in A and C, will be homoplasious. Strictly speaking, it is not characters that are homologous or homoplasious, but *matchings* of characters. Whether a character is homoplasious depends on the objects whose matching is at issue.[40]

An example of this sort of relativity is afforded by the character of *bearing live young*. This trait is believed to be a homology *within* the mammals but to have arisen independently in some species of fish and snakes. With respect to a species of mammal and a species of fish, the matching is homoplasious. With respect to human beings and chimps, the matching counts as a homology. Flying within the birds and between birds and insects provides a similar example.

Another complication arises when we apply the distinction of homology and homoplasy to a character that is itself a complex ensemble of simpler traits. Consider the "wing" found in birds and bats. Some aspects of skeletal structure are homologous, since they were inherited (it is believed) from the forelimb of a common ancestor, but the modifications of that structure for flying evolved independently in the two lineages.

It also is important to realize that the distinction between character and character state is relative to the phylogenetic level of analysis. Within the primates, walking may be a character, whose states are upright and nonupright gait. However, within a broader cladistic unit, walking might count as a character state, whose alternative states are other forms of locomotion. The hierarchy here will be familiar to philosophers accustomed to drawing the determinable/determinate distinction.

Besides surveying some needed terminology, I have tried to show how a simple (if implausible) assumption about character evolution provides a justification for the methodology called cladistic parsimony. If characters change at most once in the passage from root to tips, then synapomorphies will infallibly pinpoint monophyletic groups, while symplesiomorphies can give no such assurance. If we make multiple origination and reversion very improbable rather than out-and-out impossible, then synapomorphies seem to provide very good evidence of relatedness and symplesiomorphies very poor evidence thereof. I have not proved this last claim, but merely suggest it as intuitively plausible (its more rigorous discussion must await chapter 6). We have not examined whether overall similarity will be a reasonable method, though the reader may perhaps imagine that a model of evolution can be invented in which that

---

40. In counting homoplasies for the purposes of calculating parsimony, one counts the number of *extra* originations. In the above example there is one homoplasy in this sense, though there are four pariwise matchings among the terminal taxa that are homoplasious.

method fulfills whatever requirements we might impose. Indeed, I conjecture that any method, regardless of how plausible it is, can be equipped with a process model that renders it the very soul of reason. But this parlor trick promises to offer little insight into the problem of phylogenetic inference.

A more promising approach would be available if we had confidence that a single detailed process model were correct for the set of taxa under investigation. But, as noted earlier, we often are as much in the dark about process as we are about pattern. In this case, it would be natural to investigate how logically weak the assumptions of a process model can be made while still permitting phylogenetic inference to proceed. But like Aesop's farmer, who killed a cow while trying to see how little food is required to keep it alive, we must realize that the strategy of weakening process assumptions must eventually terminate. At some point, pattern will be irretrievable, because our process assumptions will have become too meager.

However, before we descend any further into the details of the biological problem, it will be helpful to develop a more general perspective on the kind of inference problem we here confront. Parsimony, a central idea in phylogenetic inference, has been discussed as a constraint on nondeductive inference in general. Chapter 2 is devoted to this standard philosophical topic. In Chapter 3, I take up another philosophical lead that promises to illuminate the biological problem. The *principle of the common cause* has been recommended as a plausible constraint on how we should reconstruct the causal ancestry of observed effects. Identifying this principle's strengths and limitations will provide additional purchase on the question of how genealogical relationships are to be ascertained. With these two chapters of philosophy under our belts, we shall take a fine-grained look at the systematic issues beginning in chapter 4.

Chapter 2

The Philosophical Problem of Simplicity

2.1. Local and Global Parsimony

In the first chapter, I explained the method of phylogenetic inference called cladistic parsimony. That method maintains that synapomorphies (matches with respect to derived characters) are evidence of genealogical relationship, but that symplesiomorphies (matches with respect to ancestral characters) are not. Equivalently, it holds that the best-supported phylogenetic hypothesis is the one that requires the fewest homoplasies. This latter formulation shows why the method has come to be called "parsimony." The idea is that the best explanation of the data is the one that minimizes a particular quantity.

My main purpose in chapter 1 was to raise a question without answering it: What must be true of the evolutionary process if one is to be rational in using parsimony to make phylogenetic inferences? We have seen that the nonexistence of homoplasies is a *sufficient* condition for parsimony to be right in its judgment that synapomorphies have a significance that symplesiomorphies do not possess. However, sufficiency is not necessity. We have yet to see what cladistic parsimony presupposes. The suspicion may present itself that parsimony actually requires that homoplasies are rare, but so far this is only a suspicion.

Discussion among biologists of cladistic parsimony has in some ways recapitulated discussion of parsimony and simplicity among philosophers of science. Philosophers standardly observe that in any research context, there will be many possible alternative hypotheses that are each consistent with the observations. How is one to choose among them? Philosophers and scientists as well have often claimed that it is part of the scientific method to prefer simple, parsimonious hypotheses. A question then arises: What does this preference presuppose? In particular, does appeal to simplicity commit one to thinking that nature is simple?

In this chapter, I shall trace some of the philosophical ideas that have been developed in answer to this question. The idea that the use of simplicity in scientific inference requires substantive assumptions about the physical world has fallen into disrepute. In this century, virtually all writers in the philosophy of science have rejected this thesis as mistaken or confused. It was not always so. An earlier tradition interpreted the use of a simplicity criterion as resting on a substantive thesis about the nature of the world (section 2.3). We must see why that "ontological" position[1] has been replaced by the idea that parsimony is "purely methodological" (section 2.4). I shall argue that all is not well with this now rather standard philosophical position; other work in the philosophy of science, not explicitly addressed to the nature of parsimony, forces us to reopen the question (section 2.5).

The reader will notice that little will be said in this chapter that is specific to the problem of phylogenetic inference. The reason is that philosophers have tended to discuss parsimony as a *global constraint* on scientific reasoning.[2] They usually have thought that there is a single principle of parsimony—one that finds multiple applications in physics, in biology, and, indeed, in all fields of human inquiry.

A powerful impetus behind this assumption about scientific inference is its plausibility in the case of deduction and the attractiveness of the analogy between deduction and induction. In a deductively valid argument, if the premises are true, then the conclusion must be true as well. In an inductively strong argument, the truth of the premises confirms, makes probable, or provides considerable support for the truth of the conclusion. Philosophers often see deduction as a limiting case of induction—one in which the premises provide maximally strong reasons for the conclusion.

This analogy has not gone unchallenged. But even those philosophers who find flaws in it usually maintain that there is another analogy that is persuasive. A valid deductive argument is valid in virtue of its form, not its subject matter. The following two arguments are both valid. Moreover, they are valid for the same reason, even though their subject matters are entirely disjoint:

| All fish swim. | All particles have mass. |
All sharks are fish.	All electrons are particles.
All sharks swim.	All electrons have mass.

Logicians represent what these arguments have in common by schematizing them in the following way:

1. An "ontological" thesis is one that is about the way the world is—hence my use of this term for the view that the use of parsimony or simplicity presupposes something substantive about the way the world is.
2. Hesse's review article [1967] is a useful guide to the philosophical literature. In addition to the theories she discusses, proposed by Jeffreys [1957], Popper [1959], Kemeny [1953], and Goodman [1958], more recent work includes Quine [1966], Friedman [1972], Sober [1975], Rosenkrantz [1977], and Glymour [1980].

All B's are C.

All A's are B.

_____

All A's are C.

The letters are placeholders for which any term of the appropriate gram-matical type may be substituted, thus yielding a deductively valid argu-ment. Rules of valid deduction thus seem to be invariant over change in subject matter. They are *global*, in that they apply to arguments in *all* sciences.

When philosophers, scientists, and statisticians discuss principles of non-deductive inference, they generally assume that those principles will also be global. Open any statistics text and you will find recipes for calculating confidence intervals, likelihood ratios, measures of goodness-of-fit, etc., that are supposed to apply to any empirical subject matter. The text may discuss the example of estimating the average height in a population of giraffes, but everybody knows that this is only an example. The rules are global, applying to the problem of estimating the mean of *any* attribute in *any* population of objects.

Thus, it is entirely natural for those who believe that parsimony is part of the scientific method to think that it is a global principle. Correctly understood, the principle of parsimony is sufficiently abstract to apply to a problem of adjudicating between competing hypotheses, no matter what those hypotheses are about.

This assumption about parsimony may be correct. But I must stress that it is an assumption. In the case of deductive inference, we are on much firmer ground when we claim that there are valid global principles of infer-ence. The reason is that we can actually state rules of deductive inference that are plausible and then point out that they are invariant over changes in subject matter. But no one yet has been able to formalize a global con-cept of simplicity that is completely plausible as a constraint on all scien-tific inference. This does not mean that simplicity is not global, only that our understanding of nondeductive inference is far more rudimentary than our grasp of deduction.

Whatever opinion the reader may have on this matter, the status of cladistic parsimony is much clearer. Cladistic parsimony is stated in terms of the ideas of synapomorphy, symplesiomorphy, and homoplasy. It ap-plies to hypotheses about genealogical relationship, not to hypotheses concerning other subjects. Cladistic parsimony is a *local* principle of non-deductive inference.

How, then, is the global notion of parsimony, which is discussed in the philosophy of science, related to the local notion of parsimony used in phylogenetic inference? That is an important question, which I shall leave open for now. We shall see in chapter 4 that some biologists have suggested that cladistic parsimony is a consequence of global parsimony. The idea is that since the scientific method says that simple hypotheses are preferable to complex ones, systematists should use cladistic parsimony to infer phylogenetic relationships. At this juncture, I take no stand on the correctness of this claim. My present point is to note that it requires an argument: we must begin with *two* notions of parsimony—one local, the other global—and then try to see what connection there is between them.

For now, I shall concentrate on the global notion. Why think that the scientific method[3] includes a principle of parsimony? And does this principle assume anything substantive about the physical world?

This chapter will proceed genealogically. In the next section, I describe the historical origins of the way philosophers in this century have come to think about parsimony and simplicity. Here the focus will be on what such methodological criteria say, not on what they presuppose about the way the world is: I shall try to describe those characteristic forms of inference that have been thought to involve appeals to parsimony and simplicity. In section 2.3, I take up the question about presupposition by describing an older tradition of thought, not now much in vogue, according to which parsimony is a reasonable device to use in scientific inference only because the world has certain contingent properties. The idea that the principle of parsimony is substantive, not purely methodological, has met with criticism, which will be detailed in section 2.4. So the result to this point may seem to favor the idea that parsimony is purely methodological rather than substantive. However, in section 2.5, I develop reasons for reversing this verdict. In the end, I reach a conclusion that parallels the hunch introduced in the previous chapter: *Whenever a scientist appeals to parsimony to justify the conclusion that one hypothesis is more reasonable than another in the light of observational data, substantive assumptions about the world must be involved. In practice, parsimony cannot be "purely methodological."*

2.2. Two Kinds of Nondeductive Inference

Discussion of simplicity in twentieth-century philosophy of science traces back to two main sources: one philosophical, the other scientific. This dual ancestry is important, in that the issues stemming from the problem's

---

3. In referring occasionally to "the" scientific method, I may perhaps give the impression that I hold that there is a single corpus of methods that all scientific disciplines have used at all times. I hold no such thing. Indeed, the conclusion I shall reach about the status of simplicity will point to one way in which a science's methodology must be informed by its substantive picture of the world. At this point, however, I shall assume, just for the sake of argument, that there are global and invariant canons of method.

philosophical roots differ markedly from the ones that emerged from the problem's scientific context.

The philosophical provenance of current thought about simplicity goes back to Hume's problem of induction. In discussing whether induction could be rationally justified, Hume gave prominent place to an idea he called the Principle of the Uniformity of Nature. Twentieth-century philosophers who differed over many points of detail often agreed that nondeductive inference exploits a principle of simplicity. Hume's Principle of the Uniformity of Nature was an ancestor of this idea; the thought that what we observe in the local places and times to which we have access also applies to other regions of space and time—perhaps even to the universe as a whole—is the idea that the world is simple in a certain way. Uniformity—the idea of homogeneity through space and changelessness through time—is a kind of simplicity. In thinking that what we locally observe has a more global application, we are making a simple extrapolation from the observed to the unobserved.

Although a genealogical connection is to be found between Hume and twentieth-century discussion, the descent did not proceed without modification. Contemporary philosophers typically thought that induction is a kind of argument in which premises and conclusion are linked by a particular rule of inference. In trying to characterize this form of argument, they took themselves to be describing a pattern of reasoning that scientists and everyday people frequently follow in the process of attempting to learn about the world.

Hume, on the other hand, thought of induction as a habit, not as an inferential process at all. In the *Inquiry* he says that "the most ignorant and stupid peasants, nay infants, nay even brute beasts, improve by experience and learn the qualities of natural objects by observing the effects which result from them" (Hume [1748, p. 52]). In the cases Hume cites, induction does not involve drawing conclusions from premises that include the assumption that nature is uniform. For Hume, inductions of this sort are not reasoned inferences at all. Hume held that the habit of expecting the future to resemble the past in particular respects is like a knee-jerk reflex. Your leg kicks when the physician hits your knee with a hammer, but no inference and no assumption about the uniformity of nature mediates the transition from stimulus to response.

Although Hume thought that induction often proceeds without the aid of inferential argument, I take it that he did not want to claim that we *never* self-consciously reason from past to future by appeal to the uniformity principle. The examples that Hume cites notwithstanding, it is arguable that we do this in scientific controversy and when our beliefs are challenged in everyday life. Hume's point was that it overintellectualizes what we do to interpret expectations about the future as *always* arising psychologically by a process of inference.

At the same time that Hume derided the idea that our expectations about the future are typically mediated by inference, he also claimed that induction assumes that nature is uniform. Indeed, this latter idea is the core of what is now regarded as Hume's skeptical argument about the rational justifiability of induction. How do we know that the sun will rise tomorrow, based on our observations that it has regularly risen in the past? Hume argues that any attempt to justify this expectation by way of reasoned argument must appeal to the assumption that the future will be like the past. But the thesis that it *will* be—the Principle of the Uniformity of Nature—is not something for which we have empirical evidence. Any attempt to use past observations to support this principle must, thought Hume, beg the question. Nor can the uniformity principle be known by reasoning alone. The principle, Hume concludes, is neither *a posteriori* nor *a priori* justifiable. Hume's question about induction led him to a skeptical conclusion: Our inductive practices rest on habit and custom, and cannot be justified by rational argument.[4]

Thus, Hume held that inference about the future presupposes a uniformity principle, even though he did not think that this is a premise assumed by all who have inductive expectations about the future. But how can *induction* assume something that many, if not all, *inducers* do not even believe? Here we must appeal to a distinction that became quite standard in twentieth-century philosophy of science, between the *context of discovery* and the *context of justification*.

The psychological processes by which people come to hold the beliefs they do about the future are part of the context of discovery. Once those beliefs are formulated, we may inquire into their rational foundations. We may ask what the best arguments are that could be offered on their behalf. When people reason badly or not at all, it will emerge that the arguments proposed in answer to this latter question do not describe the psychological processes of discovery. But if our interest is in the question of justification, this need not matter. We want to find the best case that can be made for the belief in question, whether or not this was what drove the agent to that belief in the first place.

---

4. Hume did not suggest that we abandon this habit. This we cannot do; the making of inductions, Hume thought, is as much a part of human nature as breathing. Nor did he espouse the anarchistic position that all empirical beliefs are equally irrational; Hume criticized superstition (e.g., he derides belief in miracles) and set forth principles for distinguishing strong inductive inferences from weak ones. However, this rejection of "anything goes" occurs within a context. If we accept as legitimate and unobjectionable the idea that we have inductive expectations, we then can separate strong inductions from weak ones. But once we step back from this inevitable part of life and ask what justifies it, we are bound to find that no rational argument can be produced in its behalf.

Hume's skepticism was a conclusion he reached about the context of justification. Our beliefs about the future are not rationally justifiable. The best argument that can be offered in their favor, Hume thought, was as follows. The premises include observations on the one hand and the Principle of the Uniformity of Nature on the other. Taken together, these license our belief that the sun will rise tomorrow or that tomorrow's bread will nourish just as today's did. That this argument rests on a premise that cannot itself be rationally defended shows that the demand for justifying arguments has gone too far. It does not show that anything is radically amiss in our inductive practices as a whole. This, I take it, is how Hume's "naturalism" combines harmoniously with his "skepticism." The skepticism concerns the possibility of a certain sort of reasoned justification, not the legitimacy of this unavoidable aspect of human life.

In what follows, I shall set aside two elements in Hume's views on induction, important though they may be. First there is Hume's psychological opinion that individuals do not standardly formulate arguments when they form inductive expectations. This claim about the context of discovery will not occupy me further. Nor shall I be much concerned with Hume's skepticism about the rational defensibility of inductive inference. Never mind whether his analysis of inductive inference leads to skepticism. My interest will be in a logical structure I shall call Hume's *rational reconstruction of induction*. This is what Hume took to be the "best case" that could be made for the thesis that our expectations about the future are rationally justified. Hume held that the best rational reconstruction of an inductive inference rests on an assumption—the Principle of the Uniformity of Nature. He held that observations by themselves do not suffice to make one inductive conclusion more reasonable than any other that also is consistent with the observations. An extra premise is needed. Hume's suggestion was that this additional ingredient is a simplicity (uniformity) criterion; once this is added, present observations can be brought to bear on what our future expectations ought to be.

The way Hume formulates his uniformity principle is worth noting. He says that inductive arguments assume something about *the world*: they presuppose that *nature* is uniform or that *the future* will resemble *the past*. Twentieth-century formulations have usually preferred to leave the world out of it. Now a principle of simplicity would probably be formulated by saying that we prefer simple *hypotheses* over complex ones. Given that the sun has risen each day in the past, it is simpler to think that the sun will rise tomorrow than that the sun will fail to rise. It is hypotheses, not nature itself, that now are said to be simple. Eventually we must consider whether this switch from world to words makes any difference. Does using the principle about *hypotheses* require us to believe that *nature* is itself simple?

I have presented Hume's rational reconstruction of induction in terms of an inference from observations of past events to a conjecture about the future. But this is not entirely accurate, nor is it sufficiently general. The past is as much beyond our observations as the future is. What we may rely on, according to this Humean point of view, is our *present* observations and mental states. We seem to remember previous sunrises; we use these present memory traces to ground our expectation about tomorrow. But one might just as well ask why our present memories are reliable indicators of what actually happened in the past. After all, memory is fallible. Our beliefs about the past, if they are rationally justified at all, must be justified in virtue of our present mental states. This is what grounds our belief that the sun has risen each day that we have bothered to make an observation.

And, of course, there is the *distant* past as well: there is the past that happened before any of us made any observations at all. Rather than infer tomorrow's sunrise from ones in the present and the recent past, one could equally ask how we infer a prehistoric sunrise from this same data. Hume's problem embraces knowledge of the past just as much as it does knowledge of the future. And equally caught in its grip are our beliefs about generalizations. If we believe, to change the example, that all emeralds are green, based on the fact that all the emeralds we have examined are green,[5] we might ask why the observations justify belief in the generalization.

According to this Humean picture, we begin with observations of the here and now and our present memory traces as data and then try to infer beyond them. There are three sorts of hypotheses (at least) that we might come to believe on this basis. In each case, our conviction that the available data provide evidence for the conclusion we reach depends on the assumption that nature is uniform. This structure is shown below.

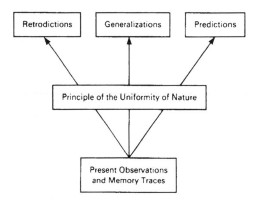

5. Here and in what follows, use of the example of inferring that all emeralds are green will assume that it is not a definitional truth that all emeralds are green.

Many modern philosophers of science have thought that an analog of Hume's insertion of a simplicity (uniformity) criterion into the rational reconstruction of induction is to be found in the so-called curve-fitting problem. Suppose we want to infer the general relationship between two empirical quantities—the pressure and temperature in a chamber of gas, say. To begin with a simple experiment, we might place a sealed pot on the stove and insert a thermometer and a pressure gauge. We then could heat the pot to various temperatures and record the corresponding pressures. The resulting data could be recorded on Cartesian coordinates, each data point representing a single observation. The problem of guessing the general relationship between pressure and temperature in this system then takes the form of deciding which curve to draw. If we are certain that our measurements are perfectly precise, we might demand that a curve pass exactly through each data point. If we are less confident, we instead might require that a curve minimize how much it departs from the data points (this being spelled out by some goodness-of-fit measure). We saw that Hume's problem can be formulated for three sorts of hypotheses—retrodictions, predictions, and generalizations. A parallel multiplicity applies to the curve-fitting problem. We may consider the problem of inferring a general curve from data points or we may focus on issues of interpolation or extrapolation. Instead of asking for the general relationship, I might simply want to know how much pressure the pot would contain if it were heated to some temperature different from the ones I have already produced experimentally.

Philosophers have often used this inference problem to argue for the importance of simplicity in science. Any curve that passes through the data points is consistent with everything we have observed. But there are infinitely many such curves. To choose between them, one must invoke a reason beyond consistency with the evidence. Here it has been customary to invoke simplicity. Smooth curves are simple. Scientists, in preferring the smoothest curve, exhibit their preference for simplicity. The structure of the curve-fitting problem is shown in figure 7.

In both Hume's problem and in the curve-fitting problem, the philosophical thesis has been advanced that a principle of simplicity bridges the gap between observations and hypotheses. However, it might be suggested that a quite different kind of answer should be given to the problems just formulated. When asked how we know that the sun will rise tomorrow, why not appeal to our well-confirmed theory of planetary motion? When asked about the pressure a closed chamber would exhibit if it were heated to a given temperature, why not answer by appealing to our theory of gases? These theories allow us to make predictions, but without any mention of simplicity. If this sort of answer is plausible, our reason for

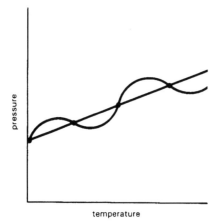

Figure 7.
The curve-fitting problem: Infinitely many curves can be drawn through the data points. Preference for a smooth curve is said to reflect scientists' implicit use of a simplicity criterion in hypothesis evaluation.

thinking that inductive inference must involve an appeal to simplicity seems to have disappeared.

The standard philosophical reply to this suggestion is to ask what justifies our theories of planetary motion and of the kinetics of gases. These ultimately must rest on observations, so Hume's problem must eventually be faced. By appealing to empirical theories, we just postpone having to recognize the use of simplicity in inductive inference. We begin with observations; all our theories, predictions, and retrodictions ultimately trace back for their justification to them and to them *alone*. This conception of how inductive inference works I shall call the *Principle of Empiricism*.[6]

So far I have considered the Humean provenance of modern discussions of simplicity. But there is a second reason that philosophers have had for thinking that simplicity is a central criterion for evaluating hypotheses. It is to be found in that other main source of our present understanding of scientific inference—namely, the arguments found in science itself. Einstein's theories of relativity and the scientific and philosophical discussions of the geometry of physical space that preceded Einstein's work (for example, the writings of Riemann, Gauss, Mach, and Poincaré) exerted a powerful influence on twentieth-century philosophy of science as well.

Rather than attempting to describe the way parsimony figured in Einstein's development of the special and general theories of relativity, I

6. Empiricism is not the truism that the senses are an indispensable source of information about the world. Rather, it is the nontrivial claim that, roughly speaking, observation is a sufficient rational basis for the beliefs we have. See, for example, Popper [1963, p. 54].

shall describe an influential thought experiment of the sort that convinced many writers in the modern period that parsimony crucially influences the kind of picture of the world we construct. Hans Reichenbach [1949, 1951] describes an experiment that Gauss proposed for determining which of the various mathematically consistent geometries is true of the physical space we inhabit. In Euclidean geometry, a triangle always has an angle sum of 180°. However, in Riemannian geometry, the angle sum is greater than 180°. whereas in Lobachevskian geometry the angle sum is less than 180°; in these last two cases, the amount of departure from the Euclidean value is a function of how large the triangle is.

According to Reichenbach, Gauss had tried to solve the question about physical space by measuring the angles of a triangle he set up between the tops of three mountains. The sides of his triangle were light rays. Gauss could detect no departure in his experiment from the Euclidean prediction. On the face of it, this may have been because space really is Euclidean, or because the departure from the Euclidean value was too small to detect, given the size triangle considered and the measurement devices used.

But Reichenbach argued that the problem of testing a geometry is more subtle. Even if Gauss had found a significant departure from the Euclidean value, the possibility would still remain that the light rays did not move in straight lines. For example, if they were acted on by some force that bent them from rectilinear motion, the measurement would not have the implication that Gauss envisioned.

This, too, might seem like a straightforwardly testable matter. After all, in principle we could take a meter rod and see whether the path followed by each light ray is the shortest possible path between the vertices they join—the path traversed by the smallest number of meter rods laid end to end would count as straight. But this suggestion, also, is open to challenge: suppose there were a strange force that not only perturbs light from straight line motion, but also affects the length of our measuring rods. After all, in checking to see if the light moved in straight lines, we assumed that the rods remain the same length as we move them about in the process of measuring.

Suppose this experiment is carried out for a very large triangle, and that the perturbations of all known physical forces are taken into account. We correct for the known physical ways that the signal ray may be affected, and find that the angle sum still departs significantly from 180°. According to Reichenbach, we would then face a choice: we could accept the physical theory we now have at hand, and conclude that space is non-Euclidean. Or we could maintain that space is Euclidean by supplementing our physical theory with a hypothetical force, one that is carefully described so that it cannot be detected by any empirical procedure. This newly postulated force would have no independent confirmation; it is introduced simply to save Euclidean geometry from refutation.

Consider the two total theories we now confront. Each conjoins a geometric claim and a physical one. Reichenbach held that the two theories are *observationally equivalent*; any observation consistent with one is consistent with the other. They may differ, he conceded, in their simplicity. Arguably, it is unparsimonious to postulate an undetectable force. But this difference in parsimony, Reichenbach claimed, is merely aesthetic, since no observational test could ever decide which of the two total theories is true.[7]

Reichenbach's argument might appear to be basically the same as Descartes's puzzle about the evil demon. I take it you believe that you now are seeing a printed page before you. Descartes might ask what justifies this belief as opposed to the hypothesis that your senses are now being misled by an evil demon. If we set up the "normal" and the "evil demon" hypotheses carefully enough, we can ensure that they will be *experientially equivalent*: any experience consistent with one will be consistent with the other. Paralleling Reichenbach, we might remark that it is unparsimonious to think that there are evil demons and then ask why this should count as a reason for thinking one hypothesis true and the other false.

If there were nothing more to Reichenbach's puzzle than this, it would show us nothing *special* about the status of geometry. We would not have discerned a *special* sense in which geometric hypotheses are "conventional" or "untestable" that does not apply with equal force to any hypothesis (such as "there is a printed page before me").

However, for better or worse, twentieth-century philosophy of science did accord such arguments a special significance. It was widely held that choice between empirically equivalent theories on the basis of parsimony was at the core of Einstein's reasoning to the special and general theories of relativity. Although Descartes' problem was a purely philosophical one, it was thought that the family of problems of which the Reichenbach puzzle is an example bore scientific fruit.

The correctness of this argument and its pertinence to scientific ques-

---

7. The hypothesis that the sun will rise tomorrow and the hypothesis that it will not are both consistent with my *past* observations. But this does not make them observationally equivalent in the intended sense. Though they agree over what has been observed to date, they do not agree over all *possible* observations. Likewise, hypotheses that agree over the present but disagree about the distant past may be observationally nonequivalent, if a suitably situated observer back then could have gathered pertinent data. The idea of its being "possible" to test two competing hypotheses observationally certainly requires elucidation; philosophies that depend on this idea (like logical positivism) have been heavily attacked for the unclarity of this idea. However, since our purpose here is just to grasp the background of philosophical discussion of simplicity, I shall not pursue this matter further.

tions about the two theories of relativity need not detain us. Whether questions like Reichenbach's show something special about physical theories of space, time, and geometry, or merely show that Descartes' puzzle can be applied to anything, is an important issue I shall not address. I mention this line of argument because it is the second factor that shaped twentieth-century thinking about simplicity. Philosophers and scientists had for a very long time acknowledged the idea we now call Ockham's razor—that "entities should not be postulated without necessity." This methodological maxim took on heightened importance for modern philosophy of science when it was seen as a crucial element in scientific work of the first importance.

From Hume, philosophy of science in our century learned the importance of simplicity in induction;[8] from Mach, Poincaré, and Einstein, it learned the importance of parsimony in theoretical explanation. Reichenbach's [1938, 1949] treatment of these two themes is rather typical in this regard. For hypotheses that are not observationally equivalent—which disagree over some possible observation, whether we shall ever make it or not—a difference in simplicity is a reason for thinking one hypothesis true and the other false. It is simpler to expect the sun to rise tomorrow just as it has in days past, and this counts as a reason for expecting it to do so. However, when the hypotheses differ over no possible observation—as in the case of Descartes' evil demon or, if Reichenbach was right, in the case of total theories of geometry plus physics—we have here a conventional, rather than a substantive, difference. According to Reichenbach and many others, there is no question of deciding which of these hypotheses is true or more plausible, but only of saying which is more convenient.[9]

---

8. Even those philosophers who saw themselves as opposed fundamentally to Hume's views about scientific inference were very much influenced by his ideas about uniformity. Thus, Popper [1959] rejects the idea of "induction," but sees simplicity as an indispensable device for comparing competing hypotheses each of which is consistent with the observations. Instead of thinking of induction as a process leading from observations to generalizations, Popper thinks of some generalizations as being better "corroborated." When two generalizations are both consistent with the observations, Popper holds that the simpler is better corroborated in his sense. It was not just "inductivists" who thought simplicity important. Popper's views will be discussed in chapter 4.

9. If simplicity is a reason for thinking one hypothesis true and another false in the case of observationally nonequivalent hypotheses, why does it suddenly become a merely aesthetic consideration when the hypotheses are observationally equivalent? The logical positivists had an answer in their verification theory of meaning: Observationally equivalent hypotheses are synonymous, so assigning different truth values to them would be absurd. However, for those who reject this theory of meaning, the question is a pressing one; I see no reason to think that simplicity is a reason in one kind of problem but not in the other (Sober [1975]).

Puzzles in the philosophy of physics about observationally equivalent theories have no ready analogs in the case of phylogenetic inference. Competing genealogical hypotheses of the kind discussed in chapter 1 are not observationally equivalent, in the sense in which philosophers use that term. So problems peculiar to the case of observationally equivalent hypotheses need not detain us. Nevertheless, the two sources of modern thought about parsimony and simplicity are still both relevant to our inquiry.

Humean ideas about a principle of uniformity pertain to *inductive* arguments. We observe a sample of objects and describe their properties; we then wish to extend that description to objects not in the sample. So, for example, Hume would picture us as noting that each observed *emerald* is *green*, and then asking whether this makes it reasonable to hold that all *emeralds* are *green*. Note that the vocabulary present in an inductive conclusion is already present in the premises. Inductive arguments have this characteristic feature; simplicity as uniformity has been thought to be a maxim that guides this kind of inference.

Parsimony, on the other hand, is not on the face of it a principle concerning smooth extrapolation. It concerns what we should postulate. It applies, not to induction, but to a variety of inference that C. S. Pierce called abduction—to inference to the best explanation. Here we imagine ourselves to confront some observations and to ask which of sereral competing hypotheses best explains them. The hypotheses considered may be stated in a vocabulary that is not already present in the observations. Parsimony in abduction says that one hypothesis is *ceteris paribus* preferable to another when it postulates fewer entities or processes.

Both these simplicity principles have been sketched in only their vaguest outlines. I have not said with any precision how uniformity is to be measured, or how paucity of explanatory machinery is to be gauged. This question of what simplicity is has yet to be answered successfully in any philosophical work. However, it will emerge in what follows that our pressing problems about this philosophical concept can be addressed without a detailed and precise description of what makes one theory, hypothesis, or explanation simpler than another. This is because the main problem for understanding simplicity is not to give a theory that measures this concept with precision, but to describe how simplicity functions within the broader context of hypothesis evaluation.

So, to use a biological formulation, our interest in simplicity will be more in its function than its structure; we want to know what simplicity *does*, not what it *is*. And a point of the first importance has already emerged. Despite the fact that philosophers have not successfully defined uniformity or parsimoniousness, they have in their discussions ascribed to simplicity a very definite methodological role. Whether the problem is inductive or abductive, the role of simplicity is inevitably described as follows: Two hypotheses are both consistent with the observations. Simplicity is then cited as a reason for preferring one to the other. Simplicity plus consistency with the observations is cited as a dual criterion. This description of the role played by a principle of simplicity in scientific inference, we shall see, is pregnant with implications as to whether simplicity is "purely methodological" or demands substantive assumptions about the way the world is.

2.3. A Lapsed Ontological Tradition

If one is attracted to the analogy between induction and deduction, and thinks of simplicity as a crucial ingredient in inductive inference, then the idea that simplicity is "purely methodological" may be almost irresistible. It is part of the scientific method, which, like deduction, is a method that is reasonably used to investigate the empirical world, no matter what that world in fact is like. We do not have to understand empirical facts about the subject matter we are investigating before we can use deductive rules of inference. Goodman [1967, pp. 348–349] nicely describes the parallel view about simplicity as holding that "the uniformity required is not in nature's activities but in our account of them. . . . In this version, the Principle of Uniformity does not tell nature how to behave but tells us how to behave if we are to be scientific."

Perhaps the idea that simplicity is "purely methodological" is now the majority view. Be that as it may, matters were not always thus. Hume, I have noted, formulated his principle in terms of the way the world is. The proposition that nature is uniform he regarded as contingent—there being no contradiction, he thought, in its denial. Hume went on to argue that we have no rational justification for this basic ontological assumption. But before Hume, philosophers frequently articulated ontological grounds for the simplicity principles they espoused.

Rather than attempting a full historical account of this ontological tradition, I shall describe one of its most influential practitioners. Newton's views on scientific method assign fundamental importance to maxims of parsimony and simplicity. As we shall see, Newton did not hesitate to justify the use of such principles by appealing to structural features of the world.[10]

10. Another, perhaps more idiosyncratic, representative of this ontological tradition was Leibniz, who held that God created the world so as to maximize the diversity of its phenomena and the simplicity of its laws. The actual world is the best of all possible worlds in this sense. Leibniz extracted detailed methodological advice from this ontological thesis: science was to represent natural phenomena as minimizing or maximizing some relevant quantity, since such "extremal" laws are simplest.

In the *Principia*, Newton lists four "Rules of Reasoning in Philosophy"—
the first two emphasizing parsimony, the second two uniformity (Newton
[1953, pp. 3—5]):

> 1. *We are to admit no more causes of natural things than such as are both
> true and sufficient to explain their appearances.* To this purpose the phi-
> losophers say that Nature does nothing in vain, and more is in vain
> when less will serve; for Nature is pleased with simplicity and affects
> not the pomp of superfluous causes.
>
> 2.   *Therefore to the same natural effects we must, as far as possible, assign
> the same causes.* As to respiration in a man and in a beast, the descent
> of stones in Europe and in America, the light of our culinary fire and
> of the sun, the reflection of light in the earth and in the planets.
>
> 3. *The qualities of bodies, which admit neither intensification nor remission
> of degrees, and which are found to belong to all bodies within the reach of
> our experiments, are to be esteemed the universal qualities of all bodies
> whatsoever.* For since the qualities of bodies are only known to us by
> experiments, we are to hold for universal all such as universally agree
> with experiments, and such as are not liable to diminution can never
> be quite taken away. We are certainly not to relinquish evidence of
> experiments for the sake of dreams and vain fictions of our own devis-
> ing; nor are we to recede from the analogy of Nature, which is wont
> to be simple and always consonant to itself . . . .
>
> 4. *In experimental philosophy we are to look upon propositions inferred by
> general induction from phenomena as accurately or very nearly true, not-
> withstanding any contrary hypothesis that may be imagined, till such time
> as other phenomena occur by which they may either be made more accurate
> or liable to exceptions.* This rule we must follow, that the argument of
> induction may not be evaded by hypotheses.

The biological reader may find especially interesting Newton's remark
in the second rule about "respiration in a man and in a beast." It would be
an absurd anachronism to ask whether Newton meant that all similarities
are evidence of common ancestry or that only some of them (synapomorphies) are. But we can see here a general principle finding immediate application in the task of explaining organic similarity. Of course,
when Newton proposed that respiration in man and beast be traced back
to a common cause, he had God in mind, not an ancestral species. But this
passage perhaps shows how natural it can be to think that principles of
phylogenetic inference flow directly from fundamental principles of scientific method. The idea that matching characteristics cry out for explanation
in terms of a common cause will be discussed in chapter 3. For now, I only
wish to note that Newton's idea implements an Ockhamite principle of

parsimony: Similarities are better explained as stemming from a single (common) cause than as the result of multiple (separate) causes.

Newton, as I said, had God in mind, not descent with modification, as the proper explanation of organic similarity and adaptedness. Like many intellectuals of the time, he saw the design argument as a powerful proof of God's existence (Newton [1953, pp. 65−66]):

> Can it be by accident that all birds, beast, and men have their right side and left side alike shaped (except in their bowels); and just two eyes, and no more, on either side of the face; and just two ears on either side [of] the head; and a nose with two holes; and either two forelegs or two wings or two arms on the shoulders, and two legs on the hips, and no more? Whence arises this uniformity in all their outward shapes but from the counsel and contrivance of an Author? Whence is it that the eyes of all sorts of living creatures are transparent to the very bottom, and the only transparent members in the body, having on the outside a hard transparent skin and within transparent humors, with a crystalline lens in the middle and a pupil before the lens, all of them so finely shaped and fitted for vision that no artists can mend them? Did blind chance know that there was light and what was its refraction, and fit the eyes of all creatures after the most curious manner to make use of it? These and suchlike considerations always have and ever will prevail with mankind to believe that there is a Being who made all things and has all things in his power, and who is therefore to be feared. . . .

I have placed two passages from Newton side by side. In the first, we find that methodology flows from fundamental facts about Nature; in the second, we find that perfection of organic adaptation flows from God. In the following exemplary passage from the *Optics*, Newton traces the perfection (simplicity) of nature in general and the perfection of organic adaptation in particular back to a common source (quoted in Burtt [1932, p. 284]):

> The main business of natural philosophy is . . . not only to unfold the mechanism of the world, but chiefly to resolve these and such like questions. What is there in places almost empty of matter, and whence is it that the sun and planets gravitate towards one and another, without dense matter between them? Whence is it that nature doth nothing in vain; and whence arises all that order and beauty which we see in the world? To what end are comets, and whence is it that planets move all manner of ways in orbs very eccentric, and what hinders the fixed stars from falling upon one another? How came the bodies of animals to be contrived with so much art, and for

what ends were their several parts? Was the eye contrived without skill in optics, or the ear without knowledge of sounds?... And these things being rightly dispatched, does it not appear from phenomena that there is a being incorporeal, living, intelligent, omnipresent . . . ?

Here we see Newton claiming that God is the univocal explanation of the mechanism of gravitation, the principle of parsimony, and the adaptedness of organisms. For Newton the perfection of organisms is only part of a larger perfection, one that forms the foundation of the scientific enterprise as a whole.

Newton's view was that the existence of God *suffices* to make science possible; because God created a simple and parsimonious Nature—one that is uniform in space and time and that "does nothing in vain"—methodological maxims of simplicity and parsimony are to be followed. To my knowledge, though, Newton never considered how science would proceed in a Godless universe. Because of this, I abstain from attributing to Newton the view that these methodological principles *presuppose* that God structured the universe in the way He did.

In chapter 1, we saw that a process in which homoplasies are impossible suffices to justify cladistic parsimony. However, from this it does not follow that cladistic parsimony presupposes that homoplasies are rare or nonexistent. The vital distinction was between sufficient conditions and necessary ones. An analogous point arises in the case of Newton's God; Newton asserts a sufficient condition for the use of a global concept of parsimony in scientific method. *If* God created a simple world, then it would seem that science will succeed in uncovering the truth about that world by appeal to a criterion of simplicity. This sufficient condition can be generalized a bit, in that there is no need for *God* to be part of this theory. *Any* process shaping the phenomena we investigate that has the property of making those phenomena simple would suffice. But just as in the case of cladistic parsimony, we must recognize that sufficient conditions need not be necessary. We have no reason, as of yet, to think that global parsimony depends on this assumption about contingent underlying processes.

When Descartes asked how we can know about the world external to the mind on the basis of our experience, he found it necessary to argue for the existence of a God who is no deceiver. Those who reject Descartes' answer must solve his problem in some other way. In similar fashion, we must take seriously the problem that Newton posed, even if we do not accept his theological solution. It is hard to see why we should treat the simplicity of a theory as any indication of its truth unless the processes whereby the phenomena were produced were somehow inclined to make them simple.

The challenge, then, for those who wish to defend the view that parsimony and simplicity are "purely methodological" is to show that these constraints on inference make sense, no matter how the world happens to be structured. How modern philosophy has risen to this challenge we now shall see.

2.4. The Methodological Critique

No contemporary philosopher of science would be satisfied with Hume's formulation of the Principle of the Uniformity of Nature. It has become part of the received wisdom in the subject to think that the idea that "nature is uniform" is too vague and amorphous as it stands. This objection, moreover, has accompanied a widespread doubt about the ontological form that Hume gave to his principle. It is not just that the sentence "nature is uniform" is too vague to be worth much; part of the problem, so this consensus concludes, is that Hume tried to describe the presuppositions of induction in terms of some structural feature of the world at large.

Even a first pass over this three-word slogan shows that it is incapable of doing the work in induction that Hume thought it would do. It is quite clear that we do not believe that nature is uniform *in all respects*.[11] The uniformity principle must be refined: how are we to express the expectation of uniformity that supposedly underlies the very activity of trying to learn about the world?

We cannot solve this problem by dividing properties into two classes—the ones we expect to change and the ones we expect to stay the same. We believe that color is constant for emeralds and variable for leaves. On the other hand, if we describe our expectations in a more fine-grained manner, we run the risk of merely restating the inductive beliefs we happen to have. In the case of our belief that all emeralds are green, we are trying to identify the assumption that leads us to think that this hypothesis is well confirmed by the observation of many green emeralds. The "assumption" cannot be that all emeralds are green, at least not if we think that observation has played a nonredundant role in the grounds we have for the belief. Perhaps, then, the presupposition of induction in this case is that emeralds are uniform in color. Given this, even the observation of a single green emerald will lead us to the conclusion that all emeralds are green.

Is it plausible to think that the entire enterprise of inductive inference presupposes that emeralds are uniform in color? This is scarcely credible. It is not hard to imagine how we might come to believe that emeralds are

---

11. Nor *could* the laws of nature imply that nature is uniform in all respects, a point brought home by Goodman's [1965] grue paradox.

heterogeneous in color. Given the right background beliefs, the observation of green emeralds might lead us to think that green is one among several colors—not the only color—these stones possess.

Even if we withdraw from the hyperbole that the whole inductive enterprise presupposes that emeralds are uniform in color, we still might suspect, more modestly, that if green emeralds are to confirm "all emeralds are green," then one must assume that emeralds are uniform in color. But this also is implausible. For example, the observations would confirm the generalization if one held, instead, that emeralds probably vary in color, but that if one of them is green, the rest probably are too.

The difference between sufficiency and necessity again comes into play. If the vagueness of the idea that nature is uniform could be dispelled, it might be true that an assumption of uniformity would *suffice* for inductive inference to go forward. So, for example, if we were prepared to assume that emeralds are all the same color, then we could see why observing a green emerald would support the generalization that all emeralds are green. But sufficiency is not necessity. We have yet to turn up a shred of evidence for thinking that induction *presupposes* any of uniformity assumptions formulated so far.[12]

This first challenge to Hume's claim that induction presupposes the uniformity of nature I shall call *the respects problem*. We do not even believe that nature is uniform or simple in all respects, so it is difficult to see how all inductive inference presupposes any such thing. If it is replied that the enterprise of induction presupposes that nature is uniform in certain specific respects, this would seem to mean that we cannot use induction to show that nature fails to be uniform in those respects. But this looks quite implausible as well: name any hypothesis that says that nature fails to be uniform in some respect, and it will be possible to show how we could come to have empirical evidence that it is true. And even when we move from trying to formulate a presupposition of *all* inductive inference to the more modest project of trying to specify the presuppositions of a *single* inductive inference, it is hard to see how uniformity is forced on us as an assumption. How, then, can Hume's formulation be even an approximation of anything that deserves to be called a presupposition of all inductive inference?

To the respects argument, I add another, which also makes it implausible to think that Hume was on the right track in saying that inductive arguments always assume that nature is uniform. I shall call this the *no*

---

12. Here I merely restate a long-standing line of argument, endorsed by many writers—for example, by Mill [1859], by Cohen and Nagel [1934, p. 268], and by Salmon [1953, p. 44], who puts the point well when he says that "every formulation of the principle of the uniformity of nature is either too strong to be true or else too weak to be useful."

upper bound argument. A standard picture of inductive inference is that we prefer the hypothesis that is the simplest one consistent with the observations. This suggests that in any inductive inference problem, we formulate a list of hypotheses ordered in terms of their complexity. We then run down the list beginning with the simplest and discard hypotheses inconsistent with the observations until we reach one that is not refuted. This hypothesis is then judged to be more reasonable than the other, more complex, items on the list that also are consistent with the observations.

The important feature of this crude model of how induction proceeds is that it places no upper bound on the complexity of the hypotheses we may have to consider before we find one that is consistent with the observations. It may be the tenth, the hundredth, or the thousandth entry on the list that is the first to go unrefuted. So the hypothesis we prefer by appeal to simplicity may be very complex indeed. In fact, there need be no last entry on the list we are prepared to inspect; for each hypothesis we may consider, we can always construct another that is more complex, yet not beyond the pale.

The idea that nature is simple, if it could be clarified, presumably would imply that there is an upper bound on how complex nature is. But if simplicity functions in hypothesis evaluation in the way just sketched, then its use involves no assumption of an upper bound. This casts further suspicion on Hume's thesis that inductive inference assumes that nature is simple.[13]

The respects argument and the no upper bound argument each suggest that the role of simplicity in hypothesis choice is not happily described by attributing to all inductive inferences the assumption that "nature is simple." But a suspicion may linger: perhaps the idea that the use of simplicity presupposes something substantive about the way the world is can be defended, once this three-word slogan is elaborated.

This brings me to the third argument we need to consider—one that turns on the fact that our inductive practices are enormously *flexible*. If we learn that nature is not uniform in some respect, we incorporate that fact into our set of beliefs and then make inferences in accordance with that knowledge. The idea that simplicity is a criterion in hypothesis choice is quite consistent with the fact that simple hypotheses are often rejected because they clash with observations or with theoretical background assumptions. Inference can be sensitive to background knowledge that the world is a complex place, yet proceed simply and parsimoniously nonetheless.

The flexibility of our inductive practices seems to provide a recipe for refuting the suggestion that inductive inference presupposes that nature is uniform in this or that respect. Once the alleged presupposition is stated

---

13. The notion of presupposition deployed in this argument will be explored more carefully in section 4.4.

with reasonable precision, we can (i) conceive how empirical evidence might be mustered to show that that uniformity fails to obtain and (ii) show how the use of simplicity and parsimony in nondeductive inference will not only survive that discovery but also play an essential role in inferring that the uniformity in question fails to obtain. The idea is that no discovered complexity can undermine the use of the simplicity criterion, properly understood.

This fact about flexibility suggests that Hume's principle of uniformity is flawed, not just because it is short on details, but because its fundamental outlook is misguided. The source of the problem seems to lie in the fact that Hume's formulation is ontological in character. If so, the way out of the problems we have just surveyed may come with seeing that simplicity involves no assumptions at all about the way the world is. The alternative idea is that simplicity is "purely methodological"; it guides the way we allow observations to shape our judgments about the plausibility of hypotheses, but makes no substantive assumptions about the world those hypotheses purport to describe. The alternative to Hume's ontological formulation, then, is that simplicity, whatever its detailed character turns out to be, is an *a priori* constraint on rational investigation. Its use is consistent with any possible observation and depends on no particular way the world might be.

We have come full circle from the ontological viewpoint epitomized by Newton. That older view, detached from its inessential theological development, saw the principle of parsimony as depending for its justification on the kinds of processes that make the world the way it is. The alternative is to think of simplicity as depending on no such process story at all. This, I believe, is the status that many philosophers now assign the simplicity concept. As plausible as it may seem in the light of the respects argument, the no upper bound argument, and the fact of induction's flexibility, I shall argue in the next section that it is profoundly mistaken. The lapsed ontological tradition described in the previous section contains the germ of an important insight.

2.5. *The Raven Paradox*

Hume investigated the nature of inductive inference at a very high level of generality. Although he discussed various examples—the sun's rising tomorrow, bread's providing nourishment tomorrow, etc.—Hume tried to find one assumption about the world that underlies *all* inductive inference. It was this search for a universal principle that led him to the idea that all induction assumes that nature is uniform.

In the previous section, we found that the substantive principle Hume proposed is seriously flawed. This engendered the suspicion that the principle of simplicity implies nothing about the way the world is, but only constrains how we must reason if we are to be rational.[14]

I now propose to criticize this idea—that simplicity is "purely methodological." However, my line of argument will be strategically different from Hume's. Rather than showing that there is one substantive assumption underlying all inductive inference, I shall suggest that every nondeductive inference from observations to hypothesis must involve substantive assumptions about the world. When we infer tomorrow's sunrise from the ones observed in the past, an additional assumption is involved; the same is true when we infer that tomorrow's bread will nourish from the fact that the bread we ate in the past has done so. But the assumption about sunrises will almost certainly be quite different from the one about bread. Hume went wrong in thinking that there is a *single* uniformity principle that must link premise to conclusion in every inductive inference.

My argument will not focus specifically on simplicity, but will apply to any principle that is said to involve nondeductive inference from observations to hypotheses. Simplicity may be thought to mediate our extrapolation from data to generalization (or to prediction or retrodiction). But even if a connecting principle is described without reference to simplicity, my point remains: *A set of observations confirms, disconfirms, or is irrelevant to a hypothesis only relative to a set of empirical background assumptions.* Confirmation is a three-place relationship between hypothesis, observations, and background assumptions. The same lesson applies to the concept of differential support: *A set of observations supports one hypothesis better than another only relative to a set of empirical background assumptions.*

The bearing of these general claims about confirmation and support on the concept of simplicity is this. Regardless of how simplicity is formulated in detail, it has usually been understood from Hume down to the present as playing a certain epistemological role. *Simplicity has been understood as a principle that takes us from observations to hypotheses.* Given a set of competing hypotheses, simplicity and consistency with the evidence determine which of these hypotheses is to count as "best." My claim is that whenever simplicity performs this function, it embodies empirical assumptions about the way the world is. Explicit mention of empirical background assumptions is often suppressed when an argument appeals to simplicity

14. Not only has this view been widely endorsed as a specificity about simplicity; it also has found support as a claim about induction as a whole. For example, Strawson [1952, pp. 261–262] has argued that "the rationality of induction, unlike its 'successfulness', is not a fact about the constitution of the world. It is a matter of what we *mean* by the word 'rational' in its application to any procedure for forming opinions about what lies outside of our observations. . . ." This is not a universally accepted view, but it is a common and influential one.

or parsimony, but substantive background assumptions there must be nonetheless.[15]

Since confirmation is a three-place relation, there is nothing intrinsic to a set of observations that settles whether they favor one hypothesis rather than another. A background theory T may be constructed that implies that the first hypothesis is preferable to the second in the light of the observations, but a different background theory T' can be described that implies just the reverse. In the absense of any background theory at all, the observations are powerless to say which competing hypothesis is to be preferred. If "simplicity" or "parsimony" is invoked as the reason for preferring one hypothesis to the other, this must be understood as implicitly assuming something about the underlying background theory. *The fact that confirmation is a three-place relation tells us that simplicity cannot be "purely methodological" when it forges an evidential connection between observations and hypotheses.*

A few words of clarification are needed before I argue for this thesis about confirmation. First, it is important to be clear that the issue here is induction, not deduction. It is obvious that empirical assumptions must be added to observations about emeralds if one wishes to *deduce* that all emeralds are green. But I am not talking about deduction; my claim is that empirical assumptions must be made if we are to claim that "all emeralds are green" is confirmed by green emeralds, or that such observations better support this generalization than one that says that emeralds will change color at the year 2000. Second, the empirical assumptions I have in mind are subject matter specific. Even if "the future resembles the past" were empirical, this sort of assumption is too vague to allow observations to bear on hypotheses. What is required, in each confirmational context, is assumptions about the investigative situation and the subject matter under scrutiny.

The thesis that confirmation and disconfirmation are three-place relations has an exception, which we must identify and set aside. If hypothesis H implies an observation statement O, then the falsehood of O will refute H, there being no need to invoke a background theory that connects hypothesis to observations. Likewise, if O implies H and O is true, then so is H, no mediating background theory being required here either. But these are enormously special cases, utterly atypical of the relationship between hypothesis and observation. First, it is entirely standard that a hypothesis under test must be conjoined with auxiliary assumptions, if it is to deductively imply anything observable (Duhem [1914]; Quine [1960]). Second, often hypotheses under test, even when embedded in a back-

15. An "empirical assumption" is a proposition that could, in principle, be supported or infirmed by observations, but that, in the context of inquiry, is assumed without argument.

ground theory, do not deductively imply any observation statement. This second point is especially pertinent to testing probabilistic hypotheses, a point to which we shall return in chapter 4.

How might one attempt to show that confirmation is a three-place relation between observations, hypotheses, and background assumptions? One possibility would be to describe a fully adequate theory of confirmation and show that a consequence of that theory is that confirmation has the characteristic here attributed to it. If the one true confirmation theory were evident to all, this strategy might be useful. However, there now are a number of conflicting approaches, each confronting its own serious problems. The subject is too much in flux for this strategy to be promising. A second possibility—the one I shall pursue here—is more indirect and perhaps less compelling in its results. It involves arguing from intuitive assessments of examples. As in all such argumentation, even if my analysis of the examples in plausible, this will not force one to the conclusion I wish to draw. Rather, my analysis will take the form of a plausibility argument for the thesis I have in mind.

Earlier in this chapter, I discussed how simplicity has been thought to constrain inductive inference and how parsimony has been thought to constrain inference to the best explanation (abduction). In this section, I shall defend my thesis about the essential role of background assumptions by focusing on a problem about induction; in chapter 3, I shall defend the thesis in the context of a problem concerning inference to the best explanation.

The inductive problem I want to examine is Hempel's [1965b] much discussed paradox of the ravens. Why is it that observations of black ravens confirm the hypothesis that all ravens are black, but that observations of white shoes seem entirely irrelevant?[16] Hempel's question was a request for the specification of the rules we follow in scientific confirmation. Perhaps such rules can withstand Hume's skeptical challenge; perhaps they cannot. But quite independent of this question about justification, one would like to understand how the scientific method works.

Hempel argued that a few simple principles seem to lead to a paradoxical conclusion. Suppose that an hypothesis of the form "All A's are B" is confirmed by observing anything that is both A and B. Suppose next that if an observation confirms a generalization, then it confirms any logically equivalent generalization. So if an observation confirms "All A's are B," it also must confirm that conditional's contrapositive, namely, "All non-B's are non-A." Applying this reasoning to the raven example, we obtain the following result: If black ravens confirm "All ravens are black," they also

16. Hempel assumes for the purposes of his example that the definition of what it is to be a raven does not settle whether all ravens are black.

confirm "All nonblack things are nonravens." But this latter hypothesis is confirmed by observing anything that is neither black nor a raven. So white shoes also confirm it. It follows, finally, that white shoes confirm "All ravens are black." But this is paradoxical. Hempel set the problem of determining whether black ravens and white shoes really to differ in their confirmational significance.

Hempel's solution was to argue that both sorts of objects confirm the generalization. Appearances to the contrary he dismissed as misguided. But of greater interest to us here is the way Hempel set his problem. We are to consider the hypothesis and its relationship to the observations without assuming anything in the way of empirical background assumptions. This, Hempel [1965b, p. 20] declared, is a "required methodological fiction." Now it is patent that in science and in everyday life, we exploit empirical assumptions in evaluating how observations bear on generalizations. Why did Hempel impose this extreme idealization?

Hempel's problem took the form it did because of the Principle of Empiricism noted in section 2.2. All our knowledge must ultimately trace back to observations and to observations alone. Even if we came to know that all ravens are black for reasons far more complex than the observation of a number of "positive instances," according to the empiricist we could have learned this truth by observation proceeding from a *tabula rasa*. Armed with concepts like "raven" and "black" and with rules of scientific method, we could formulate the generalization and then confirm it by making the relevant observations. The crucial Empiricist Principle is that this is possible even if we begin with no substantive beliefs about the world.

Hempel thought that black ravens and white shoes both confirm "All ravens are black." This is perfectly consistent with saying that black ravens have *greater* confirmational value. Hempel expresses sympathy with the efforts of various workers to show why black ravens are worth more. For example, we know that the world contains fewer ravens than it does nonblack things. This might suggest that looking at a raven and seeing if it is black offers more confirmation than looking at a nonblack thing and seeing if it is a nonraven. Formal theories of confirmation have been developed to ground this intuition.

Hempel is untroubled by the suggestion that the *degree of confirmation* afforded by black ravens as opposed to white shoes depends on an empirical fact about ravens—e.g., that ravens are rarer than nonblack things. But Hempel insisted on his methodological fiction when it comes to the question of whether black ravens and white shoes confirm at all. For him, both sorts of observations confirm the generalization, without the need of any background assumptions. For Hempel, this is a matter of the "logic of confirmation."

Good [1967] argued that whether black ravens confirm, disconfirm, or are neutral depends on what else one believes. He posed the following thought experiment. Suppose we believed that either there are lots of ravens, of which 99% are black, or there are very few ravens, of which 100% are black. This background assumption entails that the more black ravens we observe, the *less* confidence we should have in the hypothesis that all ravens are black. Good thought this showed how a black raven could *disconfirm* the generalization; it does so by reducing the amount of confidence we are entitled to have in the truth of the hypothesis. The title of Good's article was his conclusion: the white shoe is a red herring.

Good also argued that things that are neither *A* nor *B* can disconfirm "All *A*'s are *B*," provided that the problem is embedded in the right background context. His example showed how white crows can *disconfirm* the hypothesis that all ravens are black. Suppose we believe that crows and ravens are biologically related, so that polymorphisms found in one are evidence that they also are present in the other. If we see that crows are sometimes white, this disconfirms the hypothesis that ravens are always black. Good intended a general lesson here: No observation has confirmational meaning, save in the context of a background theory.

Hempel's [1967] reply was that Good's examples fail to address the problem as posed. In the first, Good assumes that we know something about ravens and their color and then shows why black ravens will disconfirm "All ravens are black." In the second, Good assumes we know something about the relationship of ravens and crows and then shows that white crows will disconfirm the generalization that all ravens are black. But Hempel demands that we indulge in his methodological fiction: knowing *nothing* empirical, we are to say whether black ravens and white shoes are both confirmatory.

What would it mean for confirmation to be a relationship between observations and hypothesis alone? In his reply to Hempel, Good [1968] confesses that

> [t]he closest I can get to giving [a two-place confirmation relation] a practical significance is to imagine an infinitely intelligent newborn baby having built-in neural circuits enabling him to deal with formal logic, English syntax, and subjective probability. He might now argue, after defining a crow in detail, that it is initially extremely likely that all crows are black, that is, that *H* is true. "On the other hand," he goes on to argue, "if there are crows, then there is a reasonable chance that they are of a variety of colors. Therefore, if I were to discover that even a black crow exists I would consider *H* to be less probable than it was initially." I conclude from this that the herring is a fairly deep shade of pink.

This exchange does not definitively settle the matter of whether confirmation is necessarily a three-place relationship. One might suggest that even though confirmation typically proceeds in the presence of substantive background knowledge, it also must be able to proceed in the absence of such. This claim, central to Hempel's formulation of his problem, is highly conjectural. What is more, it forces the empiricist to defend a peculiarly asymmetrical position. When it is pointed out that observing black ravens can favor the hypothesis that ravens are *heterogeneous* in color, the empiricist will demand to be shown what background assumptions underwrite this surprising extrapolation. Yet, when the extrapolation is from black ravens to the hypothesis that ravens are *homogeneous* in color, the empiricist will see no need to be shown why this "natural" extrapolation makes sense. But why should this be so? Why think that there are extrapolations that are reasonable without there needing to be any background beliefs that make them reasonable? This conviction is based largely on the philosophical faith that empiricism must be true.

It is noteworthy that reasonably developed theories of confirmation that in one way or another exploit the notion of probability all imply that confirmation is a three-place relation.[17] It is perhaps even more noteworthy that theories of confirmation that treat the relation of observation and hypothesis as purely "logical" and presuppositionless have had a dismal track record indeed. I conjecture (following Good [1967] and Rosenkrantz [1977]) that the indispensability of a background theory is a basic fact about confirmation.

If it is a fact, then it is highly significant for our inquiry into the notion of parsimony, in both its global and its local forms. Whenever observations are said to support a hypothesis, or are said to support one hypothesis better than another, there must be an empirical background theory that mediates this connection. It is important to see that this principle does not evaporate when a scientist cites simplicity as the ground for preferring one hypothesis over another in the light of the data. *Appeal to simplicity is a surrogate for stating an empirical background theory.*

How should we understand the idea of a "background theory" in the above principle? We can begin by saying something negative: it is not a set of observation statements. The positive characterization that will suffice for now is vague: a background theory describes how the hypotheses under test and the possible observations are "related," given the design of the experiment. As noted before, we assume that observations do not by themselves deductively ensure the truth or falsity of the hypotheses under test. In the same way, the background theory, in describing the

17. Eells [1982, pp. 58–59] uses a Bayesian analysis of confirmation to isolate a simple empirical assumption that suffices for a positive instance to confirm a generalization.

"relationship" of hypotheses to observations, does not have its truth or falsehood definitively settled by observations either.

In Good's first example, the background theory describes the probability of finding something that is black and a raven, if all ravens are black; in the second, it describes the probability that all ravens are black, if not all crows are black. The "relationships" between observations and hypotheses described by these background theories are probability relationships; these are not given to us a priori, nor are they properly treated as mere summaries of the observations we have made. I use the term "background theory" to mark the idea that the assumptions that allow observations to bear on hypotheses are not themselves mere observations.

Hume thought that the Principle of the Uniformity of Nature suffices to connect observations to hypotheses inferentially. But this principle, even if its vagueness could be dispelled, is at far too lofty a level of generality to be of much use in inductive inference. If black ravens confirm "All ravens are black," it is not because nature is uniform, but because of some far more specific assumptions about ravens and about the process of sampling.

Hume's problem, like Hempel's, is formulated in such a way that this important relativity to background assumptions is suppressed. This empiricist formulation has encouraged philosophers to believe that confirmation is consistency with the evidence plus simplicity, where "simplicity" is given a purely methodological construal. But once we see the implications of the idea that confirmation is a three-place relation between hypothesis, observations, and a background theory, we see that simplicity must do the work of a background theory; and like a background theory, the use of simplicity in a given context of inference must carry with it substantive implications about the way the world is.

The redescription of inductive inference offered here has consequences for the skeptical argument that Hume advanced. Hume's argument depends on the idea that there is a principle that cannot be justified by reason alone, which is required in all inductive inferences. Because it is required by all inductive inferences, it cannot be justified by any of them. And so we reach Hume's skepticism: the principle must be used in induction, though it cannot be justified either a priori or empirically.

I have questioned Hume's claim to have found such a principle. What we do find in any articulated inductive argument is a set of empirical assumptions that allow observations to have an evidential bearing on competing hypotheses. These background assumptions may themselves be scrutinized, and further observations and background theory may be offered in their support. When asked to say why we take past observations to support the belief that the sun will rise tomorrow, we answer by citing our well-confirmed theory of planetary motion, not Hume's

Principle of the Uniformity of Nature. If challenged to say why we take this scientific theory seriously, we would reply by citing *other* observations and *other* background theories as well.

As we pursue these questions of justification—pushing farther and farther back for the "ultimate" assumptions that underlie our empirical beliefs—will we eventually reach a stage where an empirical belief that is not strictly about the here and now is sufficiently supported by current observations, taken all by themselves? This is what the Principle of Empiricism demands. But here we see empiricism in conflict with the thesis about confirmation: If hypothesis *H* and an observation statement *O* are not deductively related (they are logically independent), then *O* confirms or disconfirms *H* only relative to a background theory *T*. The third term *never* disappears; there is no room for a simple "principle of induction" (or "principle of simplicity") that takes us directly from observations to reasonable generalizations, retrodictions, or predictions (Rosenkrantz [1977]).

To assess the bearing of this thesis about confirmation on Hume's position, we must take care to separate Hume's argument from the conclusion he reached. First, it should be clear that the *form* of Hume's skeptical argument cannot be reinstated: I see no sign of a premise common to all inductive arguments that cannot be rationally defended. However, this does not mean that Hume's skeptical conclusion is off the mark. If Hume required that we show how present observations all by themselves provide reasonable support for our predictions, retrodictions, and generalizations, he was right to conclude that they do not. The thesis that confirmation is a three-place relation sustains Hume's skeptical thesis, but not the argument he constructed on its behalf.

Although my arguments based on the raven paradox concern induction, I believe they apply with a vengeance to many abductive arguments as well. If empirical background assumptions are needed for observations to have confirmational significance for *observational* generalizations, still more are they needed to connect observations with statements whose vocabulary is not wholly observational.

In the next chapter, we shall consider a principle that has considerable plausibility as a guide to inference to the best explanation: If two events are correlated, then it is better to explain them by postulating a single common cause than by postulating two separate causes. This principle deserves to be viewed as a version of the parsimony idea: One cause is preferable to two. We shall see that this principle depends for its plausibility on empirical background assumptions. This result will help substantiate my claim that the conclusions reached in the present chapter about induction apply to abduction as well.

And, of course, phylogenetic inference is a kind of inference to the best explanation. The general thesis that I have defended about simplicity and parsimony will receive further support if I can show that the power of observations to discriminate among competing genealogical hypotheses depends on the assumptions about the evolutionary process one is prepared to make, and that this is no less true when parsimony is cited as the principle that connects observations to hypotheses. This biological issue will occupy our attention in chapters 4–6.

2.6. Hume Was Half-Right

Hume did not err when he thought that an inductive inference from observations to predictions, retrodictions, or generalizations must be supplied with a "missing premise." One cannot cite one, two, or many green emeralds as reason enough for thinking that all emeralds are green, or for thinking that this hypothesis is better supported than one that says that emeralds will remain green only until the year 2000.

In saying this, I am not making the trivial and obvious point that one cannot *deduce* the generalization, prediction, or retrodiction from the observations. A number of commentators have seen Hume as making a point no more important than this, and have gone on to block his skeptical argument as follows. Hume wants to conclude that observations do not rationally justify our beliefs about the future. If Hume's argument for this conclusion is just that one cannot deduce such beliefs from present observations alone, then he must assume that only deductive arguments provide reasons. But this is both question-begging and radically implausible.

My view is that Hume was right in a more significant way. Even granting that nondeductive arguments provide reasons, I still maintain that observations alone are not enough to ground inductive conclusions. Hume was on the right track when he thought some extra ingredient is required.[18]

However, Hume's description of what this additional element must be was defective in both its details and its general character. I see no way of making sense of the idea that "nature is uniform" or that "the future will resemble the past" in such a way that these slogans deserve to be viewed as presuppositions of all inductive inference. What is more, I very much

18. Stove [1973, p. 43] adopts a "deductivist" reading of Hume's argument, according to which induction is said to presuppose the uniformity principle on the grounds that one cannot deduce the conclusion from the observations without it. Beauchamp and Rosenberg [1981] defend the related exegetical thesis that Hume's chief point is that ampliative arguments cannot be demonstrative; however, they also maintain that Hume was not a skeptic about induction. Stroud [1977, pp. 53–77] argues that Hume is better seen as claiming that observations cannot count as reasons—whether deductive or nondeductive—unless the uniformity principle is correct. My gloss of Hume's argument owes a substantial debt to Stroud.

doubt that one can fill in the extra assumptions needed for observations to have an evidential bearing on hypotheses at the level of generality that Hume sought. Hume's mistake was to think that since each inductive inference requires assumptions additional to observations, there must be an additional assumption that every inductive inference requires (see Edidin [1984, p. 286]). Logicians describe this fallacy in terms of the order of quantifiers. "Every person has a birthday" should not be confused with "there is a day on which every person was born." Yet, something like this confusion gives rise to the conviction that inductions about the rising of the sun, the nourishment of bread, and the color of emeralds must share a common premise.

As mentioned earlier, I do not maintain that each inductive inference is utterly unique—that there are no general patterns that the philosopher or statistician can hope to codify. This would be mystery mongering and also contrary to what one can see merely by opening a statistics textbook. A sampling problem about emerald color and one about the nutritional value of bread may have a common structure. But I do not detect in this common structure a general empirical assumption that must be made by all inductive inferences, which therefore cannot be defended by empirical evidence.[19]

Hume's skeptical conclusion concerning the justifiability of induction by a reasoned argument can be reformulated in the light of this criticism of his reconstruction of how inductive inference proceeds. I have argued that each inductive argument must rely on some premise or other whose truth is not guaranteed by present experience and memory traces (or deductions therefrom). The background assumptions required to show how observations have an evidential bearing on hypotheses go beyond what is observed in the here and now. Hume challenged us to show why present observations play the evidential role they do without our assuming additional propositions that require an inductive justification. But this, quite simply, cannot be done. Present experience is no guide to the future, except when it is augmented with contingent assumptions about the connection of past to future. To hold true to the Principle of Empiricism—that beliefs about the future must be justified in terms of present observation *alone*—is, as Hume rightly saw, to be led straight to skepticism.

The bearing of this conclusion about induction on the use of simplicity in scientific inference is indirect but important. Scientists have at different times and in different disciplines used simplicity as a reason for discrimi-

19. I am not advancing here the stronger thesis that every element in our inductive practices is justifiable in some interesting way. Perhaps there are "primitive postulates" of a logical or mathematical variety that are so ultimate that they elude nontrivial justification. This position concerning the likelihood concept will be discussed in section 5.4.

nating between competing hypotheses each consistent with the observations. Nothing said here shows that this appeal to simplicity is illegitimate. However, I do think that such appeals to simplicity must be seen for what they are. Whenever a nondeductive inference goes from observations to an evaluation of the plausibility of competing hypotheses, empirical assumptions must be involved. This thesis does not dissolve when simplicity or parsimony is given as the principle that brings observations to bear on hypotheses. Appeals to simplicity must count as highly abstract and abbreviated summaries of background assumptions about the empirical subject and inference problem one faces. Such appeals should not be viewed as unmediated applications of some perfectly general and *a priori* principle of scientific reason.[20]

This conclusion does not contradict the earlier observation that our inductive practices are highly flexible. If it is suggested that induction presupposes that nature is uniform in some specific respect, we can usually show how the negation of that "assumption" is something we can gather evidence on and eventually assimilate into our stock of beliefs; if a principle of simplicity is part of inductive practice, it can facilitate our learning this alleged nonuniformity as well. This suggests that there is no substantive assumption about the world that *all* applications of a principle of parsimony require. But it hardly vindicates the idea that a given application of parsimony to an inductive problem proceeds without substantive assumptions. Again, the order of the quantifiers is at the heart of the resolution I am proposing of the dispute as to whether simplicity is substantive or "purely methodological."

I began this chapter by asking whether the use of parsimony in science makes substantive assumptions about the way the world is. With other philosophers, I have been skeptical of the idea that the use of simplicity assumes that nature is simple. But this does not mean that the use of simplicity requires *no* assumptions—only that the simplicity of nature is not one of them. We have moved away from an overly simple version of the thesis that the use of simplicity has substantive presuppositions; we no longer need formulate this idea as holding that *every* use of simplicity or parsimony must make the *same* assumption. To pursue this matter further, we must descend to a less lofty level of generality; we must see how the use of simplicity in specific scientific inference problems involves nontrivial assumptions. The phylogenetic inference problem is the case study that will flesh out this more general inquiry into the nature of scientific inference.

20. Lyell's defense of uniformitarianism within geology is a nice example of how simplicity can be used to make contingent subject matter specific assumptions look like they are direct consequences of *a priori* methodological principles. See Hooykaas [1959], Rudwick [1970], and Gould [1985] for discussion.

Chapter 3
The Principle of the Common Cause

In the previous chapter, I described two kinds of nondeductive inference, each with its associated notion of simplicity. Induction—inference from an observed sample to an unobserved containing population—has been thought to depend on an assumption of uniformity. Abduction—inference from observation to postulated explanation—has been thought to require a principle of parsimony.

The main result of the previous chapter was a claim about the notion of confirmation, whether it occurs in the context of induction or abduction. I argued that observations confirm or disconfirm hypotheses, or support one hypothesis better than another, only in virtue of associated background assumptions. This thesis was presented as a plausible diagnosis of the problem posed by Hempel's raven paradox (section 2.5); yet, it was advanced as embracing induction and abduction alike.

In the present chapter, I shall argue the importance of applying this idea about confirmation to a central issue concerning abduction. Ockham's razor says that it is vain to postulate more causes when fewer suffice to explain. We saw in section 2.3 that this general idea found expression in Newton's second rule: *To the same natural effects we must, as far as possible, assign the same causes.* Indeed, even as early as section 1.2 we saw that evolutionists take the (near) universality of the genetic code to be evidence for a common origin of all present-day organisms. Parsimony seems to direct us to trace back all species to a single (common) origin rather than trace them back to multiple (separate) originations. Parsimony favors explanations that posit a common cause over ones that postulate separate, multiple, causes.

Appeals to parsimony have not figured centrally in contemporary philosophical discussion of how common cause and separate cause explanations should be compared. Hans Reichenbach [1956] espoused and Wesley Salmon [1975, 1978, 1984] elaborated a *principle of the common cause* without exploring that principle's bearing on parsimony. Even so, the principle they defended is quite germane to the issue of parsimony in general and of phylogenetic inference in particular.

The basic idea behind Reichenbach and Salmon's principle is that cor-relations should be explained by postulating a common cause. Consider an example of Salmon's [1984, p. 159]. Two university students submit philo-sophy essays to a professor that are word-for-word identical. This *might* be due to the students' having developed precisely the same essays in-dependently. But it is far more plausible to think that the similarity is due to the students' having plagiarized from the same source—a book in the library, for example.

Phylogenetic inference offers a tempting analogy: the remarkable simi-larity of human beings and chimps *might* be due to their having indepen-dently derived their characters from separate ancestors. But it is far more plausible to think that the resemblance is due to their having obtained the traits as homologies from a common ancestor. Inferring common ancestry is a case of postulating a common cause. Hence the problem of phyloge-netic inference is a test case for the principle that Reichenbach and Salmon espoused.

One goal of the present chapter is to explore the strengths and limi-tations of this abductive principle. Another is to develop some basic prob abilistic machinery that will come into play in the chapters that follow. To defend the claim that one genealogical hypothesis is better than another in the light of available evidence, or that one method of phylogenetic infer-ence is better than another, we must make precise what we mean by "better." Evaluating the principle of the common cause will allow us to take up this important problem.

Before I turn to the details of the principle of the common cause, it will be useful to attend to some simple features of the phenetic idea that overall similarity is a proper basis for inferring propinquity of descent. To be sure, the Reichenbach idea takes correlation of characters to be the sign of a common cause (ancestor), and correlation and similarity are different. But correlation and overall similarity have a common feature, one that should set alarm bells ringing before we look at the specifics of the philo-sophical idea.

3.1. Two Pitfalls for Pheneticism[1]

Let us imagine that we can score *all* the characters possessed by each of two species and then compute the percentage of characters with respect to which the species match. This presumes that the set of all characters is a well-defined (and finite) totality; for this to make sense, we would obvi-ously have to delimit what we are prepared to count as a character. We

1. The pitfalls discussed here concern the use of overfall similarity to infer phylogenetic relationships, not the use of that concept in constructing classifications. The difference be-tween these two undertakings was noted in section 1.2.

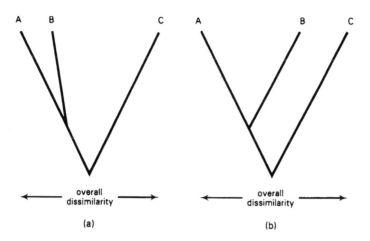

Figure 8.
In (a) overall similarity reflects propinquity of descent; in (b) use of overall similarity to infer genealogical relationship would probably mislead.

might stipulate that the sequenced genome is the description of interest, or, perhaps, that some large finite list of measurements is to count, for practical purposes, as a "complete" description of each species. The percentage similarity within this totality of characters I shall term the two species' *overall similarity*.[2]

In figure 8 we see phylogenetic trees in which the horizontal distance between terminal taxa represents their overall dissimilarity (i.e., with respect to all characters). The two trees agree that taxa A and B are more closely related to each other than either is to C. However, they differ over whether overall similarity reflects phylogenetic relationship.

In figure 8a, A and B are more similar to each other than either is to C. In figure 8b, however, it is B and C that are more similar to each other than either is to A. Systematists sampling at random from the characteristics exhibited by these three species and using overall similarity to reconstruct phylogenetic relationships would probably reach the truth if matters were as represented in 8a, but would probably reach a false genealogical hypothesis if 8b were true.

There are two reasons why overall similarity may fail to track phylogenetic relationships. First, there is the phenomenon of *homoplasy*, illustrated in figure 9a. In this illustration, the horizontal dimension does not represent overall dissimilarity; instead, I use the length of a branch to represent how probable it is that a branch will end in a state different from the one in

2. I shall not discuss the various detailed methods that have been proposed for making the notion of overall similarity precise, on which see Sneath and Sokal [1973].

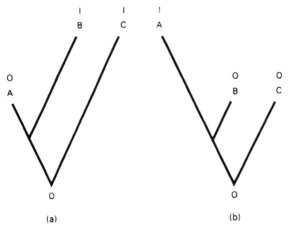

Figure 9.
Two ways in which overall similarity may fail to reflect propinquity of descent. (a) If homoplasy is abundant between B and C while the lineage leading to A is highly conservative, 011 characters may occur more often than characters exhibiting a 110 distribution. (b) If A frequently evolves autapomorphies while the lineages leading to B and C are highly conservative, 100 characters may occur more frequently than characters exhibiting a 001 distribution.

which it began. If B and C frequently exhibit the derived character state (represented by a "1") while A usually retains the ancestral state (represented by a "0"), then B and C will show far more synapomorphic resemblance than A and B will. This possibility will mislead the method of overall similarity, but so too will it mislead the method of cladistic parsimony discussed in chapter 1. That method, recall, takes synapomorphic resemblance as evidence of common descent; when shared apomorphies are in fact homoplasies, cladistic parsimony will misjudge phylogenetic relationships.

The other phenomenon that can mislead overall similarity in its attempt to recover genealogy is *autapomorphy* (a unique derived character). In figure 9b, we see that taxon A alone has the derived form; the lineages leading to B and C, we are imagining, were highly conservative. If we judged the plesiomorphic characters that B and C share but A does not to be evidence that B and C have an ancestor that is not an ancestor of A, we would be misled. Notice that this possibility is not a source of error for cladistic parsimony, since that method holds that symplesiomorphies are devoid of evidential meaning.

The point to bear in mind here is that overall similarity covers both apomorphic and plesiomorphic resemblance. As such, it is vulnerable to the two pitfalls just mentioned. If systematists studying a set of taxa believed that homoplasies and autapomorphies like those shown in figure 9 were the rule rather than the exception, they would quite rightly be skeptical about the merits of overall similarity as a method for phylogenetic reconstruction.

These points have long been recognized by pheneticists. Sneath and Sokal [1973, p. 321] consider the question of what evolution must be like if phenetic methods are to be used to reconstruct phylogenetic relationships. They formulate their requirement as follows:

> Those who would largely use phenetic similarity as evidence for recency of cladistic ancestry must assume at least some uniformity of evolutionary rates in the several clades, although Colless [1970] has shown that the requirements need not be as stringent as is commonly thought. . . . We stress here uniform rather than constant rates of evolution. As long as rates of evolution change equally in parallel lines it is unimportant whether these rates are constant through an evolutionary epoch. We may use the analogy of multiple clusters of fireworks, smaller clusters bursting from inside large clusters, a familiar sight to most readers. While the small rays of the rocket have not "evolved" at all until the small rocket exploded, their rates of divergence from the center of their rocket are identical but not constant, since they were zero during the period of the early ascent of the rocket.

The idea here is that all the branches in each generation of the process depicted in figure 2 (p. 16) have the same proportion of characters undergoing evolutionary change. Rates *at any given time* are uniform, though rates may vary *through time*.

Colless [1970] suggests a different sufficient condition for overall similarity to be a good estimator of genealogical relationship. It is enough (i) that later stocks not evolve for substantial periods at rates much greater than in earlier stocks, (ii) that sister species diverge appreciably before undergoing further splitting, and (iii) that later lines not converge upon each other less than upon earlier lines. Colless's claim is that *if* these conditions are met, overall similarity will yield a "reasonable estimate."

Sneath and Sokal describe a condition that they regard as (at least approximately) *necessary* for phenetic methods to make sense; Colless, on the other hand, develops a set of conditions that he sees as *sufficient*. Sneath and Sokal [1973, p. 321] are pessimistic when it comes to the question of whether the condition they specify will generally be satisfied in nature. They say that "clearly all the evidence at hand indicates evolutionary rates in different clades are not uniform. Different lines do evolve at different rates." Colless, on the other hand, seems to be rather more confident that lineages will generally, if not universally, conform to his conditions.

The question of how often evolution will satisfy conditions conjectured to be necessary and/or sufficient for a given method is extremely important. One does not "justify" a method by showing that there is an extremely special case in which it does its work well; nor does one "refute" a method by showing that there is another special case in which it makes a hash of things.[3] But prior to the empirical problem of relative frequency, there is another, more conceptual, question to which we must attend: What does it mean to say that a given method "requires" that a given condition be satisfied? Once this is described, an argument must be provided that shows precisely when the method will measure up to the standards adopted.

Sneath and Sokal [1973] do not address these questions in the passage just quoted. No conditions of adequacy are formulated, nor is any argument given there that overall similarity requires that evolution have the property they demand. Colless [1970], on the other hand, carries out a calculation to show that his conditions imply that A and B are more closely related to each other than either is to C precisely when the similarity of A and B exceeds the similarity of the other two pairs. But here again, a general condition of adequacy is presupposed rather than explicitly stated.

Let us briefly consider, then, what a reasonable criterion of adequacy might be for a method of phylogenetic inference. A first pass at this seemingly simple question might yield the following reply: The use of overall similarity requires a given condition if the violation of that condition would make it possible for the method to fail to yield the truth when the method is applied to a finite data set. This answer, it should be clear, requires too much. Perfectly sensible inference rules can be *fallible*; when they generate false conclusions, they may be reasonable nonetheless. If overall similarity is said to depend for its justification on this or that assumption, some other reason must be provided for saying so.

Consider the analogous problem of estimating the bias of a coin by examining the results of repeated independent tosses. If we find that six out of ten tosses have yielded heads, the "best" point estimate afforded by the data is that the probability of heads is 0.6. This is a "reasonable" estimate, though it may be false. One does not show that a method presupposes something just by demonstrating that the method can yield false estimates if the "assumption" goes unsatisfied.

A more promising explication might focus on the idea of repeated sampling. Using the sample mean in the coin toss case as the best estimate of the coin's probability has this to be said for it: if we take larger and larger

---

3. This is not to deny that isolated counterexamples can refute sweeping and unconditional claims for a method's validity, a point to which I shall return in chapter 5.

samples of tosses, and continue to use this method, we shall converge on the truth.[4]

This provides a new reading for the idea that a method requires a given assumption: the method will not be convergent unless the assumption is true. This idea is in harmony with the fact that no method can be expected to be infallible. Even if the pairwise overall similarity of A, B, and C is as shown in figure 8b, it still is possible that a few sampled characters might have A and B more similar to each other than either is to C. Such characters will be "unrepresentative," but they are not impossible. So if a phylogeny like that shown in figure 8b is a problem for phenetic methods, this is not because it ensures that *every* data set will lead phenetic methods into error. Rather, the idea is that an estimate based on a randomly sampled set of characters will *probably* be mistaken. This idea, in turn, can be characterized in terms of the notion of convergence.

In chapter 5, we shall carefully scrutinize the idea that a method presupposes those propositions that must be true for the method to be convergent. For now I simply note that it is a *prima facie* plausible construal of why pheneticists have held that rate uniformity is required.[5]

I have noted that overall similarity will not be a sensible method to use, if you know that closely related species will be *less* similar than distantly related ones (as in figure 8b). That it is in principle possible for evolution to sometimes produce phylogenies of this sort is not in serious doubt: simply stipulate rate inequalities of the kind illustrated in figure 9, and characters that mislead phenetic methods will occur more often than ones that lead those methods to the truth. So no matter how strongly justified the method of overall similarity might be, we see here a thin red line that it cannot cross. It follows immediately that it is a mistake to say that scientists may legitimately use the method of overall similarity *regardless of whatever else they believe about the evolutionary process*. No biologist would

4. Convergence will be defined more rigorously in section 5.3. The sample mean also happens to be the estimate of maximum likelihood in the coin example; it confers a probability on the observations greater than any other. Likelihood will be explained later in this chapter. Whether the sample mean is the "best" estimate because it is asymptotic, or simply because it is most likely, we shall consider in chapter 5.

5. More precisely, the above reconstruction at most shows why rate uniformity would *suffice* for the use of phenetic methods, not why it is necessary. Overall similarity might be convergent when rates are nonuniform, if speedups at some times compensated for slowdowns at others. Perhaps the idea is that this evolutionary arrangement is too improbable to be worth considering. Nevertheless, the point remains that uniformity is, at best, sufficient; it is not *necessary*. In section 6.1, we shall see that the assumption of rate uniformity, while guaranteeing that overall similarity is convergent in the model there investigated, guarantees that parsimony is convergent as well. Hence no *preference* for one method over the other is mandated by the assumption of rate uniformity.

venture so sweeping and unconditional an endorsement. From this caution, philosophy has much to learn.

3.2. Correlation, Common Cause, and Screening-Off

As noted in section 2.3, Newton held that a principle of the common cause plays a central role in scientific inference: "To the same natural effects, we must, as far as possible, assign the same causes." Newton then cites some examples. He mentions "respiration in a man and in a beast, the descent of stones in Europe and in America, the light of our culinary fire and of the sun, the reflection of light in the earth and in the planets."

Stones falling in Europe and those falling in America owe their similarity to a common cause—the earth, which exerts a gravitational force on each. In similar fashion, we might observe (although Newton, of course, would not have) that respiration in human beings and respiration in chimps trace back as homologies to a common ancestor.

But the last example Newton cites is quite different: light coming off my sons' baseball (illuminated by a flashlight in a darkened room) and that reflected by the planet Jupiter do not trace back to a common source of illumination. Each has its own source; those sources produce their effects in similar ways. This last example, we might say, involves an analogy, not a homology.

We may express this difference in the philosophical jargon of *type* and *token*. A token event is unique and unrepeatable; a type event may have zero, one, or many instances. If you and I own the same shirt, this may mean same *type* of shirt or same *token* shirt. The latter requires joint ownership; the former does not. In all four of Newton's examples, pairs of token effects have a common *type* of cause. In the first two, but not in the last, it is plausible to think that they trace back to a common *token* cause.

Besides concealing this ambiguity (on which more later), Newton's brief formulation is flawed in a second way. A moment's thought shows that there are many similarities that are not plausibly explained by postulating a common token cause. The shirt I now am wearing is blue and so is the Mediterranean Sea. The judges on the U.S. Supreme Court are nine in number and so are the planets that revolve around the sun. But these are just boring *coincidences*. It is an overactive imagination that sees *all* similar token events as due to a common token cause.

This criticism of Newton's formulation is perhaps unfair, in view of the fact that he hedges his principle by saying that common causes should be postulated "as far as possible." This phrase presumably means that a common cause should be assumed only if the postulate is otherwise plausible, given everything else one believes. The trouble is that this hedge robs the principle of its teeth. The principle now seems to say only that common cause explanations should be invoked when it is reasonable to do so, all things considered . The same may be said of separate cause explanations, and, indeed, of demonic explanations.

Can the principle of the common cause be rescued from triviality? In this century Bertrand Russell [1948] and Hans Reichenbach [1956] took the entirely natural step of focusing on the idea of improbable coincidences. If two events are similar in ways that would be immensely improbable if they had separate causes, we may reasonably hypothesize that they trace back to a common cause. Plausible examples (in addition to the plagiarism case mentioned earlier) are not far to seek:

> (i) . . . several actors in a stage play fall ill, showing symptoms of food poisoning. We assume that the poisoned food stems from the same source—for instance, that it was contained in a common meal—and thus look for an explanation of the coincidence in terms of a common cause. (Reichenbach [1956, p. 157])
>
> (ii) . . . both lamps in a room go out suddenly. We regard it as improbable that by chance both bulbs burned out at the same time, and look for a burned-out fuse or some other interruption of the common power supply. The improbable coincidence is thus explained as the product of a common cause. (Reichenbach [1956, p. 157])
>
> (iii) A group of individuals simultaneously have very similar visual experiences. It is possible that each individual, independently, is hallucinating, or that the individuals happen to be looking at distinct, though similar, physical objects. But given the similarity of the experiences, it is more plausible to think that they trace back to a common cause—the individuals are all perceiving a single physical object. (Russell [1948, pp. 480ff])

Reichenbach [1956] proposed that the structure of this sort of explanation could be understood in terms of the idea of a *conjunctive fork*. This idea is specified in terms of the probabilistic relationships that obtain among a postulated cause and its joint effects. In order to explain Reichenbach's idea, I shall embellish some of the details of the first example about the acting company. The reader will note that no probabilistic details were provided above.

Let us follow this theater troupe for several years and record the days on which the various actors experience gastrointestinal distress. We observe that the leading man and the leading lady each become ill about once every hundred days. This might lead us to infer that the probability of becoming sick on any given day for each actor is 0.01. If one actor's sickness were probabilistically independent of the other's, we could calculate the probability that the two actors become sick on the same day; it would be

$(0.01) \times (0.01) = 0.0001$. But suppose we observe that the two actors get sick together far more frequently than this would suggest. Just to make things graphic, imagine that their states of health almost perfectly covary: there is an almost perfect match in the two actors' sick days. The suspicion thereby arises that the individual actors do not become sick independently.

Reichenbach's theory says that common cause explanation begins with a correlation that requires explanation. Correlation means probabilistic dependence.[6] In the case at hand, the first actor's becoming sick (A_1) is positively correlated with the second's becoming sick (A_2):

(1) $\Pr(A_1 \ \& \ A_2) > \Pr(A_1) \times \Pr(A_2)$.[7]

The idea may then suggest itself that the actors always share their meals together and that this is a common cause that may explain their correlated illnesses. We hypothesize that when their food is tainted (T), the probability of becoming sick is quite high; however, when the food is not tainted (not-T), the probability of becoming sick is quite low. This is,

(2) $\Pr(A_1/T) > \Pr(A_1/\text{not-}T)$.

(3) $\Pr(A_2/T) > \Pr(A_2/\text{not-}T)$.

In addition, Reichenbach thought that the causal factor (eating spoiled food or eating fresh food) would have the following probabilistic property. If the two actors eat spoiled food, the probability that they both will take sick will be the product of the probabilities that each becomes ill. That is, the state of the food renders the states of the actors conditionally independent:

(4) $\Pr(A_1 \ \& \ A_2/T) = \Pr(A_1/T) \times \Pr(A_2/T)$.

(5) $\Pr(A_1 \ \& \ A_2/\text{not-}T) = \Pr(A_1/\text{not-}T) \times \Pr(A_2/\text{not-}T)$.

Reichenbach saw that (2)–(5) imply (1); a cause that is positively correlated with each effect [(2)–(3)] and renders them conditionally probabilistically independent [(4)–(5)] implies that the two effects will be correlated [(1)].

If two effects are correlated, the one provides information about the other. In the example, one actor's state of health provides a basis for predicting the other's. But once we know whether their food was tainted or not, discovering whether one actor gets sick provides no *additional* predictive help for saying if the other gets sick as well. In such cases, the cause

6. We are here considering properties that come in just two states; an actor is either sick or not, for example. In this case, the concepts of correlation and probabilistic dependence are equivalent. However, if we consider quantitative characters (as in, for example, the claim that height and weight are positively correlated in a population), we must be more careful. In that case, probabilistic independence implies that the correlation is zero, but not conversely.

7. This may be expressed equivalently as $\Pr(A_1/A_2) > \Pr(A_1)$.

is said to *screen-off* one effect from the other, since conditions (2)–(5) also imply that

$$Pr(A_1/T) = Pr(A_1/T \& A_2).$$

When a cause screens-off one effect from the other, the triplet of events is said to form a *conjunctive fork*.

It is a striking fact that the correlation (probabilistic dependence) of two effects can be explained by invoking a cause that renders them uncorrelated (probabilistically independent). There is no magic here—only the difference between unconditional probability and conditional probability. Just to demystify this simple idea completely, I shall flesh out the example with a set of hypothetical probabilities, corresponding to (2)–(5), and see what they imply about (1).

We began by observing that the two actors take sick about once every hundred days, which led us to estimate the probability of illness for each as 0.01. Similarly, since they almost always take sick together, we estimated that the probability of them both being ill is something quite close to 0.01, which is much greater than the product (0.0001) of the separate probabilities. We now shall postulate some further probabilities that allow us to deduce the facts just mentioned.

Besides the conditional independence assumptions (4)–(5), we might conjecture that

$$Pr(A_1/T) = Pr(A_2/T) = 0.95,$$
$$Pr(A_1/\text{not-}T) = Pr(A_2/\text{not-}T) = 0.0,$$
$$Pr(T) = 1/95.$$

I expand the expression for the probability of each actor's getting sick as follows:

$$Pr(A_i) = Pr(A_i/T)\,Pr(T) + Pr(A_i/\text{not-}T)\,Pr(\text{not-}T).$$

This has a value of 0.01. So our postulated structure predicts a probability of illness for each actor that precisely coincides with the frequency we have observed.

Next, I expand the expression for the probability that the two actors get sick together as follows:

$$Pr(A_1 \& A_2) = Pr(A_1 \& A_2/T)\,Pr(T) + Pr(A_1 \& A_2/\text{not-}T)\,Pr(\text{not-}T).$$

The assumption that the presence or absence of the hypothetical causal factor (T) renders the two effects conditionally independent allows this expression to be rewritten as

$$Pr(A_1 \& A_2) = Pr(A_1/T)\,Pr(A_2/T)\,Pr(T)$$
$$+ Pr(A_1/\text{not-}T)\,Pr(A_2/\text{not-}T)\,Pr(\text{not-}T).$$

It follows that the probability that both actors are sick on a given day is 95% of 0.01. Again we see that the postulated probability coincides closely with the observed frequency. I hope this helps the reader see how a cause that raises the probability of its effects and renders them probabilistically independent of each other implies that those effects will be correlated.

So far I have simply noted a set of possibilities. When two events are correlated, this *can* be explained by postulating a common cause that induces a given set of probabilistic relationships. However, Reichenbach [1956] and Salmon [1971, 1975] took the further step of conjecturing that this possibility was in fact a necessity. Their Principle of the Common Cause took the following form:

> Given two correlated events E_1 and E_2, there is some prior event C, which is a cause of E_1 and is also a cause of E_2, and which renders them conditionally probabilistically independent.[8]

Reichenbach and Salmon thereby gave the principle an *ontological* cast. It says that for every pair of events of a certain sort, there *exists* a third event with certain properties. This is quite different from the epistemological reading one might expect if the principle were a rule of nondeductive inference. In that case, one might expect the principle to read, if two events are correlated, then *it is reasonable to postulate* a common cause of a certain sort. The difference between these two formulations will have some importance in what follows.[9] The ontological formulation would be refuted if we could find a single pair of correlated events that lacks a screening-off common cause. The latter principle, on the other hand, need not be touched by such a result. Just as we saw in section 3.1 in connection with the problem of estimating a coin's bias, an inference rule can be *reasonable* without being *infallible*. The principle of the common cause may give reasonable advice, even if it occasionally errs. So refuting the epistemological formulation may be harder than refuting the ontological one.

Another thing to notice about Reichenbach's principle is that it does not value common cause explanations for their own sake, but rather because they induce a particular sort of probabilistic relationship. Common causes are to be prized because they screen-off one effect from the other. To see if

8. In this formulation, it is assumed that E_1 is not a cause of E_2 and E_2 is not a cause of E_1. Otherwise, the principle would have to be formulated by saying that correlated events must possess a screening-off common cause, or else one must be a cause of the other. Note that the principle applies to events that are negatively correlated as well as to those that are positively correlated.

9. A principle is said to be "ontological" in character when it has implications about what exists; this follows the usage of that term introduced in chapter 2. On the other hand, a principle will be said to be "epistemological" if it merely describes what it is reasonable to think exists.

this is plausible, we must determine whether other forms of explanation can do the same. Can an explanation in terms of separate causes screen-off? It is notable that the principle of the common cause as stated by Reichenbach and Salmon is not formulated in terms of this *comparative* question, even though both authors use the principle to compare common cause and separate cause explanations. This comparative issue is vital, if we expect the principle of the common cause to have epistemological import.

Finally, it is important to note that Reichenbach's principle begins with correlations as the relevant data. Even if correlations do cry out for common cause explanation, we must ask whether other kinds of data might not do so as well. This last question does not challenge the soundness of the principle, but raises the issue of its completeness.

In what follows, I shall argue that each of these questions reveals important limitations in the common cause principle, construed epistemologically. The criticisms I shall develop are therefore quite different from the one advanced by Suppes and Zinotti [1976] and Van Fraassen [1980, 1982], who have seen quantum mechanics as the source of difficulty. Their challenge undermines the principle as a general ontological thesis, but leaves it virtually untouched as an epistemological one. My criticisms, on the other hand, center on the standing of the principle as a guide in nondeductive inference. However, before I catalog these epistemological defects, I first shall describe how Reichenbach's principle came to grief as an ontological claim.

3.3. An Ontological Difficulty

Reichenbach's principle does not say that every common cause of correlated events must screen-off each from the other. It says that every such pair of events has a screening-off common cause. The logical difference here is not hard to grasp; there is all the difference in the world between saying that every pair of twins has a parent who looks after them and saying that every parent of twins looks after them.

This is a good thing, since many (nay, most!) common causes do not screen-off. Consider the device depicted in figure 10. A roulette wheel is spun. If the ball lands on 00, a signal is sent to a coin toss mechanism. A fair coin is then tossed; if it lands heads, a deterministic signal is sent to each of two bells that causes them to ring. Without the coin's landing heads, the bells remain silent. And without the ball's falling 00, the coin is not tossed.

The ball's landing 00 is a common cause, in Reichenbach's sense, of the bells' ringing; whenever the bells ring, this joint event traces back to the ball's landing 00. However, the thing to notice is that this common cause does not screen-off one bell's sounding from the other's. The states of the two bells are perfectly correlated. Though each sounds (approximately)

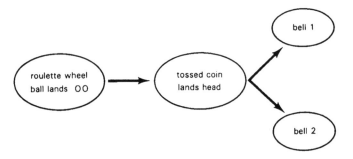

Figure 10.
A causal chain from distal cause to proximal cause to joint effects. If the ball drops 00, the coin is tossed; if the coin lands heads, the two bells ring.

once every seventy-six times the wheel is spun, they always sound together. This means that

$$\Pr(B_1 \,\&\, B_2) = \Pr(B_1) > \Pr(B_1) \times \Pr(B_2).$$

If we conditionalize these two events on the ball's landing 00, we obtain

$$\Pr(B_1 \,\&\, B_2/00) = 0.5 > \Pr(B_1/00) \times \Pr(B_2/00) = 0.25.$$

The ball's landing 00 *raises* the probability of the bells' sounding from what it was before (i.e., from what it was, simply given that the wheel was spun). However, the 00 does not render the two effects conditionally independent. Here is a common cause that fails to screen-off the joint effects from each other.[10]

In this process, there *is* a screening-off common cause. It is the coin's landing heads. If the coin lands heads up (H), both bells will sound:

$$\Pr(B_1 \,\&\, B_2/H) = \Pr(B_1/H) \times \Pr(B_2/H) = 1.0.$$

Although I have arranged this example so that the last link in the causal chain is deterministic, this is not essential. Suppose, instead, that heads confers on each bell a probability of sounding of 0.9. In this case $\Pr(B_1 \,\&\, B_2/00) = (1/2)(0.9)(0.9)$, which is greater than $\Pr(B_1/00)\Pr(B_2/00) = [(1/2)(0.9)]^2$. The distal cause does not screen-off, though the proximal one does.

Let us imagine that part of the causal process just described (with the last link deterministic as stipulated initially) is hidden from view. We observe the roulette wheel's behavior and the sounding of the bells, but nothing in

10. Salmon [1984, pp. 168ff] describes other examples in which a common cause fails to screen-off one effect from the other. Reichenbach [1956, p. 161] also recognized this possibility.

between. The bells ring only if 00 is produced. When the ball lands on that number, the bells sound about half the time. But their states are perfectly correlated. Reichenbach's principle codifies the idea that this correlation cries out for explanation. The ball's landing 00 *helps* explain the correlation, but it seems to be incomplete in the illumination it offers.

Reichenbach's principle instructs us to postulate a hidden variable. There is something that intervenes between the roulette wheel's state and the states of the bells that fully explains the correlation. Not only does it seem "reasonable" to think that some such mechanism exists. In addition, Reichenbach's principle reflects the deeper conviction that the world must be so constituted. Correlations of this sort cannot be ultimate and inexplicable.[11]

One of the most striking conceptual innovations of quantum mechanics is that it has forced us to reconsider this heartfelt ontological assumption. The original puzzle was posed by Einstein, Podolsky, and Rosen [1936] in a thought experiment they thought showed that quantum mechanics is incomplete. Since then, there has been a series of increasingly more powerful "no hidden variable" proofs, culminating in the paper of Bell [1965]. These arguments provide powerful reasons for thinking that certain sorts of correlations cannot have screening-off common causes; a strong case can be made for holding that the sort of completeness that Einstein, Podolsky, and Rosen demanded is not to be had. The technical details of these arguments need not detain us here. Nor shall I attend to the important differences that distinguish the various results from each other. Nevertheless, I shall outline one epistemological lesson that flows from Bell's result and sketch how his theorem is derived.

It may be thought that the principle of the common cause cannot be undermined by any observation. The idea is that if our current theory fails to provide a screening-off common cause for a pair of correlated events, this simply means that the theory is *incomplete*; if one detailed common cause hypothesis fails to pan out, another can be constructed in its stead. It therefore might appear that any and all observations are compatible with Reichenbach's principle. If so, the Reichenbach principle is untestable; the principle would be *a priori* and metaphysical—one that guides scientific inquiry without being vulnerable to the testimony of experience.

One of the lessons of Quine's [1952, 1960] work on the notion of *a priori* truth is that the empirical consequences of a proposition are often quite unexpected, depending as they do on the kinds of background assumptions in which the proposition can be embedded. A principle may appear to be untestable because it is very difficult to see how it might be tested; here the

---

11. It is here assumed that repeated trials have allowed us to discount the possibility that the observed correlation is a "mere accident"—i.e., the result of sampling error.

seeming invulnerability to observation reflects our own (one hopes temporary) lack of imagination, not some special epistemological status that the principle possesses.[12] Bell's result is an example of this sort: the Reichenbach principle may appear to be untestable, but it can be shown to issue in testable consequences when further plausible assumptions are conjoined.

Imagine an experiment in which two particles are produced by a common source. Call these the left particle (L) and the right (R) one. We can perform one of three experiments on each particle; these experimental settings we shall call 1, 2, and 3. On each experiment there are two possible results, which we denote by "0" and "1". "Li & Rj" represents the proposition that the ith experiment is performed on the left particle and the jth experiment is performed on the right particle ($i, j = 1, 2, 3$). "Lia" is the proposition that the ith experiment was performed on the left-hand particle with result a ($a = 0, 1$). Ditto for Rjb.[13]

I have just described a kind of experimental setup. We can run many trials on devices of this type, varying the experiments we perform on the two particles and observing the results. We thereby obtain a large number of results, which show us what happens when the particles are subjected to the same experimental arrangement or to different ones. Suppose we observe that if the same experiment is run on the two particles, they never issue in the same result:

(I) $Pr(Lia \& Ria/Li \& Ri) = 0.$

We also observe that the experimental setting for one particle screens off the setting assigned to the other particle from the result achieved on the first:

(II) $Pr(Rjb/Li \& Rj) = Pr(Rjb/Rj).$

The probability statements (I) and (II) can be thought of as summaries of what we have learned from a large number of observations.[14]

So our observations tell us that the left and right particles in the system under study are perfectly anticorrelated. If we accept Reichenbach's principle of the common cause, we shall postulate a common cause that can take on different values. This parallels how we reasoned in the acting troupe example. The correlation of sick days led us to introduce a common cause (the meals taken together) that can take on two possible values—

12. This general approach to the status of *a priori* knowledge is developed in Sober [1984c, chapter 2].
13. This exposition of Bell's [1965] argument is drawn from Van Fraassen [1982].
14. A very small inferential step should be acknowledged here. Strictly speaking, we have observed the frequencies of different experimental outcomes in different experimental arrangements. We then infer the above probabilities from this large number of observations.

tainted food or untainted food. In the present case, we shall not restrict the putative common cause to two possible values, but will use Aq to mean that the factor A has value q. We shall not worry here about how many values A can assume.

This postulated common cause will be said to have three properties:

(III) $\Pr(Lia \& Rjb/Li \& Rj \& Aq)$
$= \Pr(Lia/Li \& Rj \& Aq) \times \Pr(Rjb/Li \& Rj \& Aq),$

(IV) $\Pr(Lia/Li \& Rj \& Aq) = \Pr(Lia/Li \& Aq),$
$\Pr(Rjb/Li \& Rj \& Aq) = \Pr(Rjb/Rj \& Aq),$

(V) $\Pr(Aq/Li \& Rj) = \Pr(Aq).$

Principle (III) asserts that the experimental settings for the left and right particles plus the state of the putative common cause screen-off the results obtained on the two particles from each other. Van Fraassen [1982, p. 32] explains the rationale behind principles (IV) and (V) as follows:

> ... the common cause is meant to be located at the particle source, in the absolute past of the two events, which have space-like separation. Now the choices of the experimental settings, and of the particular type of source used, can all be made beforehand, or else in any temporal order, and by means of any chance mechanisms or experimenters' whims you care to specify.
>
> To put it conversely, if the probability of a given outcome at L is dependent not merely on the putative common cause, but also on what happens at R, or if the character of that putative common cause itself depends on which experimental arrangement is chosen (even if after the source has been constructed) then I say that the two outcome events have *not* been traced back to a common cause which explains their correlation.

Although Van Fraassen treats (III), (IV), and (V) as collectively implementing the principle of the common cause, it is perhaps more accurate to see (III) as playing this role, with (IV) and (V) contributing something distinct, though no less intuitive. For a Reichenbachian explanation would be forthcoming if there were a "conspiracy" of the kind described by Clauser and Horne [1974], wherein the state of A and the experimental settings for the two particles were coordinated by some event that was a common cause of all three.

The main point to notice, however, is that (III), (IV), and (V) have great intuitive force. They are "theoretical"—they constrain what a common cause must be like, and therefore differ markedly from (I) and (II), which merely summarize the results of repeated observations.

Bell's theorem combines these five assertions to obtain an inequality stated purely in terms of observables. Let $p(i;j)$ be the probability of getting result 1 on both the left and the right particles, if the left particle is given the ith experimental setting and the right particle is given the jth. Bell's inequality then follows:

$$p(1;2) + p(2;3) \geq p(1;3).$$

Notice that this inequality can be tested by repeated experiment.

When such experiments are performed on certain quantum mechanical particle systems, the inequality is violated.[15] But since propositions (I)–(V) entail that inequality, at least one of them must be false. (I) and (II) are well confirmed by observation. So the culprit must be at least one of (III), (IV), and (V). If these last three express what is required of a common cause model in the sense of the principle of the common cause, then that principle is false.

Experimental counterexamples to Bell's inequality all seem to involve particle systems in which very peculiar "nonclassical" things occur. Thus Salmon [1984, p. 253] remarks that "all of the problematic microphysical cases seem to involve quantum mechanical 'reduction of the wave packet'—a phenomenon that has no counterpart in macrophysics, to the best of my knowledge." The idea expressed here—one that I think is widely shared by philosophers—is that Reichenbach's principle of the common cause would have been fine, had it not been for the weirdness of quantum mechanical phenomena. In the next section, I shall argue that there are numerous additional defects in Reichenbach's principle, even when it is restricted to the simplest of "classical" phenomena.

I mentioned in section 3.2 that Reichenbach and Salmon formulated their principle mainly as an ontological doctrine ("every pair of correlated events has a screening-off common cause"), although they also give the principle an epistemological reading ("when two events are correlated, it is reasonable to postulate a screening-off common cause"). Quantum mechanics offers empirical counterexamples to the ontological doctrine. What bearing do these have on the epistemological formulation?

We have just seen a context in which it can be *unreasonable* to postulate a screening-off common cause. *If* the correlation is known to be perfect and *if* you know that Bell's inequality is violated, then you have considerable room to doubt that a screening-off common cause exists. We see here yet another example of how inference to the best explanation is mediated by background information. Reichenbach's principle leads straight from an observed correlation to the hypothesis of a screening-off common cause.

15. And what is more, quantum theory correctly predicts that the inequality will be violated.

Quantum mechanics has shown how that inference can be way laid by other facts that are confirmable by observation.

Nevertheless, this is a very special case. The strange and unexpected behavior of certain particle systems has posed the problem. But perhaps the principle of the common cause involves a classical causal framework that is entirely reasonable for any science except the physics of elementary particles. Nothing said so far addresses this issue. It is for this reason that the examples from quantum mechanics do not at all resolve the problem of how we should regard the principle of the common cause as a piece of epistemology.

3.4. Epistemological Difficulties

Reichenbach's principle, which henceforth will be understood epistemologically, not ontologically, deploys three conceptual elements. These are observed *correlation*, postulated *common cause*, and *screening-off*. The principle can be decomposed into two theses. First, there is the claim that an observed correlation ought to be explained by postulating a common cause. Second, there is the assertion that common cause hypotheses should be formulated so as to induce a screening-off relation between the two correlated effects.[16]

Both these claims face serious difficulties. To begin with, it simply is not true that every correlation cries out for common cause explanation. To see why, let us consider a more general definition of the idea of correlation than the one given in section 3.2. That condition characterized correlations for yes/no properties, such as the ringing or not ringing of the bells depicted in figure 10. But suppose one considers two quantitative characters X and Y, like height and weight. The correlation coefficient, r_{XY}, can take values between -1 and $+1$ and is defined as follows:

$$r_{XY} = \frac{\overline{XY} - (\overline{X})(\overline{Y})}{\sqrt{(\overline{X^2} - \overline{X}^2)(\overline{Y^2} - \overline{Y}^2)}}.$$

"$\overline{X}$" denotes the mean value of the X's, and similarly for the other barred symbols. It is assumed that the data consist of a list of paired values—the height and weight of each of a number of people, for example. A positive correlation indicates that higher than average values of one quantity tend to be associated with higher than average values of the other. In this case, "association" means that being heavy (or light) and being tall (or short) tend to be properties that attach to the same person. The analogy with the simpler case of yes/no properties discussed earlier should be clear: If two

---

16. The formulation of the principle in terms of *two* correlated events can, of course, be generalized to any arbitrary number of correlates.

quantities (or events) are correlated, information about one provides some basis for making a prediction about the other.

The "pairing" of observed values of X and Y need not be based on their being properties of the same individual, as in the case of height and weight just discussed. One might consider two objects and the properties they exhibit at each of a number of times. Suppose that at any given time, the two bells in figure 10 could each produce any of the twelve tones in an octave. There would be a positive correlation between their states if low pitch on one bell tended to be associated with low pitch on the other bell. Reichenbach's principle applies here with the same force it has for the yes/no case: a correlation is said to demand a common cause explanation.

The trouble is that any two monotonically increasing quantities will be positively correlated. The price of bread in England has been on the increase during the past two centuries and so has the sea level in Venice. These are positively correlated; lower than average values of one are associated with lower than average values of the other. Yet no one would propose to explain this by postulating a common cause (Sober [1987]).[17]

Why is this? It is not that we think it absurd that there may be some sort of rough resemblance between the *kinds* of processes that may lie behind these two phenomena. Economic factors, broadly construed, may have played a role in each. Rather, what seems implausible is the suggestion that the two phenomena trace back to the same *token* cause. Our background beliefs tell us that it is far more natural to see each increase as fueled by a rather localized endogenous process—the one working itself out in Britain, the other in Venice.[18]

The lesson of this example is as follows: It is not just any arbitrary correlation that demands explanation in terms of common causes. Some do; others do not. Furthermore, there is no general and a priori recipe for determining whether an observed correlation is of one sort or the other. Everything depends on one's background theory about the empirical subject matter at hand.

This point is unsurprising once one takes seriously the dispute between cladistic parsimony and overall similarity as possible indicators of propinquity of descent. I described in chapter 1 how these approaches can generate different judgments as to which genealogical hypothesis is best

17. I assume that the "passage of time" does not denote an appropriate causal variable in terms of which the correlation should be explained.

18. The reader will see in this idea of independent endogenous processes a recipe for inventing a whole range of counterexamples of the Venice/Britain variety to Reichenbach's principle. Russell [1948, pp. 486–487] recognized that a separate cause explanation involving two endogenous processes "running in tandem" can generate a complex similarity among its joint effects, just as a common cause structure can.

supported by given data. It now is time to see that correlation can also disagree with parsimony.

Suppose we have coded forty characters for species A, B, and C; they fall into the following four patterns:

		Characters			
		1–10	11–20	21–30	31–40
	A	1	1	0	1
Species	B	1	0	0	1
	C	0	0	0	1

As usual, "0" means ancestral and "1" derived. Notice that cladistic parsimony will view only the first ten characters as evidentially meaningful, and so will take the entire data set as pointing unambiguously (i.e., without any character incongruence) to the phylogenetic grouping (AB)C.

If we let correlation of characters guide our judgments about propinquity of descent, we will reach a different conclusion. Recall that two yes/no variables X and Y are positively correlated precisely when $Pr(X \& Y) > Pr(X)Pr(Y)$. We shall use *covariance* to measure the strength of association; $Cov(X, Y)$ is defined as $Pr(X \& Y) - Pr(X)Pr(Y)$. Note that independent events have a zero covariance.

The singleton and conjoint probabilities in the above data set are as follows:

$Pr(A \text{ is } 1) = 3/4,$ $Pr(B \text{ is } 1) = 1/2,$ $Pr(C \text{ is } 1) = 1/4,$
$Pr(A \text{ is } 1 \text{ and } B \text{ is } 1) = 1/2,$
$Pr(A \text{ is } 1 \text{ and } C \text{ is } 1) = 1/4,$
$Pr(B \text{ is } 1 \text{ and } C \text{ is } 1) = 1/4.$

The three covariances are as follows:

$Cov(A, B) = 1/2 - 3/8 = 1/8,$
$Cov(A, C) = 1/4 - 3/16 = 1/16,$
$Cov(B, C) = 1/4 - 1/8 = 1/8.$

So a covariance approach would conclude that the forty characters do not discriminate between (AB)C and A(BC). This is also what overall similarity would conclude.[19]

A more general point can be made about the difference between cladistic parsimony and the idea of covariance. Covariance, like the notion of overall

19. Although Reichenbach [1956] and Salmon [1984] do not say so, it is natural to take the Principle of the Common Cause as saying, in the context of phylogenetic inference, that degree of positive covariance indicates degree of propinquity of descent. A model in which this holds true will be discussed in chapter 6.

similarity, accords no special significance to the distinction between ancestral similarity and derived similarity. If a covariance approach interprets a
given set of data as favoring one hypothesis over another (or as failing to
do so), the same verdict would be obtained if all the 0's were changed to 1's
and the 1's to 0's. I leave it as an exercise to the reader to verify that this is
so for the above example. This insensitivity to the difference between
synapomorphy and symplesiomorphy, of course, is worlds away from the
parsimony approach.[20]

A case in which Reichenbach's principle diverges from the dictates of
both overall similarity and cladistic parsimony arises if we imagine a data
set consisting just of characters like the first ten shown above. Parsimony
and overall similarity agree that these 110 characters point unambiguously
to the genealogical grouping (AB)C. However, no pair of species shows
a positive covariance here, since, for example, $\Pr(A$ is 1 and B is $1) =$
$\Pr(A$ is $1)\Pr(B$ is $1) = 1.0$. The covariance idea does not instruct us to
postulate a common ancestor of the matching taxa in this case.

A final example worth pondering is the data set obtained by adding ten
more characters showing the 100 pattern to the forty displayed above.
Cladistic parsimony will continue to prefer (AB)C, even though B and C
are now the pair with the highest covariance (as well as being the pair with
the greatest overall similarity).

The biologically uncontroversial point that can be made about the dispute between phenetic measures and cladistic parsimony is quite devastating to Reichenbach's principle. If there are circumstances in which cladistic
parsimony is to be used in preference to phenetic measures, then Reichenbach's principle is mistaken as a generality. Correlation at times will be the
wrong basis on which to postulate common causes.

Hempel held that observed black ravens confirm the generalization that
all ravens are black in a circumstance in which we know nothing at all
about the empirical phenomena under investigation (section 2.5). Reichenbach held that correlated events should be explained by postulating a
common cause. These principles have a common defect. They propose too
direct a connection between observations and inferred hypotheses. Only in
the context of a background theory does an observation have evidential
meaning. Reichenbach's principle, just as much as Hempel's, is flawed by its
implicit reliance on the Principle of Empiricism—that hypotheses ultimately trace back for their support to observations and to observations
alone.

The second ingredient in Reichenbach's principle—that common causes

20. Forster [1986] elaborates a covariance treatment of cladistic parsimony. Although it
is presented as a reconstruction of the cladistic idea, the above-mentioned property of
covariance places Forster's treatment in the context of a phenetic approach.

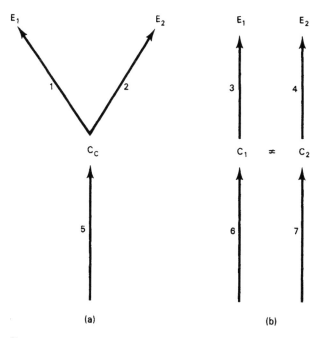

Figure 11.
If E_1 and E_2 are event types, their correlation may be explained (a) by postulating a common cause or (b) by postulating separate causes. If E_1 and E_2 are event tokens, their matching may be explained in either way. In both cases, probabilities attaching to branches 1–7 must be specified if the two explanations are to say how probable the observations are.

are to be postulated *because* they can screen-off correlated effects from each other—fares no better. Notably absent from Reichenbach's principle is the idea that hypothesis evaluation is a *comparative* task. If a principle tells us to construct a certain sort of explanation, there must be some rationale for why we should construct that kind of account *rather than some other*. If common cause explanations are preferable because they have a given probabilistic property, this must be because alternative forms of explanation cannot deliver the same benefits.

But this is a mistake. *Separate cause explanations* can screen-off correlated effects from each other. Suppose we observe that events E_1 and E_2 are correlated. Reichenbach's principle instructs us to explain this correlation by postulating a common cause, C_c. This explanation is shown in figure 11a. If screening-off is what we are after, we may formulate the common cause hypothesis so that the common cause is said to render the two effects conditionally independent.

Figure 11b shows how the observed correlation of E_1 and E_2 can be explained by postulating separate causes. But here again, if screening-off is what we want, we may stipulate that the two *distinct* causes C_1 and C_2 are perfectly correlated and that the states of these causes screen-off the state of one effect from that of the other. This separate cause explanation will then satisfy Reichenbach's four conditions:

(2') $Pr(E_1/C_1 \& C_2) > Pr(E_1/not\text{-}(C_1 \& C_2))$,

(3') $Pr(E_2/C_1 \& C_2) > Pr(E_2/not\text{-}(C_1 \& C_2))$,

(4') $Pr(E_1 \& E_2/C_1 \& C_2) = Pr(F_1/C_1 \& C_2) \times Pr(E_2/C_1 \& C_2)$,

(5') $Pr(E_1 \& E_2/not\text{-}(C_1 \& C_2))$
          $= Pr(E_1/not\text{-}(C_1 \& C_2)) \times Pr(E_2/not\text{-}(C_1 \& C_2))$.

The effect of postulating that C_1 and C_2 are perfectly correlated is to ensure that conditionalizing on the claim that not both occur—i.e., on the event denoted above by "$not\text{-}(C_1 \& C_2)$"—is interpreted to mean that neither does.

Granted, it is often implausible to stipulate that two distinct causes exhibit a perfect correlation, though if they themselves had an immediate common cause, Reichenbach's principle would view their impressive correlation as adequately explained. This is well taken, but my point is that a separate cause explanation can be constructed that induces the same probabilistic structure that Reichenbach associated with common cause explanation. And this we now have. Postulating "lawfully cooccurring" but *distinct* causes screens-off the correlated effects from each other just as much as postulating a common cause does. If one of these explanations is preferable, it must be so on grounds other than that given by the screening-off requirement.

This idea was already visible in the example of British bread prices and Venetian sea levels. We could invent a screening-off common cause explanation, but it would have been implausible to do so. Our background information indicated that plausibility was on the side of postulating separate causes. The Britain/Venice example and the example depicted in figure 11 (with C_1 and C_2 distinct but perfectly correlated) both show that a common cause explanation does not win our hearts just because it can induce a screening-off relation.

Even though screening-off is not a unique feature of common cause explanation, there is a special property of the explanations shown in figure 11 that is noteworthy. If we stipulate that the separate causes in 11b are independent, then a common cause explanation can achieve something that a separate cause explanation cannot. We may view the two patterns depicted in figure 11 as skeletons that may be fleshed out by fixing the values of the probabilities attaching to branches 1–7. Those assigned to branches 5–7 give the probability of a putative cause; those assigned to branches

1–4 are the probabilities of an effect, given the presence or absence of a postulated cause.

Suppose we know nothing at all about what these values may be. We merely wish to invent two explanations that have the patterns given in figure 11 and then compare them. In doing this, we want to formulate the *best* possible common cause explanation and the *best* possible separate cause explanation. We shall adopt the "natural" (though hardly inevitable) stipulation that causes screen-off noncauses from effects. The goal is to explain the correlation between the two observed events, namely, that $Pr(E_1 \& E_2) > Pr(E_1) \times Pr(E_2)$. What would it mean to explain this fact, and how are we to evaluate which explanation counts as better?

Merely to deduce that the inequality is true is not enough. Suppose each of the effects occurs about half the time, but that each almost always occurs when the other does. Something is seriously amiss with an explanation of these facts that assigns to each conjunct and to the conjunction as well a probability of 10^{-10}. An inequality has been deduced, but the assignment of values to the probabilities leaves a great deal to be desired.

Clearly, an explanation of the correlation must explain the frequencies of the joint and singleton events as well as implying that a given inequality obtains. These various frequencies are explained by assigning them probabilities. What makes one assignment "better" than another?

Here likelihood suggests itself. If one of the events occurs about half the time, it considerably strains our credulity to be told that it has a probability of 10^{-10}. Far better to assign it a probability of 0.5. In this case, probability assignments are better to the degree that they approximate observed frequencies. Just as in the case of estimating the bias of a coin given data about the results of independent tosses, the sample mean is the maximum likelihood estimate of the probability.

From this, we can identify an asymmetry between the common cause and the separate cause patterns displayed in figure 11. We can assign probabilities to branches 1, 2, and 5 so that the probabilities implied for the conjoint and singleton events precisely match their frequencies. But this we cannot do with the separate cause arrangement. If C_1 and C_2 are independent, then we cannot fix the probabilities associated with branches 3, 4, 6, and 7 so that the probabilities implied for the singleton and joint events exactly match their observed frequencies. We can fix a probability for the conjoint event that perfectly matches its frequency, in which case we must fail to do this for one of the singleton events. And we can stipulate probabilities for the singleton events that perfectly match their frequencies, but in so doing, we shall fail to achieve a match for the conjoint event. The common cause pattern thereby generates a better explanation than the separate cause pattern does.

It is essential to realize that this result is a highly qualified one. It does not come close to vindicating Reichenbach's general thesis that common cause explanations are better because they alone induce a screening-off relation. Rather, what we have here is a highly conditional result: *If* one can merely stipulate values for the probabilities associated with branches 1–7, the best assignment possible under the common cause arrangement will be better than the best assignment possible under the separate cause arrangement, if postulated causes are assumed to be mutually independent. We shall discuss later in this chapter when this technique of focusing on the "best case" assignment of probabilistic parameters is a reasonable one, but a few words now may be useful for the reader to grasp one sort of limitation that is involved here.

Let us apply this result to Reichenbach's example of the two actors. Each actor gets sick about once every hundred days, but if one gets sick on a day, the other almost always does so as well. We shall flesh out the common cause and the separate cause patterns as follows. The common cause explanation says that the actors always eat together and that they eat tainted food about once every hundred days. Assume further that tainted food all but guarantees gastrointestinal distress and that the symptom rarely occurs in the absence of spoiled food. This common cause hypothesis implies probabilities that perfectly match the observed singleton and conjoint frequencies.

The separate cause explanation is fleshed out as follows. We hypothesize that the actors always eat separately and that the presence of tainted food at a solitary meal virtually guarantees the illness, which would not occur without it. Let us stipulate that each actor eats tainted food about once every hundred days, and that the state of the food that one actor consumes is independent of that eaten by the other. This separate cause explanation delivers a probability for each singleton event that perfectly matches its observed frequency, but radically fails to do this for the conjoint event.

The point to notice is that we simply invented values for the probabilities associated with branches 1–7 in figure 11. Suppose, instead, that I provide information that constrains these assignments. Imagine that joint meals, should they occur, are always rigidly scrutinized, so that the chance of the actors eating tainted food under the common cause hypothesis is one in a billion. This information may seriously diminish the ability of the common cause explanation to provide a satisfying account of the observations. Indeed, we may constrain the assignment of probabilities to the branches in such a way that the separate cause explanation comes out *more* likely than the common cause story.

So the result obtained by inventing "best cases" constitutes a *sufficient* condition for a common cause explanation to be preferable to the best separate cause explanation. This sufficient condition is highly specific, in that the asymmetry may be undermined if new background information is brought to bear. More on this later.

I want to emphasize the interpretation I have given the concept of "best explanation" in this argument. The best explanation, in a likelihood framework, is the one that makes the observations most probable. In my argument, screening-off is not a *sui generis* rationale for common cause explanation; rather, it is one in a set of assumptions that entails that common cause explanations are preferable simply because they are more likely.[21]

The earlier example in which the separate causes in figure 11b are perfectly correlated shows that screening-off cannot in general be a sufficient rationale for our preference for common cause explanations. I now want to argue that common cause explanations can be reasonable and well confirmed even when they fail to induce the screening-off relation. So screening-off is not necessary, either.

The Rube Goldberg device depicted in figure 10 has already alerted us to the fact that a common cause (the ball's landing 00) can fail to screen off one effect from the other (the two bells' ringing). The structure here is quite general. Let us call the coin's landing heads *the proximal cause* and the roulette wheel's showing 00 *the distal cause*. We have here a process from distal cause (C_d) to proximal cause (C_p) to two correlated effects $(E_1$ and $E_2)$.

Let us suppose (i) that the proximal cause screens-off the effects from each other, (ii) that the proximal cause screens-off the distal cause from each effect, (iii) that all probabilities are intermediate (i.e, between 0 and 1, non-inclusive), and (iv) that the proximal cause makes a difference to the probability of each effect. In this rather general circumstance, the distal cause will not screen-off the effects from each other.[22]

---

21. In the next section, we shall see how likelihood is not the only factor affecting an explanation's plausibility.

22. To prove this claim, I begin with the following probabilities:

$$Pr(C_p/C_d) = p,$$
$$Pr(E_1/C_p) = a,$$
$$Pr(E_1/-C_p) = b,$$
$$Pr(E_2/C_p) = x,$$
$$Pr(E_2/-C_p) = y.$$

Conditions (i) and (ii) imply that $Pr(E_1 \& E_2/C_d) = Pr(E_1/C_d)Pr(E_2/C_d)$ precisely when

$$pax + (1-p)by = [pa + (1-p)b][px + (1-p)y],$$

which simplifies to

$$p(1-p)ax + p(1-p)by = p(1-p)ay + p(1-p)bx.$$

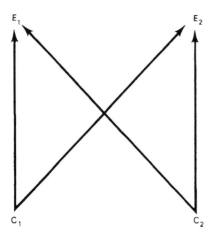

Figure 12.
C_1 and C_2 are each common causes of E_1 and E_2. See the text for a general condition under which neither common cause screens-off one effect from the other.

This fact about causal chains has a direct bearing on the claim that screening-off is a necessary feature of plausible common cause explanations. Scientists sometimes develop evidence for the existence of a distal cause, which they believe helps explain the correlation of two effects. In this case, their postulated common cause may fail to render the correlated effects conditionally independent. But the absence of screening-off does not prevent the explanation in terms of a common *distal* cause from being superior to an explanation in terms of separate causes. It is hardly uncommon for a common cause to be distal as opposed to proximal. If so, it can hardly be unreasonable for a scientist to be skeptical about a common cause hypothesis in which the common cause screens-off one effect from the other. Common causes may be plausible, but screening-off common causes will often be too good to be true.

A similar lesson follows from the fact that where there is one common cause of two effects, there may well be another. Figure 12 illustrates the kind of causal setup I have in mind. E_1 and E_2 are correlated effects, each having *two* common causes—C_1 and C_2. Let us suppose (i) that the total state of both causes (i.e., a specification of the presence or absence of each) screens-off each effect from the other, (ii) that all probabilities are intermediate, and (iii) that the probability of each effect is an increasing function

---

Given assumption (iii), this becomes

$$a(x - y) = b(x - y),$$

whose falsehood is guaranteed by (iv), which says that $a \neq b$ and $x \neq y$.

of the number of causes that are present. In this case, neither cause taken alone will screen-off one effect from the other.[23]

Suppose one is investigating the presence of a common cause on the assumption that if there is one common cause, there probably is another. In this case, it will be *unreasonable* to formulate one's description of the common cause under study so that it screens-off. But surely the existence of this putative common cause is confirmable nonetheless. It follows that the hypothesis of a common cause can be confirmed even when the postulated cause fails to screen-off. So screening-off is not necessary (and can actually be undesirable) if a common cause explanation is to be plausible.

The preceding arguments concerning distal causes and multiple common causes invite the following objection. Reichenbach's principle does not say that *every* common cause must screen-off; it says only that it is reasonable to postulate a screening-off common cause. So much was obvious from our discussion of figure 10. If so, the principle's relevance to cases of the sort just described is rather minimal: all the principle says is that a complete specification of *all* the causal facts would screen-off. But partial specifications cannot be expected to do this.

In reply, I must note that this last way of understanding the principle robs it of much of its relevance. Reichenbach and Salmon viewed their principle as guiding the construction and evaluation of explanations. But the ongoing process of inquiry never reaches the point (except, perhaps, in the quantum domain) where researchers fancy that they have laid out *all*

---

23. To prove this, let

$$Pr(C_i) = c_i,$$
$$Pr(E_i/C_1 \& C_2) = w_i,$$
$$Pr(E_i/C_1 \& -C_2) = x_i,$$
$$Pr(E_i/-C_1 \& C_2) = y_i,$$
$$Pr(E_i/-C_1 \& -C_2) = z_i,$$

for $i = 1, 2$. Condition (i) implies that

$$Pr(E_1 \& E_2/C_1) = w_1 w_2 c_2 + x_1 x_2 (1 - c_2),$$
$$Pr(E_1/C_1) = w_1 c_2 + x_1 (1 - c_2),$$
$$Pr(E_2/C_1) = w_2 c_2 + x_2 (1 - c_2).$$

C_1 screens-off E_1 from E_2 precisely when

$$w_1 w_2 c_2 (1 - c_2) + x_1 x_2 c_2 (1 - c_2) = w_1 x_2 c_2 (1 - c_2) + x_1 w_2 c_2 (1 - c_2).$$

Condition (ii) allows this to be simplified to

$$w_1 (w_2 - x_2) = x_1 (w_2 - x_2).$$

Condition (iii) says that $w_i > x_i, y_i > z_i$ ($i = 1, 2$), which guarantees that the equality is false.

the causal facts. If the principle says only that the absence of screening-off shows that explanation is incomplete, then the above comments do not pertain to it. However, I understand the principle to have a positive message—it enjoins us to formulate common cause explanations so that they induce the screening-off relation. It is this imperative that the previous remarks are meant to temper.

I have already emphasized that an epistemological principle of the common cause must be stated as a *comparative* claim: conditions must be specified under which a common cause explanation should be judged *more plausible than* a separate cause explanation. However, there is another structural feature that such a principle should possess, at least if the problem of phylogenetic inference is any guide. The problem of choosing between a common cause explanation and a separate cause explanation is often underspecified if we simply ask whether two events have a common cause. In the phylogenetic case, the question is whether they have a common cause *that some third event lacks*. In another context, the question might be whether two events have a common cause *that occurred after a certain date*. But the simple question about the existence of a common cause, full stop, I suggest, is often too trivial to be worth posing.

Two premises suffice to show why the systematist's problem of determining common ancestry should not be formulated in terms of just two species. The ancestral relation is *transitive*. That is, if x is an ancestor of y and y is an ancestor of z, then x is an ancestor of z. What is more, the species whose genealogies we may be called upon to infer all trace back along ancestor/descendant chains to a single species. It follows that any two such species must possess a common ancestor.

This argument may be generalized. I claim, first, that the relation of causality between *token* events is transitive.[24] If the window's breaking traces back to the baseball's being thrown, and if the ball's being thrown traces back to the pitcher's wanting to show off, then the window's breaking traces back to the pitcher's wanting to show off. Second, suppose for the sake of argument that all the events we may be called upon to explain ultimately trace back on cause/effect chains to a single event. This may be the Big Bang, or something more modest and proximate, perhaps. If this is right, then it is trivially true that any two events we observe must have a common cause.

24. There is another concept of cause, relating *types* of events in a population, which is not transitive. "Harry's smoking caused him to have a heart attack" is a claim of token causality. "Smoking is a positive causal factor for heart attacks among U.S. adults" is a claim of property (type) causality. For discussion of some differences between these two concepts and an explanation of why transitivity fails for type causality, see Eells and Sober [1983] and Sober [1984c, pp. 295ff].

My point here is not to assert that the Big Bang theory is true, but to point out that the problem of discriminating between common cause and separate cause explanations would still be a real one, even if there were a Big Bang. This shows that real questions about common causes almost always have more structure than is evident in the simple formulation "Do A and B have a common cause?" One way for the question to become nontrivial is to think of common causes as "relative to an outgroup."

Do human beings and bears have a common ancestor? Trivially, yes. But acknowledging the relativity of questions about common descent allows us to raise a number of nontrivial questions: Do human beings and bears have a common ancestor that chimps do not share? No. Do they have a common ancestor that trout do not share? Yes. Whether two species share a common ancestor in this nontrivial sense is relative to the choice of an outgroup.

Do English bread prices and Venetian sea levels have a common cause? If the Big Bang theory is true, then, trivially, yes. But if we acknowledge the relativity of questions about common causes, we can pose a number of nontrivial problems. Do English bread prices and Venetian sea levels have a common cause that neither shares with French industrialization? Perhaps not. Do English bread prices and Venetian sea levels have a common cause that neither shares with Samoan migrations? Perhaps yes. The search for common causes requires that the events in question be placed in a context that specifies the "level of resolution" at which the causal inquiry is to proceed.[25]

I began this section by noting that Reichenbach's principle of the common cause connects three elements—an observed correlation, a postulated common cause, and the screening-off relation. I then criticized this principle on several grounds:

> Not every observed correlation is plausibly explained by invoking a common cause.
>
> Common causes are not the only sorts of explanations that can induce the screening-off relation.
>
> A common cause explanation can be plausible and well confirmed even when the postulated cause does not screen-off the correlated effects from each other.

25. The use of an outgroup to focus questions about common causes is one technique, not the only one, for making these questions nontrivial. A different method is used in the theory of inbreeding. We wish to know whether two alleles found in a population are "identical by descent." To make this question precise, we specify a "zero time" such that if the alleles have no common ancestor more recent than the zero time, they are judged unrelated. *Time* can make questions about common cause nontrivial, just as the specification of an outgroup can. Russell [1948, p. 487] mentions this kind of temporal relativity.

Furthermore, I have argued that Reichenbach's formulation fails to include two structural features that any epistemological principle of the common cause must possess:

> A principle of the common cause must be *comparative*; it must say when common cause explanations are preferable to separate cause explanations.
>
> A principle of the common cause must acknowledge the *relativity* of the search for common causes; a nontrivial question about common causes (usually) cannot simply ask if two events have a common cause.

Despite these criticisms, a sufficient condition was developed that salvages at least part of the plausible insight on which Reichenbach's principle rests. I identified a circumstance in which a common cause explanation will be more likely than the best competing separate cause explanation. A rather different sufficient condition for preferring common cause explanations will be described in the next section.

3.5. Likelihood and the Problem of Nuisance Parameters

Reichenbach [1956] and Salmon's [1984] informal description of what drives us to postulate common causes has something to be said for it. Both notice that a correlation between two events might be explained by postulating two separate and independent causes, *but that this explanation would make the correlation too improbable.* A common cause explanation is preferable because it makes the observations less of a miracle; it is more plausible because it strains our credulity less. The operative idea here is *likelihood.*

Likelihood helps illuminate the way we reason in the plagiarism example mentioned earlier. The two students could have independently produced the matching philosophy essays, but independent processes would make the correlation nothing short of a miracle. However, if we postulate a common cause—a book from which they both copied, for example—the matching is much more probable. The likelier hypothesis is by far the more plausible one.

Statisticians recognize that a hypothesis's likelihood is often not the only thing that affects its overall plausibility. Edwards [1972, p. 202], as stalwart a defender of the centrality of likelihood as there is, observes that hypotheses of deterministic divine intervention can confer on any observation you please a maximum probability of unity. If we find such hypotheses less than fully compelling, this must be for reasons separable from their likelihood.

Another avenue of evaluation is the hypothesis's probability. Many statisticians and philosophers hold that hypotheses have probabilities only if they describe possible outcomes of a chance process. Hypotheses about an offspring's genotype or about the roll of some dice have probabilities, but Newton's law of gravitation and Darwin's theory of evolution do not. Bayesians disagree, claiming that probabilities represent *degrees of belief*; these we may reasonably have even in the absence of a model of a chance process. My point here is not to decide this issue, but to make a point on which there is consensus. Hypotheses of common cause and hypotheses of separate cause can be evaluated for their probabilities *if* they describe possible outcomes of chance processes. Likelihood helps determine the plausibility of common cause explanations, but it is not always the whole story.

It is easy to confuse these two considerations when we consider the degree to which a proposed explanation makes an observed correlation a "miracle." Let us return to the example of the theater troupe to see how these two considerations can be prized apart. The common cause explanation of the covariance of sick days had two elements. First, it was asserted that the actors take their meals together. Second, probabilities were given for the occurrence of tainted food at their meals and for the occurrence of illness, given the presence and absence of spoiled food. The separate cause explanation also can be split in two: First, there is the assertion that the actors dine separately. Second, we say how probable it is that tainted food would be present at their separate meals, and how probable gastrointestinal distress is, given the presence and absence of spoiled food at such meals. In both explanations, the second element is provided by assigning probabilities to the branches in figure 11.

The likelihood issue focuses on the probability these explanations confer on the observations. The question here is how probable the observations are *if* the actors eat together and *if* they eat separately. But this is quite separate from the question of how probable it is that the actors should dine together or separately. It may be that the common cause explanation has the higher likelihood, but that it is enormously improbable that the actors dined together. If so, the common cause explanation is improbable, though highly likely.

Bayes's theorem brings together these two determinants of the overall plausibility of the common cause (CC) and separate cause (SC) hypotheses in the light of the observations (O):[26]

26. Bayes's theorem follows from the definition of conditional probability. For any propositions X and Y,

$$Pr(X \& Y) = Pr(X/Y) Pr(Y) = Pr(Y/X) Pr(X).$$

This implies that

$$Pr(X/Y) = Pr(Y/X) Pr(X)/Pr(Y).$$

$$\Pr(CC/O) = \frac{\Pr(O/CC)\Pr(CC)}{\Pr(O)},$$

$$\Pr(SC/O) = \frac{\Pr(O/SC)\Pr(SC)}{\Pr(O)}.$$

The posterior probability of a hypothesis (i.e., the probability it has conditional on the observations) is a function of the likelihood, the prior probability of the hypothesis, and the unconditioned probability of the observations. Since the denominators are the same in both the above expressions, the question of whether (CC) has the greater posterior probability reduces to the question of whether

$$\Pr(O/CC)\Pr(CC) > \Pr(O/SC)\Pr(SC).$$

All that matters, therefore, is the likelihoods of the two hypotheses and their prior probabilities.

If two hypotheses have the same prior probabilities, then the one with the higher likelihood is overall more plausible in the light of the observations. And if two hypotheses have the same likelihoods, then the one with the higher prior probability is overall more plausible. Or more generally, slight differences in one category will be swamped by substantial differences in the other.

I do not claim that Bayes's theorem completely circumscribes everything that is relevant to how observations support hypotheses. For one thing, I have taken no stand on how one handles hypotheses that do not describe possible upshots of chance processes. However, I do claim that we can understand many cases in which we wish to compare the credentials of common cause and separate cause explanations by taking likelihood and probability to be the operative concepts.

The principle of the common cause, we have already noted, suffers from several defects. Rather than trying to formulate a substitute exhibiting a comparable level of generality, the circumspection encouraged by using Bayes's theorem as an analytic tool has much to recommend it. Whether we are considering sick actors, student plagiarism, or any of the other examples that Reichenbach and Salmon used to show the attractiveness of common cause explanations, we can use Bayes's theorem to see why the common cause explanation is superior *when it is*. But of perhaps even greater importance is the fact that the theorem allows us to see in outline when a common cause explanation may be *less* plausible than a rival explanation in terms of separate causes. It violates no first principle of scientific inference that postulating a common cause may sometimes be *less* plausible than postulating separate causes. Unless we give more details, there is no more reason to give pride of place to a principle of parsimony than to a principle of plenitude.

So far I have salvaged something modest that can be called a principle of the common cause. In the previous section, I established a sufficient condition under which the common cause hypothesis has the greater likelihood. Two properties of this treatment should be emphasized. First, the argument focused on likelihood and ignored probability. Second, the bald claim that E_1 and E_2 have a common cause does not confer any probability at all on the observations.

In the light of Bayes's theorem, the first property represents an obvious limitation. We have seen that even if (CC) is more likely than (SC), it may nevertheless be less plausible, owing to its lower prior probability. The point here is just that likelihood may not be the whole story. The second property also poses a problem, internal to the issue of likelihood, whose treatment in the previous argument we now need to scrutinize.

Neither the hypothesis that the actors dined together nor the hypothesis that they dined separately confers a probability on the covariance of sick days. Hence, as baldly stated, the hypotheses cannot be compared for their likelihoods. The claim of common cause has a likelihood only once something is said about the probabilities associated with the branches in figure 11. Statisticians call the probabilities involved here "nuisance parameters." We wish to compare the likelihoods of two hypotheses, but cannot do so without further information about these parameters. This is a nuisance, since our goal is not to estimate their values, but to test the hypotheses of common and separate causes. We do not care how often the actors ate tainted food; our interest is simply to find out whether they dined together or separately.

This problem was circumvented in the previous section by simply stipulating values for the nuisance parameters. We allowed ourselves to assign values that maximize the probability of the observed frequencies of the singleton and conjoint events. We found the "best case" for the common cause pattern and the "best case" for the separate cause pattern, and then compared these.

I stressed before that this procedure was being followed in a situation of considerable ignorance; if one has no notion of what counts as a plausible assignment of values to the various nuisance parameters, finding "best cases" for the two hypotheses may make sense. It now is time to see how this procedure can be unsatisfactory when more information is available.

A simple example will show the dangers of the "best-case strategy" used before. Suppose one knows that a given individual, Smith, voted for Ronald Reagan during the 1984 U.S. presidential elections. The question is whether this information better supports the hypothesis that Smith is a Democrat or a Republican. To use likelihoods here, one would want to know how probable that vote would be under the two hypotheses. If most

Republicans voted for Reagan and few Democrats did, then likelihood would favor the hypothesis that Smith is a Republican.[27]

However, suppose that this information is not available. Rather, what one knows is that there is another characteristic of voters that influenced whether they voted for Reagan. N is a nuisance parameter. Whether Smith has N affects the probability that he voted for Reagan, but we do not know whether Smith has or lacks this characteristic.

What we do know, I am imagining, is the probability of voting for Reagan, if an individual has any of the four combinations of traits described below:

		Nuisance Parameter	
		N	not-N
Party	Democrat	0.9	0.2
Affiliation	Republican	0.6	0.7

Note that N increases the probability of voting for Reagan (V) if one is a Democrat (D), but diminishes it if one is a Republican (R). We do not know the likelihood that Smith is a Democrat, because we do not know the probability of voting for Reagan if someone is a Democrat. But we do know that if Smith is a Democrat, then the probability of his voting for Reagan is greater if he is N than it would be if he is not-N (0.9 > 0.2). The "best case" for the hypothesis that Smith is a Democrat occurs if we stipulate that Smith has trait N. Similarly, if Smith is a Republican, his vote for Reagan is more probable if he is not-N (since 0.7 > 0.6). So the "best case" for the hypothesis that Smith is a Republican involves stipulating that Smith is not-N.

Now we compare these two best cases, each of which is a conjunctive hypothesis. "Democrat and N" makes Smith's vote more probable than "Republican and not-N" (0.9 > 0.7), so the former hypothesis is more likely. Can we then conclude that "Democrat" is more likely than "Republican"? It is essential to see that this *is* a further step, since now we are making a claim about the two conjuncts, not about the two conjunctions.

This further inference would be unwarranted if half the individuals in both parties had N. In that case, the real likelihoods would be $Pr(V/D) = 0.55$ and $Pr(V/R) = 0.65$. With this information about the representation of N among Democrats and among Republicans, we would conclude that it is more likely that Smith is a Republican. The same conclusion would follow if we thought that N is a rare trait in both parties. Here we see how a fuller treatment of the likelihoods can yield a result opposite to the one

---

27. In this example, I shall assume that the prior probabilities of party affiliation are the same, so that likelihood is the single vehicle of comparison.

we would obtain if we simply looked at the "best cases" as described above. That "Democrat & N" is more likely than "Republican & not-N" does not mean that "Democrat" is likelier than "Republican."

It is clear that if one has this further information about the nuisance parameter, one should use it and not simply look at the two best cases. But suppose this kind of information is not available. Should one decline to make an inference or adopt the best-case strategy as an imperfect but expedient solution?

No full answer to this problem will be suggested here. But it does seem clear that the most honest thing to do, if one wishes to make an inference in this case, is to announce that one's conclusion is conditional on an assumption—namely, that the relationship between the two (known) best cases is the same as the relationship between the two (unknown) likelihoods. To use the expedient best-case solution in this problem, one must assume that $Pr(V/D_b) > Pr(V/R_b)$ if and only if $Pr(V/D) > Pr(V/R)$, where the "b" subscript denotes the best-case assignment of values to nuisance parameters for the subscripted hypothesis. As we have seen above, this assumption is not inevitably satisfied.[28]

This helps clarify the kind of assumption we were making in the argument developed in the previous section. The analog of the problem of inferring Smith's party affiliation is inferring whether the correlation of two events should receive a common cause or a separate cause explanation. The analog of the nuisance parameter "N" in the problem about Smith is the assignment of probabilities to the branches depicted in figure 11. In discussing how one should explain the observed correlation, I argued that the hypothesis of a common cause is more likely than the hypothesis of a separate cause *if* a set of assumptions is satisfied. One of those assumptions is that it is legitimate to use the best-case expedient technique for handling the nuisance parameters.

There is another way to deal with the problem of nuisance parameters if a certain assumption, different from the one just described, is satisfied. Suppose that the value of the nuisance parameter is *independent* of which hypothesis one considers. In the example about Smith, this means that $Pr(N/D) = Pr(N/R)$. If this is true, and if being a Republican makes voting for Reagan more probable both for people with N and for people with not-N, then the evidence that Smith voted for Reagan makes it more likely that he is a Republican than that he is a Democrat.

This "dominance" argument can be represented in terms of a two-by-two table similar to the one displayed before. The four entries in the

28. For this and other treatments of the problem of nuisance parameters, see Kalbfleisch and Sprott [1970] and Edwards [1972, especially p. 110]. See also the discussion in Felsenstein and Sober [1986].

following table denote the probability of voting for Reagan, given each combination of causal factors:

		Nuisance Parameter	
		N	not-N
Party	Democrat	w	x
Affiliation	Republican	y	z

The dominance assumption is that $w < y$ and $x < z$. If it also is true that N is as common within one party as it is within the other, then we may conclude that it is more likely that Smith is a Republican, given that he voted for Reagan.[29]

This line of argument solves the problem posed by nuisance parameters, but without actually estimating their values. Notice that we do not need to know the proportion of Republicans and Democrats who have N to decide which party affiliation is more likely. Nor do we need to infer whether Smith has N. This way of handling nuisance parameters points to another sufficient condition under which common cause explanations are more likely than separate cause explanations.

To see what the parallel analysis is for figure 11, we need to shift gears resolutely from explaining correlations between *types* of events to explaining the matching of two *token* events. Do not ask for an explanation of why two types of events cooccur more frequently than one would expect if they were independent; rather, the problem is simply to explain why two token events *happened*. We shall take the labeled nodes in figure 11 to represent token events, between which probability relationships obtain. We wish to compare the common cause and the separate cause explanations with respect to their likelihoods, where the probabilities associated with the branches are constrained in the following way.

Suppose that C_1 and C_2 are independent of each other. Also assume that $Pr(C_c) = Pr(C_1) = Pr(C_2)$. That is, although the probabilities associated with branches 5–7 in figure 11 can in principle differ from one another, I adopt the assumption that they have the same value, denote by "c" (for "cause").

In addition, assume that the probabilities associated with branch 1 are the same as those associated with branch 3, and that the probabilities for branch 2 are the same as those for branch 4. That is, $Pr(E_1/C_c) = Pr(E_1/C_1)$; this probability I shall call p_1 (which is short for the probability of the first effect when the cause is *present*). The same holds for the other effect; assume that $Pr(E_2/C_c) = Pr(E_2/C_2)$, which I shall call p_2. A similar assump-

---

29. Dominance plus independence suffices, since $Pr(V/D) = Pr(N/D)w + Pr(not\text{-}N/D)x$ and $Pr(V/R) = Pr(N/R)y + Pr(not\text{-}N/R)z$.

tion governs the probability of the effect, given that the cause is *absent*. $\Pr(E_1/\text{not-}C_c) = \Pr(E_1/\text{not-}C_1) = a_1$ and $\Pr(E_2/\text{not-}C_c) = \Pr(E_2/\text{not-}C_2) = a_2$. The rough idea behind these assumptions is that the probabilities of events are *independent* of how they are assembled into common cause or separate cause explanations.

Given these assumptions, it follows that the probability of E_1 & E_2, according to the common cause hypothesis depicted in figure 11a, is

(CC) $cp_1 p_2 + (1 - c)a_1 a_2$.

The probability of the two effects, according to the separate cause hypothesis shown in figure 11b, is

(SC) $[cp_1 + (1 - c)a_1][cp_2 + (1 - c)a_2]$.

A little algebra shows that $(CC) > (SC)$ if and only if

$$p_1(p_2 - a_2) > a_1(p_2 - a_2).$$

If $p_i > a_i$ $(i = 1, 2)$, this condition is satisfied. That is, *if the postulated causes raise the probability of the effects and if the independence assumption described above is correct, then the common cause explanation has higher likelihood.*

The analogy between this argument comparing common cause and separate cause explanations and the dominance argument about Smith's party affiliation may be clarified by comparing the above two-by-two table with the following one:

		Possible Values of (c, p_1, p_2, a_1, a_2)		
		V_1	V_2	V_3 ...
Hypotheses	Common Cause	x_1	x_2	x_3 ...
	Separate Cause	y_1	y_2	y_3 ...

The entries in this table denote the probabilities that each hypothesis confers on the observations, given some specification (V_i) of values for the nuisance parameters. We have identified a sufficient condition for $x_i > y_i$, for each i; if the nuisance parameters are independent of the hypotheses considered, we may conclude that the common cause hypothesis is more likely.

The assumptions involved in this argument reflect one intuitive notion about (global) parsimony: A single (common) cause is to be preferred to two (separate) causes if the joint occurrence of C_1 and C_2 as independent and distinct events is less probable than the occurrence of the single cause C_c. However, it is well to note that the preference for fewer causes over more does not receive an unconditional and *a priori* justification from this argument. Its legitimacy here clearly depends on the way probabilities were assigned to branches 1–7.

How is this result related to Reichenbach's demand for a screening-off common cause? I have identified a circumstance in which a common cause explanation will be more likely than the competing separate cause explanation. But notice that the fact to be explained is that two token events *happened*. The phenomenon to account for is not an observed correlation of *kinds* of events. What is more, my argument goes forward, whether or not the probabilities of these two token events are known; nor does the argument estimate branch probabilities in the process of comparing the two explanations. Instead of *estimating* nuisance parameters, I *constrain* them. In consequence, the present argument provides a rationale for common cause explanations that is quite distinct from the best-case argument of the previous section in which the correlation of event types was the target *explanandum*.

Another difference between Reichenbach's idea and the approach described here is worth noting. In Reichenbach's formulation, both positive and negative correlations are to be explained by postulating a common cause. However, in the example just described, it is *matching* token events that favor common cause hypotheses and *nonmatching* events that favor explanations in terms of separate causation.[30]

Notice what a disaster it would be to use the best-case strategy where the problem is simply to explain a matching between token events. If we can merely stipulate values for the branches shown in figure 11, we can formulate best cases for the common cause and the separate cause patterns that both have likelihoods of unity. Comparing the two best cases thereby obtained, we find that we cannot discriminate between them. But this is absurd, if in fact we have knowledge that constrains the nuisance parameters in the way described above.

3.6. Concluding Remarks

Reichenbach drew our attention to an extremely important pattern of scientific explanation. However, he mistook a contingent and highly specific pattern for a necessary and universal one. In this he was not alone; it is a characteristic failing of empiricism to see too direct a connection between observations and the hypotheses those observations are supposed to support. Observing an object that is both *F* and *G* does not always confirm the hypothesis that all *F*'s are *G*; nontrivial further assumptions are needed to establish this connection. Observed correlations between event types are

---

30. This latter claim I leave as an exercise for the reader: Suppose that E_1 occurred but that E_2 did not, with branch probabilities associated with the common cause and separate cause explanations stipulated as before. Show that the common cause hypothesis is *less* likely than the separate cause hypothesis, relative to the observed *mismatch*.

not always best explained by postulating a common cause. Nor is the matching of event tokens always best handled in this way either. Whether the observations favor a common cause explanation depends on further background assumptions. In this chapter, I have described two sets of background assumptions, each of which suffices for a common cause explanation to be preferable to an explanation in terms of separate causes.

A Bayesian framework allows us to organize the questions we need to ask in comparing a common cause and a separate cause explanation. First, there is the issue of prior probability. Granted, the actors' covariance of sick days might be quite probable *if* they dined together, but how probable is it that they in fact shared their meals? Second, there is the issue of likelihood and the attendant problem of nuisance parameters. To see how probable the covariance in sick days is on the hypothesis that the actors dined together, we want to know how probable it is that their food was tainted and how probable sickness is in the presence and absence of tainted food.

When the fact to be explained concerns the correlation of event *types*, a best-case solution to the problem of nuisance parameters makes sense if one is prepared to make an assumption about the relation of these best cases to the likelihoods of interest. When the fact to be explained concerns the matching of token events, an independence-plus-dominance assumption suffices to solve the problem of nuisance parameters. Here, then, are two sufficient conditions that ground Reichenbach's idea that a common cause explanation is preferable to a separate cause explanation.

I do not anticipate that Reichenbach's principle will be replaced by anything of comparable generality. I doubt that much can be said *in general* about the circumstances in which common cause explanations are to be preferred beyond general remarks about priors and likelihoods. What more there is that needs to be said must come from specific empirical theories, not from general philosophical ones. It is the separate sciences that provide the background theories that show how observations have evidential meaning. It is these that ultimately decide whether a common cause explanation is better supported than a separate cause explanation.

The general thesis that correlations or matchings always require common cause explanation need detain us no longer. Viable principles of causal explanation must be more conditional in form. The task now is to examine in detail what biologists have said about the problem of phylogenetic inference. Even if common cause explanation is too broad a category to be justified within a single format, it remains open that reconstructing genealogical relationships is a species of that genus on which some additional light can be thrown.

Chapter 4

Cladistics and the Limits of Hypothetico-Deductivism

In this chapter, I begin investigating the strengths and weaknesses of cladistic parsimony. The major result of the previous two chapters will repeatedly come into play: we shall constantly be on the lookout for assumptions about the evolutionary process that are said to sustain or undermine the use of parsimony as a tool for bringing character data to bear on phylogenetic hypotheses. The ideas on likelihood and probability developed in chapter 3 will not be used much in the present one, though they will occupy center stage in the next. The reason is that the arguments to be considered in this chapter (for the most part) do not treat phylogenetic inference as a probabilistic phenomenon; rather, the guiding idea behind these arguments is that phylogenetic hypotheses have deductive consequences that permit those hypotheses to be evaluated for their plausibility.

It is crucial in what follows that the reader keep a certain simple distinction clearly in mind. Criticizing the logic of an argument is quite different from criticizing that argument's conclusion. Most of my discussion in this chapter and the next will involve the first kind of project. I shall suggest that many of the arguments that biologists have formulated concerning cladistic parsimony are unsound. Some of these arguments have been justificatory; others have been critical. In criticizing the justificatory arguments, I shall not conclude that parsimony is not the method of choice. In criticizing the critical arguments, I shall not conclude that the method is entirely beyond reproach. That an argument is flawed does not mean that its conclusion is false.

So the general drift of this chapter and the one that follows will be rather negative. I shall claim that the biological literature has not succeeded in fully justifying cladistic parsimony; nor has it succeeded in showing that the method is incorrect. This is not to say that that literature has been useless. The problem is difficult and multifaceted. And though the arguments do not always establish everything they claim to, they often throw considerable light on the difficulties that remain to be addressed. In methodological discussions about science just as much as in science itself, theories may enhance our understanding even when they do not prove to be entirely satisfactory.

4.1. The Problem Emerges

Systematists who now use the method of phylogenetic inference called cladistic parsimony usually trace back this idea to the writings of Willi Hennig. In identifying Hennig as the inventor of cladistic philosophy, they are undoubtedly correct; the reason, though, is not a matter of dates. It is true that the original German of Hennig's principal theoretical work predated other descriptions of parsimony in the systematics literature; it also is true that Hennig's work became widely known to Anglophone systematists only after it was translated, by which time other biologists had already formulated the parsimony idea.[1] However, the reason Hennig is properly viewed as the source of cladistic parsimony is to be found at least as much in *how* he described it as in *when* he did so.

Before Hennig's book appeared in English, the parsimony idea was formulated by two systematists who expressed considerable skepticism about it. Camin and Sokal [1965] considered the idea that the best evolutionary hypothesis is one that minimizes the number of evolutionary changes. Though Sokal is a founding father of pheneticism, this did not stop him and Camin from describing this phylogenetic approach. However, they described it only to assert its inadequacy. They claimed that parsimony "depends on the assumption that nature is indeed parsimonious" (pp. 323–324), an idea they found biologically implausible.

It is noteworthy that Camin and Sokal [1965] produced no argument that shows that parsimony rests on this assumption; like Sneath and Sokal's [1973] later claim that overall similarity assumes that rates are uniform (discussed in section 3.1), the thesis is simply asserted. Perhaps they thought the thesis was too obvious to require an independent argument. Or perhaps it was insider's knowledge of a much discussed thought experiment that drove them to this conclusion.

During the early 1960s, Camin simulated an evolutionary process by drawing a set of hypothetical organisms and representing their evolution by tracing them from one page to another with less than perfect fidelity. The genealogical relationship and evolutionary processes underlying the evolution of these Caminalcules, as they came to be called, their designer kept to himself. Camin gave his colleagues at the University of Kansas the puzzle of inferring phylogenetic relationships from the organisms he had constructed. Commenting on this problem, Camin and Sokal [1965, pp. 311–312] observed that "those trees which most closely resembled the true cladistics invariably required for their construction the least number of postulated evolutionary steps for the characters studied." Perhaps the fact

---

1. Hennig [1966] was a translation into English by D. Davis and R. Zangerl of Hennig's revision of his earlier (1950) *Grundzüge einer Theorie der phylogenetischen Systematik.*

that Camin made evolution proceed parsimoniously in his thought experiment (ie., by having his organisms achieve a given end state via a fairly minimal number of changes) led him and Sokal to think that nature must do the same, if the use of parsimony is to make sense.

In contrast with Camin and Sokal's assessment, the idea that the presuppositions of parsimony are less than transparent appears in another early formulation of the parsimony concept, one to which Camin and Sokal refer in their paper. Cavalli-Sforza and Edwards, both students of R. A. Fisher, had taken up the project of considering phylogenetic reconstruction as a problem of statistical inference. The goal was to compare phylogenies in terms of their *likelihoods*. Technical difficulties prevented them from taking this project to completion. As an alternative, they considered the consequences of adopting a *principle of minimum evolution*: "The most plausible estimate of the evolutionary tree is that which invokes the minimum nett amount of evolution" (Edwards and Cavalli-Sforza [1963]).

These statistically minded biologists were consistently circumspect in their judgment about what that method presupposes. Although they thought the minimum principle "intuitive," they remarked that (Cavalli-Sforza and Edwards [1967, p. 555]; square brackets mine)

> [t]he assumptions underlying this method are not too clear; it may go some way towards handling ... [situations in which parameter values needed for explicitly statistical estimation are unknown], but its success is probably due to the closeness of the solution it gives to the projection of the "maximum-likelihood" tree. The extent of the similarity merits further investigation, and experience with simulated trees should clarify its logical status. It certainly cannot be justified on the grounds that evolution *proceeds* according to some minimum principle, as recently suggested by Camin and Sokal....

In contrast to the pheneticist's rejection of parsimony and the statisticians' circumspection about it, we find in the works of Willi Hennig a positive endorsement of ideas that lead naturally to the principle of parsimony, even though Hennig, to my knowledge, never called his idea by that name. It is for this reason that the systematist's genealogy of methods tends to trace present-day use of cladistic parsimony back to Hennig, not to phenetic or statistical ideas. In terms of identifying ancestors, it is the defense of an approach, not its formulation, that sometimes determines perception of intellectual lineages.

Hennig's critique of overall similarity and his defense of synapomorphy as the key to genealogical reconstruction are developed in his main theoretical work, *Phylogenetic Systematics* (Hennig [1966]). His discussion in that work follows much the same pattern it does in his summary review article (Hennig [1965]). In both cases, the starting point was to dissect the con-

characters

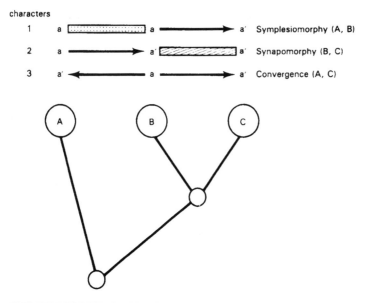

1   a [::::::::::::::::::] a ———————————▶ a′ Symplesiomorphy (A, B)

2   a ———————————▶ a′ [/////////////] a′ Synapomorphy (B, C)

3   a′ ◀——————————— a ———————————▶ a′ Convergence (A, C)

Figure 13.
Hennig contrasted three kinds of similarity; only the second, he thought, provides evidence of phylogenetic relationship (from Hennig [1966, p. 147]).

cept of "resemblance." Hennig [1965, p. 608; 1966, p. 147] uses the diagram reproduced here as figure 13 to distinguish three kinds of similarity. In each of the three characters, *a* is the ancestral (plesiomorphic) and *a′* the derived (apomorphic) state.[2]

Character 1, Hennig says, shows how plesiomorphic resemblance can fail to reflect phylogenetic relationship: *A* and *B* are similar to each other though different from *C*; yet, the true phylogeny is A(BC). Character 3 shows how the same sort of "misleading similarity" can be generated by convergence; *A* and *C* resemble each other with respect to a derived character though neither resembles *B*. The pattern exhibited by character 2 Hennig calls "synapomorphy." This and this alone provides evidence of phylogenetic relationship.

It may strike the reader that so far I have merely summarized material already spelled out in chapter 1. But there is one difference between Hennig's formulation and the terminology I suggested there. Hennig contrasts synapomorphy with convergence. In both characters 2 and 3, two

2. Assume for the sake of argument that the most recent common ancestor of the three terminal taxa was plesiomorphic for all three characters. In section 1.3, I suggested that this does not follow from the definition of "plesiomorphic," but is a substantive assumption. However, this issue will not affect the following discussion.

of the three taxa have in common the derived character state *a'*. Yet, Hennig's usage is that character 2 alone counts as synapomorphic. Hennig is not entirely consistent on this matter, however, since he goes on to define synapomorphy to mean "common possession of derived characters" (Hennig [1965, p. 609]).

In chapter 1, I followed this definition of Hennig's, but not the usage he employs in figure 13. A consequence of my definition is that synapomorphy (a match with respect to the derived character state) is not an infallible guide to phylogeny. Synapomorphy may provide evidence, but it does not deductively determine propinquity of descent. This is because the common possession of a derived character may be homologous or homoplasious. On the other hand, if synapomorphy is defined in the way suggested by figure 13—so that it excludes the possibility of homoplasy—then synapomorphy is equivalent to *derived homology*. Real synapomorphies, on this more demanding interpretation, cannot fail to reflect phylogenetic relationships.

It is not to be doubted that one might adopt either reading and proceed consistently. I define "synapomorphy" to mean derived matching because I want it to be possible to determine which characters are synapomorphic simply by knowing which state is ancestral and which derived. The stronger reading that Hennig uses in the above figure has more packed into it; one must know, not just the character's polarity, but whether there were any changes in the branches linking apomorphic terminal taxa with their most recent common ancestor. In fact, since 011's being a synapomorphy in this stronger sense deductively implies that the genealogical relationship is A(BC), it would seem that knowing that a character is a true synapomorphy in this sense already requires one to have decided the question of what the phylogeny is.

Although I favor using synapomorphy to mean *apomorphous similarity*, there is precedent for the stronger usage according to which it means *derived homology*. Those who feel drawn to the latter definition inevitably find that they need the concept of "putative" synapomorphy (section 1.4). The reason is that "real" synapomorphies in their sense already settle the matter of genealogy, and so cannot provide evidence about phylogeny unless phylogenetic relationships are already known. To begin with *evidence* and then proceed to a logically distinct *hypothesis* requires cladistic theory to begin with the notion of synapomorphy as that concept is used here.

If this is right, though, we must return to Hennig's reason for saying that symplesiomorphy does not provide evidence of phylogenetic relationship. On the same page, Hennig says that "this arises from the fact that characters can remain unchanged during a number of speciation processes. Therefore, it follows that the common possession of primitive ('plesiomorph') characters which remained unchanged cannot be evidence of the close relationship of their possessors" (Hennig [1965, p. 609]). What is true is that one cannot *deduce* phylogenetic relationships from symplesiomorphies. But Hennig makes a more ambitious claim: he says that symplesiomorphies *do not provide evidence about* genealogical relationships.

The gap between these claims cannot be overemphasized. Think of the relationship between a symptom and a disease. If you knew that bearers of a symptom *always* have a certain disease, you could *deduce* the presence of the disease from the presence of the symptom. Symptoms rarely have this neat property, but they can provide *evidence* for the presence of diseases nonetheless.

Hennig correctly notes that shared ancestral characters can fail to reflect phylogeny. He concludes that symplesiomorphies do not provide evidence of common descent. But if this argument were correct, another would be as well: the common possession of a *derived* character may be homologous or homoplasious, and so *synapomorphies* (in my sense) do not provide evidence of common descent either.

In point of fact, neither of these arguments is sound. Character distributions—whether they involve matches of ancestral or derived character states—never allow one to deduce phylogenetic relationships. This is because the simple process model discussed in chapter 1 and its ilk are manifestly false. There is always some chance, however small, that homoplasies may arise; and there is always some chance, however small, that autapomorphies may arise in the ingroup. From this it immediately follows that the link between character distributions and phylogenetic hypotheses is not deductive.

Character 1 in figure 13 shows how a symplesiomorphy can fail to reflect phylogenetic relationship. But another symplesiomorphy—one in which *A* has the derived form and *B* and *C* the ancestral form—would succeed in reflecting the phylogenetic relationships depicted there. An adequate argument evaluating the evidential meaning of symplesiomorphy would have to consider *both* these possibilities. It is not enough to show that plesiomorphic resemblance *can* fail to reflect phylogeny.

Besides asking why synapomorphy carries *more* evidential weight than symplesiomorphy, Hennig also addresses the question of why apomorphic resemblance should count as evidence in the first place. His answer is to quote an earlier publication in which he espoused an "auxiliary principle." This asserts (Hennig [1966, pp. 121–122]; square brackets his)

> ... that the presence of apomorphous characters in different species 'is always reason for suspecting kinship [i.e., that the species belong to a monophyletic group], and that their origin by convergence should not be assumed a priori.' ... This was based on the conviction

that 'phylogenetic systematics would lose all the ground on which it stands' if the presence of apomorphous characters in different species were considered first of all as convergences (or parallelisms), with proof to the contrary required in each case. Rather the burden of proof must be placed on the contention that 'in individual cases the possession of common apomorphous characters may be based only on convergence (or parallelism).'

Hennig is obviously alive to the fact that shared derived characters may or may not reflect phylogeny.

Hennig's words echo Hume's ([1748, p. 51]) remarks about the principle of the uniformity of nature: "If there be any suspicion that the course of nature may change, and that the past may be no rule for the future, all experience becomes useless and can give rise to no inference or conclusion." The suggestion is that without Hennig's auxiliary principle or Hume's uniformity principle, one simply could not bring evidence to bear on hypotheses.

In chapter 2, I discussed Hume's claim that the principle of the uniformity of nature is an indispensable assumption. What argument does Hennig provide for thinking that apomorphic resemblances must be taken to be evidence of common descent? Hennig's remarks in both the works cited above occur after he has argued that symplesiomorphy provides no evidence about genealogy. Perhaps, then, Hennig's reason is that since plesiomorphic similarities cannot be used as evidence, phylogenetic inference would become impossible if apomorphic resemblance were discarded as well.

If this is Hennig's argument, we must see that it is undermined by his unsound argument against symplesiomorphy. *All* resemblance—whether ancestral or derived—is fallible. But this does not mean that symplesiomorphy is devoid of evidential meaning. Having failed to disqualify symplesiomorphy as a possible source of evidence, Hennig cannot claim that apomorphic resemblance is the only game in town.[3]

There is another question we must raise about Hennig's auxiliary principle—that apomorphic resemblances must be presumed innocent until proven guilty. Let us suppose that phylogenetic inferences could not be made if we doubted the reliability of apomorphic similarities. It does not follow just from this that we must assume that such resemblances are reliable. There is, after all, the option of agnosticism—we could simply

---

3. Think of the equally fallacious argument that can be run in the other direction: Since apomorphic resemblance is fallible, it cannot be used. If we were to discard plesiomorphic resemblance as well, phylogenetic inference would become impossible. Hence we must adopt an "auxiliary principle" according to which symplesiomorphies count as evidence of common descent.

maintain that the problem of reconstructing genealogy cannot be solved with the resources now available. The mere fact that an assumption is indispensable if we are to make knowledge claims is not much evidence that it is true.

And even if we grant Hennig's auxiliary assumption, we still must ask what we commit ourselves to in accepting it. What, if anything, are we assuming about the evolutionary process when we assume that apomorphic resemblance has the evidential meaning that cladism claims for it? Are there circumstances in which shared apomorphies do not have this evidential significance? Are there circumstances in which symplesiomorphies provide substantial information about common descent? If so, does acceptance of Hennig's principle mean that one must assume these circumstances rarely arise in nature?

In discussing Hennig's thoughts about resemblance, I have not used the word "parsimony," nor have I mentioned Hennig's ideas about how character incongruence is to be resolved. If only synapomorphies have evidential meaning and if all the synapomorphies in one's data set point to the same genealogical relationships, then there is no problem. In this happy circumstance, the characters collectively provide stronger support for the favored genealogical hypothesis than any of them does separately, provided that the characters are mutually independent. Just as in a court of law, adding independent lines of evidence that lead to the same conclusion increases the level of support.

On the other hand, even if shared apomorphies are regarded as the unique bearers of evidential meaning, it still may happen that different synapomorphies may conflict. This problem was discussed in section 1.4. Hennig recognized that this difficulty can sometimes be resolved by reexamining the characters—by discovering, for example, that an apparent synapomorphy is really a symplesiomorphy. In this case, one discards a character because it has been misinterpreted. But the possibility remains that different genuine apomorphic resemblances can be incongruent with each other. What is one to do then?

Although Hennig cannot be said to have led the reader by the hand through the problem of character incongruence, the implication of treating shared apomorphies as the sole, though fallible, bearers of evidence about genealogy seems clear enough. If characters with a 110 distribution favor the (AB)C grouping and if characters with a 011 distribution favor A(BC), and if the characters are accorded equal weight, then one should prefer (AB)C if and only if there are more 110 than 011 characters. This is just parsimony by another name.

My criticisms of Hennig's arguments do not mean that his conclusions are untrue. My point is just that Hennig did not succeed in justifying his conclusions. Cladists subsequently tried to fill in the details that Hennig's account did not provide. Whether they succeeded in doing this we now shall have to determine.

4.2. Falsifiability

A number of systematists have attempted to defend cladistic parsimony by linking it to ideas on scientific method developed by Karl Popper [1959, 1963]. In this section, I shall not consider whether cladists have understood the philosophical texts correctly. Cladistic ideas about the testing of genealogical hypotheses can and should be evaluated on their own terms. As we shall see, though, the problems I shall unearth are not solved by importing what is plausible in Popper's philosophy of science.[4]

Cladists often claim that cladistic parsimony is a neutral methodological tool, whose use carrries with it no substantive assumptions about the evolutionary process. For example, Wiley [1975, p. 236], in a passage that is quoted with approval by Eldredge and Cracraft [1980, p. 67], says that the testing of phylogenetic hypotheses "must be done under the rules of parsimony, not because nature is parsimonious, but because only parsimonious hypotheses can be defended by the investigator without resorting to authoritarianism or apriorism." Nelson and Platnick [1981, p. 39] similarly contend that the very possibility of evaluating competing hypotheses leads to parsimony as a methodological principle (italics mine):

> One might ask why a parsimony criterion should be used—after all, how do we know that evolution has actually been parsimonious? The answer, of course, is that we don't; we don't know whether evolution was always, sometimes, or even never parsimonious. We cannot observe the path of evolution directly, but only its results, and we can only attempt to reject some hypotheses about that path in favor of others. But there are a tremendous number of possible hypotheses; take for example, the presence of hair in mammals. It is possible that hair has been acquired independently in every species of mammal (that is, that the most recent common ancestor of any two species of mammals had no hair); it is also possible that two particular mammalian species acquired their hair together, from their own most recent common ancestor, but that all other mammals acquired their hair independently of those two and of each other. The number of such hypotheses possible for even a single character is immense, and when entire sets of characters are considered, approaches close enough to infinity to approximate it for practical purposes. None of

---

4. For criticisms and elaborations of Popper's views on method, see Hempel [1965a], Salmon [1967], Putnam [1974], Jeffrey [1975], Ackermann [1976], Rosenkrantz [1977], and Lakatos [1978].

these hypotheses can be rejected on grounds that they are impossible, but almost all of them can be rejected on grounds that more parsimonious alternatives are available. *In short, if we do not prefer the most parsimonious hypothesis, we have no basis for preferring any one of these numerous alternatives over the others.*

I hope the reader detects a shift between Nelson and Platnick's last sentence and the one just before it. Certainly, numerous alternatives can be rejected *if* parsimony is adopted as the method of discrimination. But this does not imply that alternatives may be discarded *only if* parsimony is invoked.

Gaffney [1979, pp. 97–98] advances an argument of just this sort, but then recognizes (in a footnote) that it is not successful. Gaffney seeks to connect cladistic parsimony with a broader philosophical idea:

One of the most basic ideas in the history of scientific explanation is that often called parsimony or Ockham's razor. This idea is usually stated as follows: Among two or more conflicting solutions to a given problem, the simplest solution (i.e., the one involving the smallest number of logical steps or auxiliary conditions) should be chosen, all other factors being equal. In this sense, parsimony might be considered a methodological rule, invoked only because to do otherwise could result in no choices being made and no progress possible, not because it mirrors reality in some way.

He then notes two formulations of this principle attributed to Ockham himself and concludes that "... it seems to me that parsimony, or Ockham's razor, is equivalent to 'logic' or 'reason' because any method that does not follow the above principle would be incompatible with any kind of predictive or consistent system."

Again we see the familiar idea that parsimony makes sense because without it no discriminations could be made among competing hypotheses. However, in a footnote to the first passage quoted, Gaffney [1979, p. 98] says that "strictly speaking, if the rule is used only to provide a means of escaping a dead end, then it could just as well choose the most complex alternative."

Exactly so. This suffices to undermine one proposed justification of parsimony—either in its global form as a general methodological principle or as a local constraint that applies just to the problem of phylogenetic inference. *There are other procedures that induce a ranking among competing hypotheses.* Indeed, in the case of phylogenetic inference, no great imagination is required to see this, since biologists have constructed a number of alternative methods. If the problem is just to discriminate among competing phylogenies, overall similarity succeeds in making discriminations and so do other approaches. The justification for using parsimony must be found elsewhere.

Of course, the authors just quoted recognize this point. This is why they connect philosophical ideas about parsimony with the practice of using cladistic parsimony in phylogenetic inference. This connection is meant to show, not that cladistic parsimony is the only method that can discriminate among hypotheses (however arbitrarily), but that it is the only method that in some sense makes "correct" discriminations. By this, I do not mean that parsimony always singles out the true phylogeny or that it does so more often than competing hypotheses do. As Nelson and Platnick point out, we typically have no independent access to the question of whether our methods point to the truth. Rather the thought behind saying that parsimony is "correct" is that parsimony correctly determines which phylogenetic hypothesis is best supported by the data.

I noted in section 2.1 that it is important to begin with a distinction between global parsimony and local parsimony. By the former, I mean the sort of general methodological constraint that philosophers have discussed under the rubric of "simplicity" or "Ockham's razor." By the latter, I have in mind the specifically phylogenetic idea. The authors quoted above assert an important connection between these two concepts: cladistic parsimony (the local concept) is the right method to use in reconstructing phylogeny, because (global) parsimony is a legitimate constraint in science as a whole. We now must see how this claimed connection is supported by argument.

Several cladists have claimed that global parsimony licenses cladistic procedures when additional, though modest, premises are added. Wiley [1975, p. 234] says that three axioms suffice: "(1) Evolution occurs; (2) only one phylogeny of all living and extinct organisms exists, and this phylogeny is the result of genealogical descent; (3) characters may be passed from one generation, modified or unmodified, through genealogical descent." Wiley [1981, p. 2] suggests a somewhat different formulation: "The history of speciation may be recovered when speciation is coupled with character modification or when the rate of speciation does not proceed faster than the rate of character evolution." Eldredge and Cracraft [1980, p. 4] say that "it is our position that, in the analysis of evolutionary history (i.e., pattern) in its most general form, we need only adopt the basic notion that life has evolved."Gaffney [1979, p. 86] likewise claims that modest assumptions suffice to justify cladistic parsimony:

> *Evolution: All the forms of life (i.e., taxa) have been produced by natural processes of inheritance, change, and divergence from a common origin . . . .*
> *Synapomorphy: New taxa are often characterized by new features . . . .*

Our two basic hypotheses, then, are that evolution has occurred and that new taxa may be characterized by new features. Using only these two generalizations, we can develop and test hypotheses about the geometry of descent. There is no reliance upon the 'synthetic theory' of evolution or any other particular hypothesis of evolutionary machanism, and there is no reliance on any particular model or hypothesis of speciation or the nature of species.

These modest evolutionary assumptions, plus an appreciation of the concept of global parsimony, are supposed to lead straight to cladistic parsimony.

But how? The connecting argument is sometimes expressed in terms of the concept of *falsification*; at other times, it is set forth in terms of *ad hocness*. Given a set of character distributions for the taxa under investigation, alternative phylogenetic trees[5] may be constructed. Each tree may be characterized in terms of the minimum number of homoplasies it requires if it is to generate the observations. Each of the homoplasies required by a phylogenetic hypothesis falsifies it. The best-supported phylogenetic hypothesis is the one that is least falsified by the data—i.e., the one that requires the fewest homoplasies (Gaffney [1979, p. 94]; Eldredge and Cracraft [1980, p. 70]; Wiley [1981, p. 111]).

The alternative formulation, in terms of *ad hocness* goes as follows: When a phylogenetic hypothesis is forced to say that a given character is homoplasious, this counts as an *ad hoc* assumption to which the phylogenetic hypothesis is forced to assent. The scientific method enjoins us to avoid *ad hoc* assumptions. Hence the phylogenetic hypothesis that requires the fewest homoplasies is the least *ad hoc*.

One small point is worth registering before the main issue is addressed. The principle of one homoplasy, one vote assumes that all characters should be weighted equally. Suppose we know the distribution of three characters over species A, B, and C and the polarity of each. The first two are distributed as 110; i.e., A and B are apomophic while C is plesiomorphic. The third has the distribution 011. (AB)C requires a total of four evolutionary changes to account for these characters, whereas A(BC) requires five such changes.

In other words, (AB)C requires a single homoplasy, to account for character 3, while A(BC) requires two homoplasies, one for each of the first

---

5. Or cladograms. The discussion of how parsimony is supposed to work does not turn on this difference: cladograms require the same number of homoplasies as the trees that conform to them (when these two concepts are understood in the way proposed in section 1.3), so we can compare competing trees or competing cladograms by using cladistic parsimony and get the same result. For convenience, I shall talk in what follows about trees in which the taxa under investigation are all terminal.

two characters. Suppose we grant that each homoplasy counts against the phylogenetic hypothesis that requires it. This means that (AB)C is disconfirmed by character 3 and A(BC) is disconfirmed by characters 1 and 2. So far, we have simply recorded the testimony of *each* character. How are we to assess what they mean *collectively?*

If we adopt the assumption that each character has the same evidential import as every other and that they are independent, we can merely count homoplasies. But if we suspected that character 3 disconfirms (AB)C far more than characters 1 and 2 together disconfirm A(BC), we would reach the opposite conclusion.

The fact that cladists count homoplasies has suggested to some commentators that cladistic parsimony assumes that all characters have equal weight. I myself extract a different moral. Characters must be weighted *before* any method—cladistic parsimony included—is applied. If it is maintained that character 3 deserves more weight than characters 1 and 2 together, then this should be taken into account. One expedient is to pretend that character 3 is in fact worth the weight of *five* identically distributed characters, and then count votes in a data set made of characters 1, 2, and these five "surrogates" of the original character 3 (Kluge and Farris [1969]). Parsimony, per se, does not say anything about how weighting is to be achieved.[6]

To assess the falsificationist defense of cladistic parsimony just described, we must ask what "falsify" means in this context. A number of cladism's critics have supposed that phylogenetic hypotheses falsified by a character must in fact be false. They then ask why the "least falsified" phylogenetic hypothesis should be taken seriously. If a hypothesis has been shown to be false by even one character, is that not enough to rule it out?

Two responses to this charge are possible. The first defines the falsification relation to mean "logical incompatibility." To say that a character falsifies a hypothesis just means that one of them must be false; either we must throw out the character or the hypothesis. A 011 character (as usual, with "0" meaning ancestral and "1" derived) would "falsify" (AB)C in this sense if the truth of the phylogenetic hypothesis and the distribution of the character were logically incompatible. A character may "falsify" a phylogenetic hypothesis without the hypothesis actually being false; what

---

6. Felsenstein [1981] understands methods of phylogenetic inference already to include principles of character weighting; in consequence, he considers "unweighted parsimony" and "weighted parsimony" as separate methods. I, on the other hand, see a common thread running through these two procedures, which I call "parsimony," thus leaving the weighting procedure as a separate issue. This difference is at bottom simply terminological, I suspect.

is essential is that we have to choose (Gaffney [1979, p. 83]; Eldredge and Cracraft [1980, pp. 69−70]; Farris [1983, p. 9]). I shall call this the relation of *strong falsification*.

This formulation will not be satisfactory if genuine homoplasies can occur in nature. If (AB)C is the true phylogeny, there nonetheless may be characters that exhibit the 011 distribution (where "0" means ancestral and "1" derived). If characters "falsify" a phylogenetic hypothesis, this cannot mean that the two are logically incompatible.

There is a weaker relationship that may obtain between hypotheses and observations, one which corresponds more closely to the real world of phylogenies and homoplasies. I shall say that a hypothesis H is *weakly falsified* by an observation O precisely when O *disconfirms* H. The point is that O can weakly falsify H, even though O and H are both true. The relation of strong falsification excludes this possibility.

Popper's philosophy of science is of very little help here, because he has little to say about *weak* falsification. Popper, above all, is a hypothetico-*deductivist*. For him, observational claims are deductive consequences of the hypotheses under test and the initial condition and boundary condition statements that are assumed to be true in the context of investigation. From the hypothesis H and auxiliary assumptions A, one can deduce the prediction O. If O is false and if the auxiliary assumptions A are true, then H must be false.

Deductivism excludes the possibility of probabilistic testing. A theory that assigns probabilities to various possible observational outcomes cannot be strongly falsified by the occurrence of any of them.[7] This, I suggest, is the situation we confront in testing phylogenetic hypotheses. (AB)C is logically consistent with all possible character distributions (polarized or not), and the same is true of A(BC).

This point depends on what we are prepared to accept as a plausible process model. Deductive connections between phylogenetic hypotheses and polarized character distributions would exist if we adopted the fairy tale process model of section 1.3. If homoplasies are impossible, (AB)C deductively implies that no 011 characters can evolve (where "0" means

7. Popper [1959, pp. 189−190] sees this quite clearly when he says that *"probability statements will not be falsifiable.* Probability hypotheses *do not rule out anything observable;* probability estimates cannot contradict, or be contradicted by, a basic statement; nor can they be contradicted by a conjunction of any finite number of basic statements; and accordingly not by any finite number of observations either." Popper nevertheless allows that probabilities may figure in scientific discourse; he suggests that we adopt a "methodological convention" that says, roughly, that hypotheses shall be deemed falsified when they say that what we observe is very improbable. This, of course, introduces the idea of likelihood. My present point, though, is to urge that the usual deductivist interpretations of Popper simply do not apply to the problem of phylogenetic inference.

ancestral and "1" derived). However, as soon as we abandon this process model and accept, instead, the possibility of multiple origination and reversion, the deductive connection just described simply vanishes.

The central question here is the same one raised in the previous section about Hennig's arguments. Cladistic parsimony claims that shared apomorphies confirm hypotheses of genealogical relationship but that shared plesiomorphies do not. Equivalently, we may put this point in the language of (weak) falsification: cladistic parsimony claims that a phylogeny is disconfirmed by the homoplasies it requires and that no other aspects of the data can do this. The question is, why think these claims about evidential meaning are true? What, if anything, do they assume about the evolutionary process?

The reader will notice that I have moved interchangeably between a (weak) verificationist and a (weak) falsificationist formulation of cladistic doctrine. I have pictured cladism as claiming that apomorphic resemblance is the only thing that *confirms* phylogenetic hypotheses and, equivalently, that homoplasies are the only things that *disconfirm* phylogenetic hypotheses. Doctrinaire Popperians may not be happy here, if they insist that "Science" is falsifiable, not verifiable. But we have seen that phylogenetic hypotheses are neither strongly verifiable nor strongly falsifiable by character distributions. If they are weakly falsifiable—disconfirmable—this is because character distributions support some phylogenetic hypotheses better than others. But if A(BC) is worse supported than (AB)C by given data, (AB)C is better supported. Perhaps the words "falsify" and "verify" should be discarded here, since they misleadingly suggest deductive connections where none exist. Once we replace them with "disconfirm" and "confirm" and understand hypothesis evaluation to be a comparative task, there is nothing to choose between saying that some competitors are confirmed and others are disconfirmed.[8] Popper's asymmetry has disappeared.[9]

8. A subsidiary benefit of describing cladistic parsimony in terms of the idea of weak falsification is that it becomes abundantly obvious how parsimony differs from compatibility (or "clique") analysis. If genealogical hypotheses and characters really were logically incompatible, the idea of discarding characters might make sense. However, if characters merely confirm and disconfirm genealogical groupings, then discarding characters will look more like the mistake of ignoring relevant data. This observation is not meant to refute the compatibility approach, but only to point out that the difference between it and parsimony becomes clearer if we abandon the rhetoric of strong falsification.Compatibility methods will be discussed further in chapter 5.

9. This rejection of Popper's asymmetry is quite different from Quinean appeals to Duhem's thesis (see, e.g., Quine [1960]). Suppose that a hypothesis plus auxiliary assumptions deductively implies an observation statement: $H\&A$ implies O. The Duhem/Quine point is that just as O does not allow one to conclude that H is true, so not-O does not allow one to conclude that H is false. In reply, note that an asymmetry between verification and

The fact that no character distribution strongly falsifies a phylogenetic hypothesis is sometimes obscured by talk of novelties "defining" monophyletic groups. Consider figure 14, drawn from Eldredge and Cracraft [1980, p. 25]. The caption they provide says that "each level of the hierarchy (denoted by branch points) is defined by one or more similarities interpreted as evolutionary novelties." Note that the *absence* of a novelty does not pick out a monophyletic group. Lacking an amniote egg, for example, unites perch and lamprey, but these do not comprise a monophyletic group apart from the other taxa represented.

What does "define" mean here? Philosophers and mathematicians usually require that a definition provide a necessary and sufficient condition. A square is defined as a plane figure with four straight sides of equal length, all at right angles. Do evolutionary novelties "define" monophyletic taxa in this sense? Consider Eldredge and Cracraft's [1980, p. 37] discussion:

> ... the similarity of dense body hair cannot define a set including a mouse and a lion but excluding a human, because the shared possession of dense body hair between the mouse and lion is, at that hierarchical level, a symplesiomorphy, that is, there are other organisms with dense body hair excluded from the set. As the hierarchical level is increased by adding other groups with hair, this similarity is eventually seen to define a set biologists call Mammalia, and at this level hair is a shared derived similarity, a synapomorphy.

What one needs to see here is that the definition of monophyly implies that a hairless descendant of a mammalian species would still be a mammal. So if a character "defines" a monophyletic group, this must be consistent with the possibility that some member species lack the "defining" character. If hair (or *dense body hair*) "defines" *Mammalia*, it does so in a way quite different from the way *unmarried man* defines *bachelor*.

So what could be meant by saying that traits "define" monophyletic groups? The idea we want to capture is twofold. First, monophyletic groups, like species themselves, originate with evolutionary novelties. When a parent species produces a daughter species, it is essential that the daughter have some trait not found in the parent. In this respect, begetting as a relationship between species differs from begetting as a relationship between organisms. A parental organism can produce an offspring that is identical with the parent, by cloning. But if a population in

---

falsification would be restored if we assume in the context of inquiry that our auxiliary assumptions *A* are true. A more telling limitation of Popper's asymmetry becomes visible when we consider probabilistic testing.

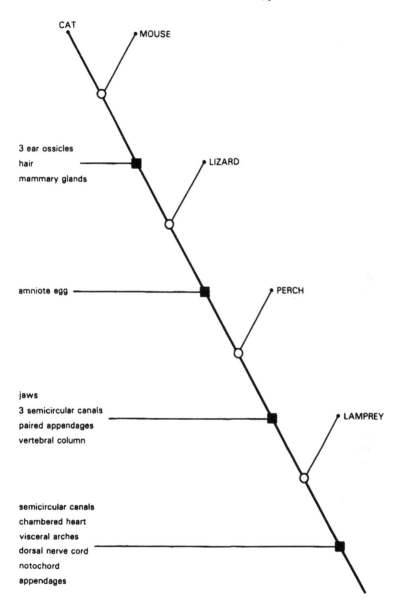

CAT

MOUSE

3 ear ossicles
hair   LIZARD
mammary glands

amniote egg   PERCH

jaws
3 semicircular canals   LAMPREY
paired appendages
vertebral column

semicircular canals
chambered heart
visceral arches
dorsal nerve cord
notochord
appendages

Figure 14.
An example illustrating the relationship of characters and monophyletic groups. A novel
character marks the emergence of a new group, but the character does not "define" that
group in the sense of providing a necessary and sufficient condition for belonging to it
(from Eldredge and Cracraft [1980, p. 25]).

one species buds off a peripheral isolate that is such that both the isolate and its descendants remain identical with the parent population, no biologist would regard this as a new species.

Each group made up of a species and all its descendants counts as a distinct monophyletic group; it follows that a new monophyletic group comes into existence every time a speciation event occurs. It also follows that if speciation requires a character change (the offspring species must differ from the parent), so does the emergence of a new monophyletic group. The first species in a new monophyletic group must differ from its immediate ancestor. This is one sense in which a novelty may be said to "define" a monophyletic group. It marks its appearance.

But that novelty may then be lost within that same monophyletic group. This is why a hairless mammal is still a mammal. Traits do not define monophyletic groups in the traditional sense of providing necessary and sufficient conditions for membership.

The second sense in which traits "define" groups—a sense that also radically differs from the classical notion of definition just mentioned—is that traits provide fallible evidence for the existence of such groups.[10] Without clearly distinguishing the two senses of definition just mentioned from the traditional notion of definition in terms of necessary and sufficient conditions, it is possible to think that the discovery of a shared apomorphy can definitively settle the question of whether the apomorphic taxa belong to a monophyletic group to which plesiomorphic taxa do not. The apomorphy may "define" a group in two senses, but not the third.

Another idea that has obscured the evidential relationship of characters to genealogical hypotheses is the suggestion that there are no "true" homoplasies. Any similarity that seems to be homoplasious can be shown, upon closer analysis, to involve different characters. So "wings" in bats and birds do not constitute a homoplasy, this argument suggests, because once we describe the appendages in greater detail, the appearance of similarity between the two groups disappears.

The trouble with this argument is that any similarity, even a genuine homology, can be made to vanish when enough details are given. Subtle differences can be detected between my arm and yours, but this should not undermine the idea that there is a shared arm structure that we inherited from a common ancestor. Whenever we perceive a similarity, we perceive a similarity that exists along with many differences. If homoplasies are defined out of existence by this expedient, the same fate will befall the

10. Consider Hennig's [1966, pp. 79–80] observation: he says his approach treats morphological characters not "as ingredients of higher categories [monophyletic groups] but [as] aids used to apprehend the genetic [genealogical] criteria that lie behind them" (square brackets mine). See Beatty [1982] for related discussion.

similarities that offer evidence of genealogy. The end result will be a set of thoroughly unique species with no similarities left on which to base hypotheses of common descent.

4.3. Explanatory Power

Farris [1983] endorses the falsificationist defense of parsimony surveyed in section 4.2, but gives it a new twist by appealing to the idea of *explanatory power*. Farris's line of argument depends on a point developed in section 1.3 about the very different relationships that a genealogical hypothesis bears to the concepts of homology and homoplasy. Besides serving to justify cladistic parsimony, this idea also, he thinks, diffuses what is perhaps the most standard objection to parsimony—namely, that the method assumes that homoplasies are rare. In section 4.4, I shall discuss Farris's attempted refutation of this criticism.

As noted in section 1.3, a genealogical hypothesis—whether it specifies a cladogram or a tree—does not by itself deductively imply that any character is a homology. Consider a tree in which the three terminal taxa exhibit the phylogenetic relationship (AB)C. How might this tree explain a character distributed as 110 (i.e., one in which A and B are apomorphic and C is plesiomorphic)? Farris observes that the tree does not imply that A and B inherited their apomorphic form unmodified from a common ancestor. It certainly is possible that the apomorphies shared by A and B are homologous; but it also is possible that the traits were independently derived.

Matters are quite different when we look at homoplasies instead of at homologies. Genealogies *do* imply homoplasies. The (AB)C tree implies that any character distributed as 011 must contain a homoplasy. Farris [1983, p. 13/680][11] summarizes these two points as follows: "The relationship between characters and genealogies thus shows a kind of asymmetry. Genealogy $((A, B), C)$ requires that the $B + C$ character be homoplasious, but requires nothing at all concerning the $A + B$ characters. The genealogy can be true whether the conforming characters are homoplasious or not."[12]

Farris then uses this asymmetry to characterize what he takes to be the explanatory power of a genealogical hypothesis (Farris [1983, p. 18/684]; italics mine):

11. The second page reference to quotations from Farris [1983] will indicate the page in a slightly abridged version of the paper reprinted in Sober [1984b].

12. Notice that in saying that the derived character shared by B and C must be homoplasious, Farris is assuming that the most recent common ancestor of the three taxa is plesiomorphic.

In choosing among theories of relationship on the basis of explanatory power, we wish naturally to identify the genealogy that explains as much available observation as possible. In general, deciding the relative explanatory power of competing theories can be a complex task, but it is simplified in the present case by the fact that genealogies provide only a single kind of explanation. A genealogy does not *explain by itself* why one group acquires a new feature while its sister group retains the ancestral trait, nor does it offer any explanation of why seemingly identical features arise independently in distantly related lineages. (Either sort of phenomenon might of course be explained by a more complex evolutionary theory.) A genealogy is *able to explain* observed points of similarity among organisms just when it can account for them as identical by virtue of inheritance from a common ancestor. Any feature shared by organisms is so either by reason of common descent or because it is a homoplasy. The explanatory power of a genealogy is consequently measured by the degree to which it can avoid postulating homoplasies.

Farris connects these ideas about phylogenetic inference to more global issues concerning hypothesis evaluation: the scientific method enjoins us to prefer hypotheses that have greater explanatory power (i.e., which require fewer *ad hoc* hypotheses—since these diminish the hypothesis's explanatory power). Hence, the above analysis of what determines the explanatory power of genealogical hypotheses leads directly to the methodology of cladistic parsimony.

Notice that Farris's argument demands a distinction between what a hypothesis "explains by itself" and what it "can explain." He says that a genealogy "does not *explain by itself*" any character distribution; yet, Farris claims that "a genealogy is *able to explain* observed points of similarity among organisms just when it can account for them as identical by virtue of inheritance from a common ancestor."

Farris's first claim seems right, if it means that genealogies, in and of themselves, do not supply "complete" explanations of any character distribution. To be told only that A and B share a common ancestor that neither shares with C leaves a great deal unsaid as to why a given character has the distribution it does. To know in addition the character's polarity (i.e., the state of the root of the tree) still leaves vast quantities of relevant information unspecified. If the root began in state 0 for some character and the tips display apomorphies unique to A and B, the question might still be posed—*why* do A, B, and C exhibit the characters they do? That this why-question remains to be answered shows that genealogies do not give complete explanations—i.e., they omit information that is explanatorily relevant.

Now we must consider Farris's claimed asymmetry—that "a genealogy is able to explain observed points of similarity . . . just when it can account for them as identical by virtue of inheritance from a common ancestor." I take it that what Farris means in saying that a hypothesis "is able to explain" a similarity is that the hypothesis *helps* to explain it—i.e., the hypothesis provides a nonredundant part of an illuminating account of the similarity.

(AB)C "is able to explain" a character distributed as 110 because the genealogical grouping can be supplemented to yield a fuller explanation. This supplementation may be represented as a deductive argument from a set of explaining premises to the character distribution that is to be explained; I follow Farris in assuming that the most recent common ancestor of the three taxa is plesiomorphic for the character in question:

> *Genealogical Hypothesis*: A and B have a common ancestor X that is not an ancestor of C.
>
> *Interior States*: X possessed the apomorphic character state and transmitted that state to A and B. The apomorphy arose exactly once and was retained on the branch leading from the root to X. No character evolution occurred on the branch leading from the root to C.
>
> *Evolutionary Mechanisms*: X possessed the derived form for evolutionary reason such-and-such. X transmitted the derived form unchanged to A and B for evolutionary reason so-and-so. No character evolution occurred on the branch leading from the root to C for evolutionary reason thus-and-so.

> *Observed Character Distribution* (110): A and B have the derived state and C has the ancestral state.

In this explanation, phrases like "so-and-so" and "such-and-such" are placeholders for which substantive evolutionary conjectures may be substituted.[13]

The (AB)C genealogical grouping helps explain the 110 character by being a part of this whole.[14] However, there are other ways to supple-

---

13. The above schema for explaining a character distribution does not mean that it is particularly easy, or even in principle possible, to know all the elements described. The point is to show how a genealogical hypothesis can be an indispensable part of a more inclusive set of premises that, if true, would explain a character distribution.

14. There is a usage of "explains" according to which assumptions cannot explain a result unless they are true. In saying above that these three premises "explain" the character distribution, I mean that they would explain it if they were true. They are "explanatory," where this property is independent of the question of whether the assumptions, in fact, are true. In just this sense, Newtonian mechanics is an explanatory theory even though it is false.

ment the (AB)C genealogical hypothesis so that it helps explain the 110 observation. For example, the (AB)C hypothesis can be supplemented by premises about interior states and evolutionary mechanisms that imply that the 110 character involves a convergence of the lineages leading to A and B. In this case just as much as in the first one, the genealogical hypothesis plays an indispensible role in explaining the observed character distribution.

Both the preceding explanations include the genealogical hypothesis (AB)C. They differ in their second and third premises, but both triplets are able to explain why the character in question is distributed as 110. If a scenario that posits a homology is explanatory, so too is one that posits a homoplasy. Again, this is not to say that they are equally plausible; I merely claim that each has the property that it would explain the distribution if it were true.

If the second scenario, which shows how a convergence in the (AB)C tree can lead to a 110 character, is explanatory, the same must be true of a scenario that shows how a 011 character evolved on that same tree. The difference between this third explanation and the second one concerns whether convergence occurs within the ingroup or between an ingroup taxon and the outgroup. Again, this kind of story explains the character distribution by showing why the convergence occurred. The genealogical hypothesis contributes to the explanation.

Farris claimed that no genealogical hypothesis "by itself" explains any character distribution, but that a genealogical hypothesis "is able to explain" just those similarities that it can interpret as homologies. I grant the first point, but not the second. I do not see a meaningful sense in which genealogical hypotheses are unable to explain the character distributions they imply are homoplasious.

It may be objected that assumptions of homoplasy are implausible and that this is why the explanatory power of a genealogical hypothesis is diminished by the homoplasies it requires. To assess this suggestion, we must decide what "implausible" means. If "implausible" means "improbable," then the suggestion is that homoplasies are improbable and so a genealogy is disconfirmed by the characters it takes to be homoplasies for just that reason. The problem with this suggestion is that many cladists, including Farris himself, have wanted to defend parsimony without recourse to this assumption; so this is not a plausible way of fleshing out Farris's argument.

The other reason this suggestion will not help Farris's claimed asymmetry is that he wants explanatory power to be a yes/no affair. He wants (AB)C to be able to explain 110 but to be incapable of explaining 011. Importing considerations of relative plausibility does not induce this yes/no notion of explanation; rather, it turns plausibility of explanation into a matter of degree. Perhaps modest premises can be found that show that (AB)C explains a 110 character *better* than it explains a character distributed as 011. But probabilistic considerations are unlikely to show that a genealogy *cannot offer any explanation whatever* of the traits it implies are homoplasies.

The difficulties I have discussed for Farris's concept of explanatory power in some ways parallel my objections to the use that cladists have made of the concept of falsifiability. If falsifiability requires a deductive relationship between genealogies and character distributions, then no genealogical hypothesis is falsified by any character distribution. If, on the other hand, strong falsification is discarded as a criterion and replaced by the weaker (and more plausible) relation of disconfirmation, then the cladistic thesis about how characters are to be interpreted may be true, but a new argument is needed to show that it is.

Explanation, like confirmation, may be given a strong and a weak reading. A genealogical hypothesis strongly explains a character distribution if the hypothesis, in and of itself, provides a complete explanation of the distribution. But as Farris rightly observes, no genealogical hypothesis strongly explains any character distribution. Alternatively, we may ask what a weaker notion of explanation might be. The suggestion I have just explored does not lead to the kind of conclusion that Farris wants to draw. A genealogical hypothesis weakly explains a character distribution if the hypothesis is a nonredundant part of a possible evolutionary explanation of why the character is distributed as it is. The problem is that genealogical hypotheses can weakly explain homoplasious as well as homologous characters.

4.4. *Minimizing Assumptions versus Assuming Minimality*

Perhaps the most common criticism of cladistic parsimony is that it assumes that homoplasies are rare. After all, the method says that the best phylogenetic hypothesis is the one that requires the fewest homoplasies. Does this not require that homoplasies be uncommon?

Farris [1983, p. 13/679] offers an interesting analogy to argue that it is not always true that "an inference procedure that minimizes something must ipso facto assume that the quantity minimized is rare ...":

> In normal regression analysis, a regression line is calculated from a sample of points so as to minimize residual variation around the line, and the choice of line has the effect of minimizing the estimate of the residual variance, but one rarely hears this procedure criticized as presupposing that the parametric residual variance is small. Indeed, it is known from normal statistical theory that the least squares line is

the best point estimate of the parametric regression line, whether the residual variance is small or not. The argument that the parsimony criterion must presume rarity of homoplasy just because it minimizes required homoplasy is thus at best incomplete. That reasoning presumes a general connection between minimization and supposition of minimality, but it is now plain that no such general connection exists. Any successful criticism of phylogenetic parsimony would have to include more specific premises.

This elegant argument is worth pondering by anyone who thinks he can simply see what parsimony assumes from the way it identifies the best phylogenetic hypothesis. I should stress that Farris's argument does not show that parsimony makes no assumption about whether homoplasies are rare; rather, the argument is intended to show that this does not follow just from the fact that parsimony says that the best hypothesis requires the fewest homoplasies.

To show that parsimony does not require that homoplasies be rare, Farris begins with a point noted in the previous section. Genealogical hypotheses do not imply that any character is a homology although they do imply that some character distributions must involve homoplasies. Farris tries to use this point to show that abundance of homoplasy never indicates that a less parsimonious hypothesis is better supported than the most parsimonious hypothesis. He considers three taxa A, B, and C and eleven characters. The first ten traits are distributed as 110; the eleventh exhibits the 011 pattern. The phylogenetic hypothesis (AB)C requires that the eleventh charater involve a homoplasy, but leaves open which of the first ten are homologies or homoplasies. The A(BC) hypothesis, on the other hand, requires that each of the first ten characters involves a homoplasy, but leaves open what is true of the eleventh. Since (AB)C requires fewer homoplasies, it is the one that parsimony prefers.

It should be clear from this that a phylogenetic hypothesis places a *lower bound but not an upper bound* on the number of homoplasies that there are in the data. (AB)C says that there was at least one; A(BC) says that there were at least ten. Neither hypothesis asserts that homoplasies were rare. *The parsimonious hypothesis minimizes assumptions; it does not assume minimality.*

I once thought (Sober [1983, p. 341]) that this observation shows that parsimony does not assume that homoplasies are rare. But this does not follow. The *hypothesis* singled out by parsimony as the best explanation of the data does not place an upper bound on the amount of homoplasy. But this, by itself, does not show that the *method* imposes no assumptions about the probability of homoplasy.

It is not uncommon for an inference procedure to exploit assumptions that do not surface as implications of the hypothesis inferred. Suppose I want to estimate the mean height in a population. If I assume that my data were drawn by random sampling from a single normal distribution, the best estimate of the population mean is the sample mean; it is, recall, the maximum likelihood estimate. Suppose I look at some data and infer by this method that the mean height is 5 feet, 7 inches. Notice that the hypothesis I select says nothing about random sampling or normal distributions. But this does not mean that the method I used made no such assumption.

Farris's distinction between minimizing assumptions and assuming minimality is a vital one. My present point is that we must look in the right place if we wish to apply this idea. The hypotheses inferred by a method may not fully reveal the presuppositions of the method itself.

Let us look more carefully at how Farris argues from the fact that parsimonious *hypotheses* minimize assumptions without assuming minimality to the conclusion that the *method* does not assume that homoplasies are rare (Farris [1983, pp. 13–14/680]; italics mine):

> The sensitivity of inference by parsimony to rarity of homoplasy is readily deduced from these observations. If homoplasy is indeed rare, *it is quite likely* with these characters that ((A, B), C) is the correct genealogy. In order for that grouping to be false, it would be required at least that all 10 of the A + B characters be homoplasious. As these characters are supposed to be independent, the coincidental occurrence of homoplasy in all 10 should be quite *unlikely.* Suppose then that homoplasy is so abundant that only one of the characters escapes its effects. That one character might equally well be any of the 11 in the data, and if it is any one of the 10 A + B characters the parsimonious grouping is correct. That grouping is thus a much *better bet* than is ((B, C), A). At the extreme, as has already been seen, if homoplasy is universal, the characters imply nothing about genealogy. In that case the parsimonious grouping is no better founded than is any other, but then neither is it any worse founded.
>
> It seems that no degree of abundance of homoplasy is by itself sufficient to defend choice of a less parsimonious genealogy over a more parsimonious arrangement; it can never shift the preference to a different scheme. In this the relationship of abundance of homoplasy to choice of genealogical hypothesis is quite like that between residual variance and choice of regression line. Large residual variance expands the confidence interval about the line, or weakens the degree to which the least squares line is to be preferred over nearby lines, but it cannot by itself lead to selection of some other line that fits the data even worse.

Farris's position, then, is that frequency of homoplasy is relevant to the *magnitude*, not the *direction*, of inequalities in evidential support.

Notice that Farris has focused exclusively on those facts about the data that can be *deduced* from competing genealogical hypotheses. (AB)C and the eleven characters *deductively imply* that character 11 involves a homoplasy. A(BC) and the eleven (polarized) characters *deductively imply* that characters 1–10 are homoplasious. Call each of these implications that a phylogenetic hypothesis has when conjoined with the data its *special consequence*. As long as homoplasies are less than universal (and assuming that each character has an equal chance of being homoplasious), then it is more probable that at least one character is homoplasious than it is that at least ten are. The special consequence of (AB)C is more probable than the special consequence of A(BC). So (AB)C, Farris concludes, is "the better bet."

At first glance, this may look like a likelihood argument. Genealogical hypotheses are judged in terms of the probabilities of their (special) consequences. But a closer look shows that this is not so. First, in a likelihood argument, one considers the probabilities that the hypotheses *confer* on observations. But (AB)C does not imply a judgment about the probability of homoplasies (or at least Farris has not shown that it does). (AB)C and the data together imply that *at least* one character is homoplasious; but this does not mean that (AB)C and the data together imply a probability for the existence of some number of homoplasies.

Second, if likelihood is to measure evidential support, it is important that the likelihoods of hypotheses be compared relative to *the same* observations. It does not make much sense to look at two hypotheses in terms of what they say about *different* observations. Yet, this is what occurs in Farris's argument: (AB)C implies that character 11 is homplasious, while A(BC) implies that characters 1–10 are.

Third, likelihoods are standardly assessed by seeing how the competing hypotheses probabilify an *observation* claim that can be independently checked. But the statement that one or another character is a homoplasy is not an observational claim.[15] To be sure, Farris stipulates that each character has an equal chance of being homoplasious and this assumption is arguably independent of the genealogical hypotheses considered. But a likelihood argument requires more than this. One needs to know what observational claims are true, not just what their probabilities are.

And finally, a likelihood calculation must take account of all the data. One must see what probability a hypothesis confers on the entire data set. But Farris's argument focuses on one of the deductive implications that the

15. No naive notion that observation statements can be established without background information is required here. The distinction between observation and hypothesis will be discussed in section 4.6.

hypotheses have when conjoined with the data. As noted above, these implications are not, properly speaking, part of the data at all.

I have already noted one defect in this argument: the assumptions of a *method* need not be implied by what the preferred *hypotheses* themselves assert; recall the simple example of estimating mean height. A second defect derives from the fact that Farris restricts his attention to the *deductive implications* that follow from the competing hypotheses together with the data. Farris says that parsimony does not assume that homoplasies are rare because parsimonious hypotheses do not deductively imply (in conjunction with the data) that this is so. But now we must ask whether the presuppositions of a method are exhausted by what it *deductively* implies. Suppose I create a method in which I stipulate that the probability of homoplasies has the following distribution:

Number of Homoplasies	0	1	2	3	...	n
Probability	1/2	1/4	1/8	1/16	...	$(1/2)^{n+1}$

From this probability assignment, I cannot *deduce* that homoplasies will be rare. After all, my method does not absolutely exclude the possibility that many homoplasies will occur in a given phylogenetic tree. But there are presuppositions here nonetheless. A method may place no absolute upper bound on how much homoplasy there may be, and still make assumptions about how much homoplasy should be expected.[16] As with falsification and explanation, presupposition must be understood probabilistically, not just in terms of deduction.

In Farris's example, the (AB)C hypothesis plus the data deductively imply that there is at least one homoplasy, whereas the A(BC) hypothesis plus the data imply that there are at least ten. These two implications about the lower bound on the number of homoplasies I termed the "special consequences" of the two phylogenetic hypotheses. The first special consequence cannot be less probable than the second: if there are at least ten homoplasies, there must be at least one (but not conversely). Can one reach any conclusion about the relative probabilities of the phylogenetic hypotheses from this fact about the relative probabilities of their special consequences?

The answer is *no*—without further assumptions nothing follows about the probabilities of the two phylogenetic hypotheses. There is a wider les-

16. This point bears on the discussion of the "no upper bound argument" in section 2.4. The practice of selecting the simplest hypothesis consistent with the observations places no upper bound on how complex the chosen hypothesis may have to be. But suppose I adopt this policy because I stipulate (as Jeffreys [1957] did) that prior probabilities are ordered by their complexity. Here my method makes a substantive assumption about the probabilities of different hypotheses, even though it does not in principle rule out any hypothesis.

son here, one not limited to the notion of probability. Popper [1959, chapters 6–7] encountered a problem of this sort in his work on falsifiability. The structure of the problem is illustrated by the following argument form, which Popper realized is invalid:

H_1 implies S_1

H_2 implies S_2

S_1 is more falsifiable than S_2

H_1 is more falsifiable than H_2

The S_i are the "special consequences" of the hypotheses in which we are interested: the idea is to evaluate the falsifiability of hypotheses H_1 and H_2 by examining the falsifiability of their special implications. But this is not in general a viable strategy.

Here is an example of Popper's that shows why. Let the S_i be conjectures about the general form that the earth's orbit around the sun assumes:

The earth moves in a circular orbit (S_1)

The earth moves in an elliptical orbit. (S_2)

Popper notes that any three data points are consistent with S_1; it takes at least four data points to falsify this hypothesis. On the other hand, S_2 is consistent with any four points; it takes at least five to falsify S_2. So S_1 is more falsifiable than S_2. Within Popper's methodological framework, this means that if both hypotheses are consistent with the observations, S_1 is preferable (better corroborated). S_1 is more falsifiable; hence, according to Popper, it is simpler.

Now let us consider specific hypotheses that describe the exact trajectory of the earth through space. Let H_1 describe a particular circular orbit; let H_2 specify a particular elliptical path. Note that H_1 implies S_1 and H_2 implies S_2. The rub is that H_1 and H_2 are each falsified by a single data point not lying on the path that the hypothesis specifies. H_1 and H_2 are equally falsifiable, even though their special consequences are unequally falisifiable. This illustrates why the above argument scheme is invalid.

The lesson about consulting special consequences as a guide to the status of the hypotheses implying them is rather general. It is not limited to the issue of reaching conclusions about probability, since falsifiability leads to the same result. In Farris's example, (AB)C and the data imply that there is at least one homoplasy, whereas A(BC) plus the data imply that there are at least ten. The special implications may be compared for their falsifiability, for their probability, or for some other property. The relationship between special consequences is no sure guide to the relationship between the hypotheses that imply them, unless further assumptions are supplied.

In summary, then, there are two main ways in which Farris's intriguing argument is flawed. First, there is the vital distinction between what a method assumes and what a hypothesis chosen by the method implies. The latter need not perfectly reflect the former. Second, even if we could ascertain the assumptions of the method by looking at what hypotheses favored by the method assert, there is the problem posed by the policy of judging hypotheses by examining their special consequences. Parsimonious hypotheses place lower bounds on the number of homoplasies that are less constraining than the lower bounds imposed by their less parsimonious competitors. In this respect, they minimize assumptions without assuming minimality. But how this translates into an overall assessment of the phylogenetic hypotheses themselves remains to be seen.

4.5. Stability

Can cladistic parsimony be justified by showing that different suites of characters often lead, via that method, to the same phylogenetic hypothesis? Nelson and Platnick [1981, p. 219] say that there are just two possible explanations for why two data sets lead via parsimony to the same cladogram: "... the agreement is either (1) an artifact imposed upon the samples by the methods of the invesigator, or (2) a reflection of some real factor that is independent both of method and investigator." This simple dichotomy illustrates, I think, why the stability of parsimony—by which I mean its ability to reach the same phylogenetic hypothesis from different data sets—is not, per se, a justification of that method.

When will two data sets both point to the phylogenetic grouping (AB)C? If one uses cladistic parsimony, this will occur precisely when (AB)C minimizes the number of homoplasies that is required for each data set, taken separately. If cladistic parsimony correctly indicated which hypothesis is best supported by the first data set, then the discovery of a second, independent suite of characters would provide additional confirmation. This is just because two sources of support for the same hypothesis are better than one (provided, of course, that they are independent).

The incontestable point is that phylogenetic *hypotheses* are better supported when additional independent data are provided that lead to the same conclusion as the initial data set. But this does not mean that phylogenetic *methods* are supported by their "stability"—their imperturbability under the addition of new characters.

Let us suppose, just for the sake of argument, that cladistic parsimony is the best method for assessing the evidential meaning of character distributions. Let an initial set of fifty characters be such that (AB)C is the best hypothesis, when parsimony is used to analyze the data. A new data set is then introduced, also involving fifty characters, and A(BC) is the most parsimonious hypothesis for this second set. The data sets disagree. If parsimony is the correct way to discern evidential meaning, this result does not in the slightest impugn that method's credentials. When different pieces of data point in different directions, it is essential to consider what *all* the data say. A natural "principle of total evidence" enjoins us to find the most parsimonious tree, relative to all one hundred characters.

Parallel remarks apply to other methods—for example, to overall similarity. Suppose a phenetic analysis of the initial fifty characters points to (AB)C as the best-supported hypothesis. It may emerge that the second batch of fifty characters points to A(BC) instead. The correct resolution of this shift in testimony is to look at *all* the data. If overall similarity is the correct method to use, then one should calculate the overall similarity of the three taxa relative to all one hundred characters.

Given that a method of inference has been chosen, agreement between independent data sets increases the overall support accruing to the *hypothesis* singled out as best. And given that we have a method of inference in hand, lack of agreement between subsets of data forces us to assess the credentials of the competing hypotheses relative to all the characters available.[17] The point is that all this is conditional on the assumption that a method of inference has already been chosen; stability bears on the standing of *hypotheses*, not on the *methods* used to select them.

There is along tradition in taxonomy of viewing stability of classification as a virtue.[18] If taxonomy simply aimed to provide a Dewey-decimal system for the living world, this would be understandable. Librarians may be able to perpetually improve the way they group books together, but for those of us who use libraries, stability is a virtue of classifications. We get the hang of old methods and would just as soon not have them change with each passing fashion in the science of information retrieval.

However this may be when the issue is classification, the desirability of stability is cast into an entirely new light when the problem is phylogenetic inference. Phylogenetic hypotheses should not be stable under the addition of new characters, if those characters in fact suffice to disconfirm genealogical conjectures that were accepted earlier. The science of phylogenetic inference should make a virtue of stability no more (and no less)

17. We also might look for points of *consensus* ("consensus trees") between the data sets: with more than three taxa there may be genealogical relationships on which the data sets concur and others with respect to which they disagree. For example, the first set of characters may select ((AB)C)D, while the second singles out ((AB)D)C. The point of consensus is that (AB) is a monophyletic group apart from each of the other two taxa.
18. See Mickevich [1978], Nelson [1979], Wiley [1981, pp. 268–271], and Sokal [1985, pp. 738ff] for references and discussion.

than any other science that aims at reconstructing objective features of the natural world.

4.6. The Distinction between Observation and Hypothesis

It is not unprecedented in the history of science that a distinction between observation and hypothesis has been important. Sometimes so-called observations become too theory-laden. An essential step toward clarification involves peeling away theoretical assumptions so that the data can become more theory-neutral. This allows the assumptions linking observations to hypotheses to be brought more clearly into view.

Perhaps the most famous example of this kind of process is Einstein's clarification of the concept of simultaneity, which was, for him, a necessary methodological prelude to his special theory of relatively. We do not "directly observe" that two distant events are simultaneous. What we do observe is that we receive a signal (a light beam, perhaps) from one event at the same or different time that we receive a signal from the other. From these data, we infer whether the distant events are simultaneous. This inference requires principles additional to the observations. By cleanly separating the *observation* of the two signals' reception from the *hypothesis* that the distant events are simultaneous, Einstein was able to investigate the theoretical principles that connect the one to the other.

We do not directly observe that taxonomic characters are homologous or homoplasious. Rather, what we observe is that species share some characters but not others. If we add an assumption about the characters' polarity, we can describe our data as consisting in two kinds of similarity—ancestral and derived. From these we attempt to infer phylogenetic relationships. The question under investigation is what additional principles we must add to these observations to evaluate phylogenetic hypotheses. The observations do not pinpoint genealogies all by themselves.

This clean division of observed similarity, conjecture about polarity, and phylogenetic hypothesis is blurred if we think of our data as consisting of synapomorphies and symplesiomorphies, where the former concept is given the strong reading discussed in section 4.1. If synapomorphy means not just *shared* apomorphy, but *homologous* apomorphy, then we no longer can talk about synapomorphies as being our data as opposed to already asserting the hypotheses we wish to evaluate in the light of the data. To describe a character as synapomorphic in this strong sense is *already* to settle the question of phylogenetic relationships. We have thereby conflated the *evidence* and the *inference* we wish to make on its basis. In doing this, we obscure the status of the *nondeductive* principles that connect observations to hypotheses.

There is a deductive relationship between the claim that a character distributed as 011 (where, as usual, "0" means ancestral and "1" derived) evolved via a single evolutionary change and the phylogenetic hypothesis (AB)C. They are logically incompatible. On the other hand, there is no deductive relationship between the claim that a character distributed as 100 evolved via a single evolutionary change and the phylogenetic hypothesis (AB)C. They are not logically incompatible. (nor does either imply the other). It is for this reason that hypothetico-deductivism in the form of Popperian falsificationism has seemed so plausible an account of the rationale behind cladistic parsimony. But the claim that a character evolved via a single evolutionary change is not part of the data. Once we see this, we should also see that hypothetico-deductivism is an insufficient analytic tool for discerning the evidential meaning of character distributions (even assuming that we know how to determine polarity). Phylogenetic hypotheses do not deductively imply or deductively rule out any character distribution.

It is now unfashionable to insist on a difference between "observation" and "theory." We are supposed to have learned that there is no neutral observation language—that all observation is saturated with theoretical assumptions. Only a naive and discredited positivism would assert that there are statements that can be conclusively verified by "pure observation"—without the need of interpretation and auxiliary background knowledge. The "myth of the given" has for a long time been seen for what it is—a myth.[19]

I am not urging a return to a discredited absolute distinction between observation and hypothesis. I am happy to grant all the above truisms, vague though they may be. I do not claim that judgments of character similarity between species are *absolutely* untheoretical. I do not claim that you can "tell by just looking" (without any background knowledge) that two species are in the same character state. Such judgments of similarity are, I will grant, highly inferential and conjectural. A biologist must learn how to recognize characteristics.

What I do claim is that it is important to separate the inferred phylogeny from the data on which it is based. Both may be "theoretical" in the broad sense that both may depend for their justification on background assumptions of one sort or another. What I object to is the kind of theoretical perspective that is introduced into the data when we describe them in terms of the concept of homology. Our description of the data may depend on some theory or other, but it had better not depend on the very hypotheses we intend to use the data to evaluate.

19. So fashionable is this incantation, that it is difficult to footnote it without mentioning most of the influential philosophers of the last forty years. Here is a partial list: Goodman [1952], Hanson [1958], Kuhn [1970], Maxwell [1962], Popper [1959], Quine [1952, 1960], Sellars [1963], and Smart [1963].

Philosophical fashion, as I have noted, has moved from one extreme to the other. Positivists like Carnap wanted to discern an observation language that is entirely "theory-neutral." Ideally, the statements formulated in that language would be conclusively verifiable. Theories in science would then be legitimized by their connection with this observational basis. Once this philosophy was rejected, the pendulum swung to the other extreme. It was then announced that no theory/observation distinction can be drawn or that a reasonably clear distinction will have no philosophical importance whatever. But surely there is a sensible middle ground that gives the distinction between observation and hypothesis its due.

As in so many other ways, discussion in systematics has tended to parallel developments in philosophy. Pheneticists originally took the strong position that no theoretical assumptions were to affect the selection and weighting of characters or the methods used for constructing classifications. Gradually, this ideal of absolute theory neutrality was seen to be as unattainable as it was undesirable (Hull [1970]). Assigning characters equal weights is as much a weighting as assigning them unequal weights. There is no such thing as degrees of similarity until a decision is made about what should count as a character.[20] Methods cannot be absolutely neutral. Pheneticists themselves developed numerous measures of overall similarity. And for any measure, different weightings of characters can produce any relation of overall similarity you please. Without some determinate objective notion of what the enterprise is about, there is no way to show that any measure of similarity is wrong or implausible or that any particular weighting assigned to characters is wrong or implausible.

Positivism in its heyday wanted observations to be absolutely theory-neutral. It was perhaps quite understandable that the reaction against positivism should swing the pendulum to the other extreme—to denying that the distinction between observation and theory makes any sense at all. Pheneticism in its heyday wanted characters to be absolutely theory-neutral. It is understandable that the cladistic reaction against pheneticism should have led to formulations in which characters are themselves construed as hypotheses.[21] This would have been harmless if it had not ob-

20. It is a shame that Goodman's [1970] pithy article on similarity never made its way into the systematics community. He shows quite simply and elegantly that every pair of objects is equally similar unless one specifies some selection principle for what counts as a character and some weighting principle for how shared characters are to affect overall similarity. Biologists had no trouble coming to see this point on their own, however.

21. This way of setting the problem of phylogenetic inference has been attractive to non-cladists as well. Meacham and Estabrook [1985, p. 431], for example, begin their exposition of the compatibility approach by saying that their method "is founded on the idea that, for the purpose of making plausible reconstructions of evolutionary relationships ..., characters are *already* hypotheses of evolutionary relationships."

scured the fact that character distributions (even granting that polarity is already known) do not bear deductive relationships to phylogenetic hypotheses.

Both in philosophy and in systematics, the question of whether observations are "theory-laden" has too often been addressed as a yes/no matter. The question is posed in terms of a dichotomy between two extremes: either observations are absolutely atheoretical or no significant distinction can be drawn between observation and hypothesis. This simplistic yes/no formulation needs to be replaced by one in which theory-neutrality and theory-ladenness are matters of degree. We should not ask whether the description of a character distribution makes theoretical assumptions, but what those assumptions are.

Synapomorphy may be a theoretical category, but seeing that it applies in a specific case should not require that one already know what the phylogenetic relationships are. Polarity is likewise a theoretical category, and biologists who assume that characters are polarized in one way rather than another are obliged to defend this with an argument.[22] But to see each of these categories as theory-laden should not lead one to collapse the problem of phylogenetic inference into a structureless whole in which everything presupposes everything else. If characters can be polarized without knowing the phylogeny of the group under study, and if similarities and differences can be ascertained in the same circumstance, then phylogenetic inference can go forward. Without this separation of observation and hypothesis, phylogenetic inference cannot get off the ground.

My wish to decouple the concept of synapomorphy from the idea of homology does not mean that hypotheses of homology are in principle unacceptable. An (AB)C tree may generate a 110 character via numerous interior paths. If a biologist has reason to think that it is far more probable that the path contain precisely one change than that it contain any greater number, this hypothesis may be stated, defended by biological argument, and taken into account when the character's evidential meaning is assessed. But without being explicit about this hypothesis, it is illegitimate to assume that synapomorphies are homologies. My suggested terminology is intended to isolate the idea of a derived matching from the process assumption about how a derived matching was obtained at the tips of the tree. This separation then allows us to ask whether interpreting a derived matching as evidence of relatedness requires the process assumption.

In the next chapter, I shall survey discussions of cladistic parsimony that have employed a probabilistic perspective. Phylogenetic hypotheses do not have deductive implications about character distributions. But perhaps

---

22. Methods for inferring character polarity will be discussed in chapter 6.

such hypotheses can be shown to confer probabilities on observed similarities. If so, the scope and limits of parsimony and other methods of phylogenetic inference may be illuminated by seeing how their correctness depends on the way trees probabilify data. This path, too, we shall see to be fraught with difficulties.

Chapter 5
Parsimony, Likelihood, and Consistency

In this chapter, I shall examine in detail the debate between Farris [1973, 1983] and Felsenstein [1973b, 1978, 1981, 1982, 1983a,b, 1984] concerning the status of cladistic parsimony, judged as a form of statistical inference. In section 5.1, I review the notion of a *nuisance parameter*, which figured in the discussion in chapter 3 of Reichenbach's principle of the common cause, and show how it arises in the problem of phylogenetic inference. In section 5.2, I consider the opening round of the biological battle: Farris [1973] versus Felsenstein [1973b]. Here the issue was the connection of parsimony and likelihood. The argumentative ground then shifts somewhat, in that Felsenstein [1978] examined parsimony from the point of view of the quite separate notion of statistical consistency. Felsenstein's argument, Farris' [1983] response, and my own evaluation of the relevance of the requirement of statistical consistency (with a detour through Descartes' evil demon problem and reliability theories of justification) form the subject of sections 5.3, 5.4, and 5.5. In section 5.6, I return to the problem of how parsimony and likelihood are connected, focusing on Felsenstein's [1979, 1981, 1982, 1983a,b, 1984] more recent work.

I use the term "battle" in the above paragraph advisedly. Tempers have run high in the systematics community for the last twenty or so years. Pheneticists challenged evolutionary taxonomists; then cladists came along and challenged pheneticists. If scientists were disembodied spirits, it might be possible for them to engage in energetic disagreements without strong emotions intruding. But, for better or worse, this has not been possible for scientists made of flesh and blood. Hull [1988] presents a detailed analysis of the twists and turns that these and related controversies have taken; he particularly emphasizes how the development of ideas interacts with changing associations of people. His is truly a *sociology of knowledge.*[1] However, the focus here and in what follows is on ideas, not on the people espousing them. The subject of this work is logic, not loyalties. I

---

1. Though not with the admixture of conceptual relativism usually associated with that term.

do not judge this approach better or worse than Hull's; they are different and complementary.

The debates I now shall trace have been charged with emotion. But the ideas can be detached (at least to some degree) from the feelings that accompanied them. As history, this treatment must be partial and incomplete. But as an effort to get clear on the correctness of various approaches to the problem of phylogenetic inference, this detachment may have something to recommend it.

5.1. The Nuisance of Nuisance Parameters

Assessing the credentials of cladistic parsimony would be easier, if a hypothesis (H) postulating one or more monophyletic groups could be conjoined with plausible auxiliary assumptions (A) to allow one to deduce character distributions (C). If the conjunction $H \& A$ implies C and C turns out false, then H must be false if A is true. If verdicts on the truth of C and A were independently available, then it might be possible in principle for all phylogenetic hypotheses, save the true one, to be refuted.

In the previous chapter, I argued that the logic of phylogenetic inference does not conform to this simple model. Hypotheses postulating monophyletic groups, when conjoined with plausible auxiliary assumptions, do not allow one to deduce character distributions. This is the essential limitation of the hypothetico-deductive approach.

A fallback position, which I discussed in chapter 3 and alluded to in passing in chapter 4, is provided by the concept of *likelihood*. If hypotheses do not imply what character distributions *will* occur, they may yet imply what character distributions will *probably* occur. Likelihood thereby provides a probabilistic analog of the concept of (strong) falsification. If two hypotheses each imply a probability for an observed character distribution, then the one conferring the higher probability is better supported by the evidence. Perhaps this idea can be used to show why different character distributions confirm and disconfirm, even if they do not strongly falsify.

However, this proposal also is too simple, and again for a simple reason. Phylogenetic hypotheses, as we have used that term, do not imply probabilities for any character distribution. Recall that phylogenetic hypotheses specify *cladograms* or *phylogenetic trees* (section 1.3). The present point is that neither cladograms nor trees by themselves imply a probability for any character distribution. Not only do phylogenetic hypotheses not deductively imply how characters will be distributed; they do not even imply how they will *probably* be distributed. This simple fact has made the probabilistic treatment of phylogenetic inference into a difficult and subtle problem.

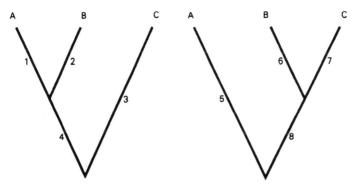

Figure 15.
If the (AB)C and the A(BC) trees are to confer probabilities on observed character distributions, then values must be specified for the transition probabilities associated with
branches 1–8. These branch transition probabilities are *nuisance parameters*.

Although a phylogenetic hypothesis fails to issue in such implications,
the same cannot be said for a logically stronger hypothesis—one in which
the phylogenetic tree is part but not the whole. *A tree conjoined with a specification of branch transition probabilities does imply a probability for each possible character distribution.* Let us consider a character that comes in just two
forms—apomorphic (1) and plesiomorphic (0). To each of the branches of
the trees displayed in figure 15, we must associate two transition probabilities. Let "e_i" (for "evolution") denote the probability that the ith
branch will end in state 1 if it begins in state 0. Let "r_i" (for "reversal")
denote the probability that the ith branch will end in state 0 if it begins in
state 1. These two numbers fix the probabilities of the other two possible
events that can occur on a branch, each of which involves the branch's
ending in the same state in which it began.[2]

If values are stipulated for the transition probabilities associated with
branches 1–8, the likelihoods of the (AB)C and the A(BC) trees may be
calculated.[3] One then could see how probable an apomorphy shared by A
and B but not by C (i.e., a character distributed as 110) would be, given
two conjunctions. There is the probability implied by (AB)C conjoined

2. Although "e_i" and "r_i" represent evolutionary changes, their complements do not necessarily imply stasis. A branch may end in the same state in which it began by undergoing
any even number of flip-flops between the two possible states.
3. Just for the sake of simplicity, I assume that the trees to be considered are such that
the most recent common ancestor of the three taxa is plesiomorphic on all characters. An
alternative formulation is embodied in the trees displayed in figure 5 (p. 30), in which it is
species Zero that is assumed to be plesiomorphic for all characters. This formulation would
complicate the calculations a little, but would not materially affect the conclusions reached.

with the values assigned to branches 1–4, and the probability implied by A(BC) conjoined with the values assigned to branches 5–8.

Which of these conjunctions will have the greater likelihood? That depends on the values stipulated for the transition probabilities. Suppose all events on all branches have a probability of 1/2. Then the probability of 110, given (AB)C and this assumption, is 1/8. In fact, the same probability is implied by A(BC) and the assumption. So if $e_i = r_i = 1/2$ (for all i), then (AB)C and A(BC) confer the same probabilities on the character distribution. They are equally likely.

Matters change if we stipulate that $e_i = r_i = 0.1$ (for all i). Given this assumption, (AB)C confers on 110 a probability that is nine times as great as the probability that A(BC) implies ($0.081 > 0.009$).

As a final example, suppose that the chance of change is virtually nill in branches 1, 2, and 4, but that change is quite probable in branches 5 and 6. I leave it to the reader to supply a numerical example of this sort. Relative to this stipulation, (AB)C will imply a much lower probability for 110 than A(BC) will.[4]

Cladistic parsimony claims that shared apomorphies are always evidence of common descent. It claims, unconditionally, that 110 supports (AB)C better than it supports A(BC). Can this thesis be represented in terms of likelihoods? We have just seen that phylogenetic hypotheses do not imply probabilities by themselves and that how we stipulate transition probabilities affects which phylogenetic hypothesis is more likely.

I do not claim that the three example specifications of values for the branch transition probabilities are plausible. For one thing, I assumed that all characters have the same suite of transition probabilities. But beyond this, there are other features of the assignments I have considered that should give pause. In the first two cases, e_1 and e_3 are assigned the same value (as are e_5 and e_6), even though these branches must differ in their temporal durations. This is not intuitively plausible, nor is it consistent with the model of character evolution to be investigated in chapter 6. In the third case, I assume that branch transition probabilities depend on genealogical hypotheses in a very idiosyncratic way. My point here is simply to note that different stipulations of values for branch transition probabilities have different effects on the likelihood comparison of (AB)C and A(BC). The plausibility of these assignments is a separate matter. It follows that parsimony will connect with likelihood only in the context of a model of how transition probabilities are assigned; it is not true that each and every such assignment conforms to the dictates of parsimony.

The present discussion of figure 15 is intended to remind the reader of

4. The reason is that (AB)C is so constrained that it is much "harder" for it to evolve a 110 character than it is for A(BC) to do so, given the way that tree is (differently) constrained.

the discussion of Reichenbach's principle of the common cause that focused on figure 11 (p. 93). Precisely the same problem arose there. The hypothesis that two events have a common cause does not imply a probability for the two events any more than (AB)C by itself implies a probability for 110. The hypothesis that two events have separate causes does not imply a probability for the two events any more than A(BC) implies a probability for 110. In the case of Reichenbach's principle, I identified two further stipulations, each of which suffices to show that the common cause hypothesis is more likely than the hypothesis of separate causes. One or the other of these stipulations may be highly plausible in a given inferential context; but each is contingent, not logically inevitable. The parallel point here is that different stipulations of transition probabilities affect whether (AB)C is more likely than A(BC), relative to the character distribution 110.

So far I have said that we could evaluate phylogenetic hypotheses by comparing their likelihoods *if* we knew the values of the relevant branch transition probabilities. This claim concerns sufficiency, not necessity. Antecedent knowledge of transition probabilities would *suffice* to render phylogenetic hypotheses comparable in likelihood. But this does not mean that such knowledge is *necessary*. Indeed, it is not; we could get by if we knew how probable the different assignments of transition probabilities would be conditional on the respective phylogenies. If (AB)C is true, we can imagine that some values for the transition probabilities associated with branches 1–4 are more probable than others. If we knew how probable these different possible assignments are, we could calculate the likelihood of (AB)C by taking these different possibilities into account.

Before the reader's consciousness clouds over at the prospect of pondering what a probability of a transition probability is, it is useful to see how this is precisely analogous to a situation that might arise in the simple inference problem discussed in section 3.5. There we were interested in determining Smith's party affiliation (Democrat or Republican); the data consisted of the simple fact that Smith voted for Ronald Reagan (V). A straightforward likelihood approach would involve comparing $Pr(V/R)$ and $Pr(V/D)$.

In the example, I stipulated that the probability of voting for Reagan is influenced by another causal factor (N) besides that of party affiliation. I considered a two-by-two table that depicts the probability of voting for Reagan, given each of the four possible combinations of factors:

		Nuisance Parameter	
		N	not-N
Hypotheses	Democrat	x_1	x_2
	Republican	y_1	y_2

My original discussion of this example focused on the case in which $\Pr(V/D)$ and $\Pr(V/R)$ are simply not calcuable from the available information. However, I now want to modify the example so that it will apply to the present point.

The hypotheses whose relative support we wish to compare concern Smith's party affiliation. Whether Smith has or lacks N is a *nuisance parameter*; it affects the likelihoods and so we must take it into account, but we do not know what its value is (i.e., we do not know whether Smith has N or lacks it.)

In the case of phylogenetic inference, one wishes to make an inference about phylogenetic relationships. Here it is the value of the branch transition probabilities that are the nuisance parameters. As we saw above, they affect the likelihoods, but their values are unknown. In the case of figure 15, we may set out a 2-by-n table of the relevant likelihoods, just to emphasize the analogy. The entries in the table denote the probabilities of obtaining a given observation (e.g., 110 on a given character), conditional on a phylogenetic hypothesis and an assignment of values to the branch transition probabilities.[5]

		Nuisance Parameters			
		N_1	N_2	$\ldots$	N_n
Phylogenies	(AB)C	x_1	x_2	$\ldots$	x_n
	A(BC)	y_1	y_2	$\ldots$	y_n

In both the case of Smith and the present problem of phylogenetic inference, the values of the x_i and y_i are known. The problem is to use that information to say something about the likelihoods of the hypotheses of interest.

If one knew whether Smith has or lacks N, then the likelihoods of the hypotheses about party affiliation would be specified by the relevant column entry. If he has N, you compare x_1 and y_1; if he lacks N, you compare the values in the other column. If you knew which suite of transition probabilities was the correct one—i.e., what the branch transition probabilities would have to be under each phylogenetic hypothesis—you could do the same. This strategy *suffices* to obtain the likelihoods, but it is not *necessary*.

If one simply knew how probable N is among Democrats and among Republicans, the relevant likelihoods would be calculable. Recall that $\Pr(V/D)$ and $\Pr(V/R)$ are expandable as follows:

5. As an expository convenience, I am imagining that each N_i specifies an array of values for all the transition probabilities that pertain to both trees.

$$\Pr(V/D) = \Pr(V/D \& N)\Pr(N/D) + \Pr(V/D \& \text{not-}N)\Pr(\text{not-}N/D),$$
$$\Pr(V/R) = \Pr(V/R \& N)\Pr(N/R) + \Pr(V/R \& \text{not-}N)\Pr(\text{not-}N/R).$$

If half the Republicans and half the Democrats have N, then, these expressions reduce to

$$\Pr(V/D) = x_1(1/2) + x_2(1/2),$$
$$\Pr(V/R) = y_1(1/2) + y_2(1/2).$$

This shows that you need not know whether Smith has or lacks N; knowing how probable N is under the two competing hypotheses suffices.

Precisely the same strategy can be pursued for phylogenetic inference. Instead of asking what the transition probabilities would have to be under the two competing hypotheses, we could get by if we know how probable the different possible values would be. This is because $\Pr[110/(AB)C]$ and $\Pr[110/(A(BC)]$ are each expandable as follows:

$$\begin{aligned}
\Pr[110/(AB)C] = {} & \Pr[110/(AB)C \& N_1]\Pr[N_1/(AB)C] \\
& + \Pr[110/(AB)C \& N_2]\Pr[N_2/(AB)C] \\
& + \cdots \\
& + \Pr[110/(AB)C \& N_n]\Pr[N_n/(AB)C],
\end{aligned}$$

$$\begin{aligned}
\Pr[110/A(BC)] = {} & \Pr[110/A(BC) \& N_1]\Pr[N_1/A(BC)] \\
& + \Pr[110/A(BC) \& N_2]\Pr[N_2/A(BC)] \\
& + \cdots \\
& + \Pr[110/A(BC) \& N_n]\Pr[N_n/A(BC)].
\end{aligned}$$

The two summations can be expressed more concisely as

$$\Pr[110/(AB)C] = \sum_i \Pr[110/(AB)C \& N_i]\Pr[N_i/(AB)C],$$
$$\Pr[110/A(BC)] = \sum_i \Pr[110/A(BC) \& N_i]\Pr[N_i/A(BC)].$$

These two expressions show how the probability of a character distribution, conditional on a phylogenetic hypothesis, can be construed as an average, the average being computed over the possible values that the branch transition probabilities might take.[6]

In the beginning of this section, I provided three examples in which one stipulates what the transition probabilities would be within each phylogeny. These three stipulations exhibited cases in which (AB)C is more likely than, exactly as likely as, and less likely than A(BC), relative to a 110 character. In the present context, we are imagining that the precise

---

6. For simplicity, I ignore the fact that branch transition probabilities vary continuously; in consequence an integral sign would be more accurate than the summation sign used above.

values of the transition probabilities are unknown. But the previous argument goes through unaffected. Simply imagine that the values stipulated before are not known point values but are the overwhelmingly probable values for branch transition probabilities within a given phylogeny. In the first case, for example, let it be almost certain (p = 0.999) that all evolutionary events on all branches have probability of 1/2. By suitably arranging that the other possible assignments of values (the ones which collectively have a probability of 0.001 of being true) do not matter, we can obtain a case in which the two phylogenies are equally likely. Similar adjustments may be introduced into the second and third examples discussed above.

We saw initially that it is a possible to stipulate values for branch transition probabilities that contradict cladism's general claim about the evidential significance of synapomorphy. The same is true when we stipulate probability distributions for the branch transition probabilities.

The discussion in chapter 4 of hypothetico-deductivism ended on a pessimistic note. You simply cannot deduce character distributions from phylogenetic hypotheses conjoined with plausible background assumptions. We now have seen that the probabilities of character distributions can be deduced from phylogenetic hypotheses, provided that we know how probable different arrays of transition probabilities are under each phylogeny. Does this allow us to proceed full steam ahead with a likelihood assessment of competing phylogenetic hypotheses? There are at least two problems that still remain—one conceptual, the other empirical.

The conceptual problem concerns what it means to talk about the probability of a branch transition probability. Like the biologists who have participated in this debate, I am reluctant to postulate probabilities that cannot be grounded in a model of a chance setup. The decay of a radioactive atom has a probability, but Newton's law of gravitation, as far as I know, does not. If the true phylogeny of the three taxa under consideration is given by the (AB)C tree in figure 15, then I suppose that for each character, there are two well-defined probabilities (e_i and r_i) associated with each of branches 1–4. But this does not mean that it makes sense to talk about the probability of a transition probability. A plutonium atom has a given half-life, but what would it mean for there to be a probability associated with different possible half-life values (other than 0 and 1, perhaps)? If half-lives for the atom were drawn from a hat, that would suffice. But, as far as I know, no such chance process underlies the phenomenon. There are first-order probabilities here (i.e., probabilities of events that are not themselves probabilistically defined), but are there second-order probabilities (i.e., probabilities of probabilities)? The transition probabilities in a tree may be well defined; but pending some specification of a chance process, I do not understand what it means to assign a probability to different possible probabilities.[7]

Even if we waive this question for the moment, an empirical problem still remains. In a phylogenetic inference problem we not only may be ignorant of the true values of the transition probabilities; in addition, we may not know how probable the different possible transition probabilities are. That is, even after we settle the conceptual problem of how to make sense of the idea of a second-order probability, we still face the empirical problem of determining the probability of different arrays of transition probabilities under different phylogenetic hypotheses.

5.2. Two Best-Case Expedients

In section 3.5, I discussed a strategy for dealing with the problem of nuisance parameters that I called "the best-case solution." This was explained via the example of inferring whether Smith is a Democrat (D) or a Republican (R), given that he voted for Reagan (V). I set up the problem by saying that one does not have the information needed to evaluate the likelihoods directly. One does not know $Pr(V/D)$ or $Pr(V/R)$. However, one does know the values of $Pr(V/D \& N)$, $Pr(V/D \& \text{not-}N)$, $Pr(V/R \& N)$, and $Pr(V/R \& \text{not-}N)$. These are the four likelihoods x_1, x_2, y_1, and y_2 represented in the table in the previous section. Although these four numbers are known, one does not know whether Smith has or lacks N or what the probability of N is among Democrats or among Republicans.

The "best-case solution" to the problem of nuisance parameters involves comparing the best case of the Democrat hypothesis with the best case of the Republican hypothesis. Given the values stipulated in the original example (p. 106), we may reason as follows. If Smith is a Democrat, then his vote for Reagan would have been more probable if he had had N than it would have been had he lacked N ($x_1 > x_2$). So the best case for the Democrat hypothesis is "Democrat and N." Similarly, if Smith is a Republican, then his vote for Reagan would have been more probable if he had lacked N than it would have been if he had had N ($y_2 > y_1$). So the best case for the Republican hypothesis is "Republican and not-N." We then compare the known likelihoods of these two best cases and find that $x_1 > y_2$; "Democrat and N" is more likely than "Republican and not-N."

---

7. A model for these second-order probabilities might elaborate the idea that the taxa under consideration possess different kinds of characters in fixed percentages, where the kinds differ in the (first-order) transition probabilities they possess. Then the second-order probability would be understood as the chance that a character, randomly selected from this totality, possessed a given (first-order) transition probability. An alternative model that renders these second-order probabilities well defined will be explored in chapter 6.

The best-case solution then leads one to conclude from this that it is more likely that Smith is a Democrat than that he is a Republican. I pointed out in section 3.5 that this inference must involve a further assumption; there is no necessary connection between one of these *conjunctions* being more likely than the other and a *conjunct* in the first being more likely than the corresponding conjunct in the second.

Notice that the best-case strategy for dealing with nuisance parameters involves findings a maximally likely hypothesis that is logically stronger than the one you are interested in and then"throwing away" some of its content to obtain a logically weaker hypothesis. You infer that "Democrat and N" is the most likely of the four alternatives and then conclude that "Democrat" is the better-supported hypothesis about party affiliation. This strategy is the one that has been exploited in likelihood treatments of cladistic parsimony. A hypothesis that is logically stronger than a phylogenetic hypothesis is identified as the one with maximum likelihood. Then the extra content in this hypothesis is discarded, with the embedded phylogenetic hypothesis declared the hypothesis of maximum likelihood.

By now the reader is well aware that this best-case strategy is not the same as a full likelihood evaluation of competing phylogenetic hypotheses in their own right. But a special feature of the biological literature on this issue is that there are different ways of using the best-case strategy, ones that have produced results incompatible with each other. It is to the details of this matter that I now turn.

In section 4.3, I discussed Farris's [1983] paper in which he proposed a hypothetico-deductive defense of cladistic parsimony. This paper was a major departure from Farris's previous thinking on the question, in that he had earlier developed probabilistic defenses of parsimony (Farris [1973, 1977, 1978]. Farris [1983, p. 17/683] subsequently rejected this whole strategy of argument—not just his own specific efforts in this vein—with the following words: "The statistical approach to phylogenetic inference was wrong from the start, for it rests on the idea that to study phylogeny at all, one must first know in great detail how evolution has proceeded. That cannot very well be the way in which scientific knowledge is obtained. What we know of evolution must have been learned by other means." Farris then argues that those "other means" involve the search for hypotheses with maximal explanatory power, where this idea is connected to parsimony via the arguments considered in section 4.3.

With this wholesale rejection of the relevance of a statistical approach, there is perhaps no more vivid contrast than the words of Farris's former self. He begins his 1973 paper as follows (Farris [1973, p. 250]):

> While it is generally agreed that the reconstruction of evolutionary trees should ideally be regarded as a problem in statistical inference,

few approaches to evolutionary taxonomy have taken into account the full implications of that premise. A statistical inference procedure can properly exist only as a method derived under a specified model and demonstrably possessing one or more optimality properties under that model. Stochastic models of the evolutionary process have seldom been discussed in the context of evolutionary inference problems, and explicit consideration of the statistical optimality properties of evolutionary inference methods has consequently been neglected. The purpose of the present paper is to construct a simple probability model of the evolutionary process and to discuss the desirability of some inference methods under that model.

This could well serve as a summary statement of the main point of chapters 2 and 3 and of the main problem of phylogenetic inference. Only in the context of a background theory does an observation have evidential meaning. The problem, then, is to develop a plausible background theory in which parsimony's claims about the evidential significance of character distributions may be evaluated.

In the passage just quoted, Farris demands that a statistical approach to the problem of phylogenetic inference provide a set of criteria ("optimality properties") by which different possible methods can be evaluated in the light of how they perform within a specified model. Farris says he will adopt a Bayesian optimality criterion. We wish to compare different evolutionary hypotheses in the light of the same data. Farris stipulates that the different hypotheses have the same prior probabilities. In this case, the ordering of hypotheses in terms of their posterior probabilities will be the same as the ordering in terms of their likelihoods.[8] So all we need do as Bayesians is consider likelihoods.[9]

Farris [1973, p. 251] then discusses general features of the model of evolution to be adopted. He begins with Cavalli-Sforza and Edwards's [1967] work on phylogenetic inference. They had adopted a likelihood framework and a model of evolution in which random genetic drift is the sole cause of evolutionary change. In their model, the probability of change per unit time is the same throughout the entire branching process; by assuming homogeneity of rates, they had employed what biologists call a "clock assumption."

Besides noting the mathematical intractability of their formulation, Farris registers an objection of principle to using this sort of model. We would like to be able to *test* clock hypotheses. To do this, we need to infer

---

8. A look at the two inversion formulae displayed on p. 104 will show why this is so.
9. Likelihoodists who look askance at Farris's Bayesian assumption of equal priors will note that priors play no essential role in his subsequent argument.

phylogenies without commitment to this assumption and then see what these phylogenies imply about the constancy or heterogeneity of the rates of change that attach to different branches of the inferred tree. To assume rate homogeneity in the construction of one's phylogeny in this context is to beg the question. Process assumptions must be kept to a minimum in the reconstruction of pattern if we are to be able to test process hypotheses against an independently determined reconstruction of pattern.

Farris then proposes a model whose assumptions he believes to be weaker and simpler than the ones exploited by Cavalli-Sforza and Edwards [1967]. A character's evolution on one branch is assumed to be independent of whether it evolves anywhere else in the tree and each character is assumed to evolve independently of every other. Character evolution is also assumed to be reversible.

Farris then supposes that the tree to be inferred has some fixed but unknown temporal duration (n). The amount of time from the root to the tips is divided into numerous small temporal units of size u so that there are $N = n/u$ time units in all. Farris then adopts a Poisson type model for the probability of character change. If we let u be sufficiently small, the probability that any character changes more than once in a given time unit is negligible. If p_{ij} is the probability that the ith character changes in the jth unit of time, then the expected amount of change in that character (s_i) is simply

$$s_i = \sum_{j=1}^{N} p_{ij}.$$

Farris [1973, p. 252] then supposes that "for sufficiently small u, s_i is independent of u for every character; that is, s_i tends to a well defined limit as u tends to zero."

Farris [1973, pp. 252–253] defends these assumptions as biologically realistic:

> ... even a character that has high probability of changing repeatedly during the evolutionary process is unlikely to change during a particular time unit, provided that the time units are sufficiently small and numerous. As each small time unit has its own probability, p_{ij}, of a change's occurring in each character, the evolutionary process is plainly not restricted to be homogeneous over time ... the restriction that s_i tend to a well defined limit as u tends to zero simply implies that this expectation does not depend upon an arbitrary choice of time intervals.

Farris then shows how these assumptions can be used to infer what I shall call, following Felsenstein [1973b], an evolutionary "pathway." This consists of a phylogenetic tree (in our sense) *plus* a specification of the character states that attach to each temporal unit in the interior of the tree. The most likely pathway, Farris demonstrates, is one that involves the fewest changes between root and tips.[10] Since "we will usually be content to infer just the shape of an evolutionary tree, rather than the complete information on sequences of changes" (p. 253), we can simply discard the part of the inference that concerns the tree's interior character states and retain the hypothesized tree. Farris thus exploits what I am calling the best-case strategy. He notes (p. 254) that "it would be mathematically more pleasing to select the estimated tree shape ... directly"—i.e., by considering not just the best case of each possible tree shape, but the full likelihood function, which covers all possible interior assignments consistent with a given tree. But this, Farris feels, would require "the imposition of additional assumptions upon the stochastic evolutionary model." The best-case strategy is preferable "in the interest of retaining as much generality as possible in the inference procedure." The conclusion of the analysis, then, is that "under the model constructed ... most parsimonious trees are also maximum-likelihood-estimated trees" (p. 254).

Farris then argues that some interesting lessons follow concerning what parsimony does and does not assume. He points out that this model does not require that the expected number of changes (s_i) for any character should be low. That is, it does not assume "that only one change in a character during the entire evolutionary sequence is more likely to occur than any larger number of changes, or that cases of parallelism are rare in nature" (pp. 254–255). This, he says, lays to rest Camin and Sokal's [1965] claim that parsimony as a rule of inference requires that evolution be parsimonious.

It is true that Farris's argument does not depend on any assumption about the expected number of changes that a character will experience in the passage from root to tips. The reason is that Farris's use of the best-case strategy makes this entirely irrelevant. Consider the (AB)C phylogeny in figure 15, relative to a 110 character. If change is improbable per unit time, then a best-case assignment of interior states for (AB)C will place a single change somewhere on branch 4 and no changes anywhere else. But now suppose we were told that there was so much time in the process that the expected number of changes is somewhere around ten. What are we to conclude about the best-case assignment we have just constructed?

10. There are many pathways that are tied for first place, though all will have the same underlying tree topology. For example, an optimal pathway for a 110 character to evolve on (AB)C in figure 15 is obtained by allowing just one change *anywhere* on branch 4 and no changes anywhere else.

The proper conclusion is that it is very improbable. But Farris's argument has nothing to do with the *probability* of the tree interiors he postulates. The best-case solution of the nuisance parameter problem does not attend to this issue; all that matters is that the values it selects are part of the hypothesis of maximum likelihood. In just the same way, a best-case solution of the nuisance parameter problem in inferring Smith's party affiliation might lead one to focus on "Democrat and N" as the conjunction of maximum likelihood, even though, unbeknownst to the investigator, it may be exceedingly improbable for a Democrat to have trait N.

Consider how Farris's procedure would handle branch 3 in figure 15, given a character that has a 110 distribution. Let us suppose that this branch is divided into 1,000 temporal units and that the probability of change in each of them is $1/100$. A best-case pathway of the kind Farris advocates will assign no change to each unit. In this way, the probability of the branch's ending in state 0, given that it began in state 0 and moved through this precise sequence of states, is $(99/100)^{1,000}$. This is a higher value than any other specific assignment; for example, if we stipulated that there is a change every hundredth interval beginning with interval #100, this specification will produce a probability of $(1/100)^{10}(99/100)^{990}$. Yet, the second *kind* of result (in which there are ten changes *somewhere or other*) is more probable than the first.

What would a full treatment of the likelihood look like here? The branch in question begins and ends in the 0 state. Given the above assumption about the expected number of changes, there is some chance (a small one) that the branch experienced zero changes in state; there is another probability that two changes occurred; and so on, for each even number of changes. A full likelihood treatment would represent the probability of that branch's ending in state 0, given that it began in the 0 state, as a weighted sum over *all the different possible pathways* that could link a 0 beginning with a 0 finish. The weighting of each possible pathway would represent how probable it is that that pathway should have occurred. The point is that Farris's best-case procedure cuts through all this. In particular, note that the best pathway for a given tree topology is the one that yields a conjunction of topology plus pathway that is most *likely*; this best pathway may or may not be *probable* in the light of the tree topology.

In emphasizing the importance of asking how probable a pathway is, given a tree topology, I am not departing from a strict likelihood framework. The question is vital to assessing the likelihood of the genealogical hypothesis and has nothing much to do with the question of what the hypothesis's prior probability is. A glance back at the summations displayed on p. 155 should convince the reader of this point.

Felsenstein [1973b] also uses the best-case expedient to investigate the connection of parsimony and likelihood. However, instead of inferring an evolutionary pathway and then throwing away the interior character states, he constructs another kind of conjunctive hypothesis. Felsenstein uses an imaginary data set consisting of the distribution of three characters over four species to reconstruct a phylogenetic tree in which branch transition probabilities are specified. After finding the conjunction of tree plus suite of branch transition probabilities that has maximum likelihood, he discards the estimated transition probabilities and reaches the tree he judges to be most likely. Felsenstein and Farris both use the best-case expedient, but implement it in different ways.

Felsenstein uses this best-case strategy to reach two conclusions. First, he argues for a quite general sufficient condition under which parsimony and likelihood will coincide. If the expected amount of change that each character will experience in the entire tree is very small, then the most likely tree is the one that requires the fewest character changes. This, he observes, "accords with intuition. If we assume that it is a priori very improbable that any evolutionary changes at all will occur, then that tree will strain our credulity least which would require the fewest of these improbable events to explain the observed data" (p. 244). More specifically, he argues that if change is very improbable, than for any data set, the most likely conjunctive hypothesis—consisting of a tree and a suite of branch transition probabilities—is such that the tree included in this favored conjunction is the one that parsimony would select.

Felsenstein [1973b, p. 245] then argues that "if we relax the assumption that the probability of change is small, there is no necessary connection between likelihood and parsimony." To show this, he discusses his four-taxon, three-character, example. Branch transition probabilities are allowed to assume any possible value and it is found that the most likely conjunction of tree plus estimated suite of transition probabilities is such that the tree included in this best conjunction is *not* the one that parsimony would select.

Instead of presenting the example that Felsenstein there develops, I shall describe a simpler one that he suggested in Felsenstein and Sober [1986] to make the same point. It involves just three species and three characters:

		Species		
		A	B	C
	1	1	1	1
Characters	2	1	1	0
	3	1	0	0

We assume that transition probabilities may vary from branch to branch, but that within any single branch all characters have the same transition probabilities. As usual, "0" denotes ancestral and "1" derived. No restrictions will be placed on the values that the estimated transition probabilities may take.

Our task is to assign values to the branch transition probabilities in the two trees in figure 15 so as to find the best case for (AB)C and the best for A(BC). After finding maxima for each, we shall compare these best cases with each other, thereby determining the maximum likelihood tree by the best-case strategy.

Felsenstein developed a computer search algorithm that tries out different possible assignments of transition probabilities until a candidate assignment cannot be improved by small changes. This heuristic is of the "hill-climbing" variety and therefore has the weakness of any such procedure. If you start on a hill and go up until you cannot ascend any farther, you are assured of having found a *local* maximum, but not necessarily the *global* maximum. However, by starting the procedure in different places, one can obtain some assurance that the global maximum has been identified.

Felsenstein's procedure yields the following suite of transition probabilities for branches 1–8. Recall that "e_i" denotes the chance of a 0-to-1 transition on branch i and that "r_i" denotes the chance of a 1-to-0 change on the ith branch:

Best Case	Best Case
Branch Probabilities	Branch Probabilities
for (AB)C	for A(BC)
$e_1 = 1.0$	$e_5 = 1$
$r_1 = 0$	$r_5 = -$
$e_2 = 0$	$e_6 = 1/2$
$r_2 = 0$	$r_6 = 0$
$e_3 = 1/3.$	$e_7 = 0$
$r_3 = -$	$r_7 = 0$
$e_4 = 2/3$	$e_8 = 1/3$

Relative to the three characters in the data set, the likelihood of (AB)C under this best case estimate of the nuisance parameters[11] is 0.02194 and that of A(BC) is 0.037037.

Thus, the best-case expedient indicates that A(BC) is more likely than (AB)C. Yet, note that cladistic parsimony will favor (AB)C over A(BC);

---

11. If one wishes to stipulate that transition probabilities must be intermediate—greater than 0 but less than 1—then the extreme values in these best-case estimates may be modified by adding or subtracting some very small quantity.

(AB)C requires no homoplasies to account for the data, whereas A(BC) requires a homoplasy to account for character 2.

An even simpler example of this sort can be concocted (Felsenstein and Sober [1986]). Simply consider the way Felsenstein's best-case strategy would handle several independent characters all distributed as 110. Cladistic parsimony, as well as overall similarity, would interpret this as strong and unequivocal evidence for (AB)C and against A(BC). But Felsenstein's best-case strategy implies something quite different. The two phylogenies have identical likelihoods of unity, relative to best-case assignments of branch transition probabilities. Simply let e_1, e_2, e_5, and e_6 equal 1 and e_3, e_4, e_7, and e_8 equal 0.

Felsenstein [1973b] and Farris [1973] reached opposite conclusions about the connection of likelihood and parsimony. Farris argued that parsimony is a maximum-likelihood method regardless of whether change is expected to be rare; Felsenstein takes himself to have established that parsimony and maximum likelihood will necessarily coincide only when change is assumed to be rare. In the second half of his argument, recall, Felsenstein does not assume that characters have high probabilities of changing on a branch, but only that the probabilities can take any value at all. The values for the nuisance parameters are estimated from the data with no prior constraints placed on what they might be.

Both Felsenstein and Farris use the best-case strategy, but implement it in different ways. Farris estimated tree plus interior character states, whereas Felsenstein estimated tree plus branch transition probabilities.[12] Given that they produced such different results about the connection of parsimony and likelihood, the question immediately arises of which procedure is better. Felsenstein [1973b, pp. 246–247] answers by invoking a criterion quite distinct from likelihood for judging inference rules. It is the idea that an inference rule ought to be *statistically consistent*. Felsenstein claims that his procedure possesses this characteristic, but that it is unclear whether Farris's does so.

Before taking up in the next section the bearing of this further consideration, we should be clear on what Falsenstein's [1973b] discussion establishes. Using his best-case expedient for handling nuisance param-

---

12. Martin Barrett (personal communication) has pointed out to me that Farris's procedure does not, strictly speaking, identify the pathway that makes the observations most probable. Assuming, as Farris does, that the evolutionary process is Markovian, any two pathways that occupy the same states at the time interval immediately before the tips will confer identical probabilities on the states at the tips. Rather, Farris computes the probability of *reaching the states at the tips via a given pathway*. This is not the probability of the observations alone, but the probability of a "mixture" of the observations with a hypothesis. This point parallels the discussion of Farris's [1983] argument in section 4.4.

eters, he provides a general argument and an example. The general argument concludes that *if* the expected number of changes in each character throughout the whole tree is low, then the most parsimonious tree will be the tree of maximum likelihood. That is, rarity of change suffices for parsimony to have a likelihood rationale. But this implies no conclusion to the effect that parsimony *requires* that changes be very imporbable. Felsenstein addresses this issue by his example, not via a general argument. The example he gives shows how permitting high probabilities of change *can* lead parsimony and likelihood to part ways. This does not mean that parsimony and likelihood *must* fail to coincide if change is not assumed to be rare.

So the possibility is left open that there is a sufficient condition for parsimony to have a likelihood rationale broader than the one Felsenstein cites. It is possible, for all we have seen so far, that rarity of change suffices, but is not necessary. However, what should be clear enough so far is that *if* we accept Felsenstein's method for handling nuisance parameters, there can be no universal and unconditional identity of parsimony and likelihood.

5.3. Statistical Consistency

Convergence—which statisticians call statistical consistency—is a property that an inference rule or estimator has in the context of a process model. A rule is convergent if larger and larger data sets will lead the method to converge on the true hypothesis. For example, suppose we wish to estimate a coin's probability of landing heads from the results of repeated independent tosses. We might adopt different rules for interpreting the data. We might decide to let the sample mean serve as our best estimate of the coin's probability, or we might decide to let some other property of the sample guide our judgment. The sample mean is convergent because the law of large numbers says that as the sample is made large without limit, the sample mean will asymptotically approach the true probability.

This may be stated more carefully in terms of probabilities: We wish to estimate the value of some parameter, θ; s_n, which is a function of the n observations in the sample, is a consistent estimator of θ if and only if the following condition obtains. For any two positive numbers d and e, a number n_0 exists such that when n exceeds n_0,

$$\Pr(|s_n - \theta| < d) > 1 - e.$$

Roughly speaking, the sample mean is a consistent (covergent) estimator of the parameter because we can be as certain as we want (make $1 - e$ as large as you like) that we are as close as we wish to be (make d as small as you like) by sampling enough.[13]

We next should define what consistency means in the context of evaluating competing hypotheses. Instead of wishing to assign a value to a parameter, we now consider the problem of selecting a policy that tells us how to discriminate between two competing hypotheses—(AB)C and A(BC) in a phylogenetic example, perhaps. Suppose I am testing a hypothesis H_0 against a competitor H_1. My test is consistent precisely when, if H_1 is true, the probability of rejecting H_0 tends to unity as the sample size goes to infinity. The common thread between consistent estimation and consistent testing is that the rejection of falsehood is a virtual certainty if the data set is infinitely large.

I mentioned above that a rule of inference or an estimator.is convergent only relative to a model. This may be less than transparent in the case of a simple coin-toss problem, but it is true, nevertheless. Suppose I propose to use the mean number of heads in a sample of tosses to estimate a coin's probability of landing heads. This is the maximum likelihood estimate; it also possesses the property of statistical consistency. Neither of these claims could be advanced without making assumptions about the sampling process; typically, one assumes that the coin has a single probability that remains unchanged throughout the sequence of tosses. One assumes that the result on one toss is independent of the result on any and all others. These are process assumptions within which one can show why the sample mean is a consistent estimator.

I say *a* consistent estimator, because the sample mean is often not the only one that guarantees consistency. Suppose one were sampling heights (with replacement) from a population of people in which heights are normally distributed. The goal is to find the average height in the whole population. One consistent estimator is the sample mean. Another is the sample median. Although these two estimators may yield different estimates for the same finite data set, each converges on the true population value as the sample is made infinitely large. This simple example shows that the convergence requirement is not enough. The fact that a rule is statistically consistent is not sufficient to show that it is the best rule to use. However, there is an influential statistical philosophy that holds that a rule must be consistent. This philosophy is the one that Felsenstein [1973b, 1978] adopts in his discussion of cladistic parsimony.

13. Fisher [1956, pp. 150–151] finds this definition less than satisfactory, since "any particular method of treating a finite sample of ... observations may be represented as belonging to a great variety of such general functions." He prefers, instead, to say that a consistent statistic is "a function of the observed frequencies which takes the exact parametric value when for these frequencies their expectations are substituted."

Felsenstein [1973b, pp. 267–267] asserts that his best case expedient for finding the most likely phylogenetic tree is statistically consistent. What does this mean? Let T_t be the true but unknown tree and P_t be the true but unknown suite of branch probabilities. We are assuming, recall, that all characters in this system have the same suite of transition probabilities. T_t and P_t then jointly specify a probability distribution for each possible kind of character distribution. In an inference problem involving three taxa in which the characters come in only two states (0 or 1), T_t and P_t together imply a probability for each of the eight possible character distributions 111, 110, 101, 011, 100, 010, 001, 000. As we sample more and more characters, the proportion of sampled characters in each of these eight categories will approach the probability associated with each. In this limiting case, Felsenstein says, his best-case expedient will lead him to infer a conjunction of tree plus transition probabilities $T_i \& P_i$. In the limit, the inferred tree T_i is almost certain to be identical with the true one T_t (i.e., the probability of this is $1 - e$, for arbitrarily small e).

Felsenstein's basis for saying this of his expedient method is that he judges that method to fall within the sufficient conditions established by Wald [1949] for maximum-likelihood estimation to be consistent. No full argument for this is presented in Felsenstein's paper.

One clause in Wald's sufficient condition is that there be a finite number of unknown parameters to be estimated. Felsenstein points out that Farris's procedure violates this condition. Recall that Farris estimates the interior states of the tree for each character. It follows that each new character introduces a new set of parameters (one parameter for each of the small intervals into which the branches are divided) to be estimated. Felsenstein concludes that this does not show that Farris's procedure is statistically inconsistent, only that it does not fall within the scope of the sufficient condition for consistent estimation laid down by Wald.

Felsenstein settles this open question in his 1978 piece, entitled "Cases in Which Parsimony or Compatibility Methods Will Be Positively Misleading." There he provides a simple example in which parsimony fails to be convergent. Since Farris's best-case expedient always yields a result that coincides with cladistic parsimony, this shows that Farris's procedure will be statistically inconsistent as well. The basic idea in Felsenstein's [1978] example (somewhat simplified here) can be illustrated by consulting the (AB)C phylogeny in figure 15 (p. 151). Assume that the true phylogeny for the taxa is (AB)C and that $0 \to 1$ transitions are possible while reversions from $1 \to 0$ are not. Assume also that the probability of change on branches 1 and 3 (denoted by "P") is much larger than the probability of change on branches 2 and 4 (denoted by "Q"). As before, all characters are assumed to have the same set of branch transition probabilities.

Given these assumptions, the question is whether parsimony will asymptotically retrieve the true phylogeny by sampling more and more characters. All character distributions are possible, so there is obviously some chance that a single character will have the 011 distribution. If we observed just one character and found it to have this distribution, we might use parsimony to infer, quite erroneously, that the true phylogeny is A(BC). But this just shows that cladistic parsimony is fallible; it can sometimes reach a false conclusion. Our present interest is whether cladistic parsimony must yield the true phylogeny when the possibility of sampling error is removed, so to speak.

Felsenstein shows that there are values of P and Q for which cladistic parsimony will be statistically inconsistent. It is easy to see why. Parsimony holds that synapomorphies alone have evidential meaning. In the present context, this means that a cladistic inference will take account of just three kinds of characters—ones that exhibit the 110, the 101, and the 011 pattern. If 110 occurs more often than 101 and 011 each do, then cladistic parsimony will judge that (AB)C is the best-supported hypothesis. Similarly, if 101 characters occur more frequently than 110 or 011 characters do, then parsimony will judge that (AC)B is best.

The simple idea behind Felsenstein's example is that (AB)C is the true phylogeny, but there are values for the branch transition probabilities that imply that a 110 character is *less* probable than a 101 character. This will be true precisely when

$$(1 - P)[Q + (1 - Q)PQ] < P^2(1 - Q)^2,$$

which simplifies to

$$P^2 > Q(1 - PQ)/(1 - Q).$$

Felsenstein [1978, p. 405/668] then shows that for each possible value of Q, there are values for P that satisfy the inequality and values that violate it. These are shown in figure 16.

Roughly speaking, when P^2 is much larger than Q, 110 characters will be less probable than 101 characters. In this case, as more and more characters are examined, the law of large numbers makes it virtually certain that 110 characters will occur less frequently in the data than 101 characters. Such values for the branch transition probabilities ensure that cladistic parsimony will converge on a false hypothesis—(AC)B. So cladistic parsimony is not statistically consistent in this case.[14]

14. Compatibility methods will be statistically inconsistent in this example as well. That approach discards the smallest number of characters that suffices to allow the remaining data to be perfectly congruent. In this example, since 101 characters will outnumber 110 characters, compatibility methods will discard the latter and select the (AC)B tree.

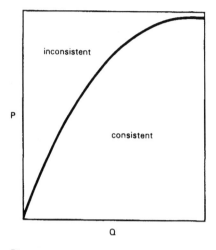

Figure 16.
Felsenstein [1978] established a sufficient condition for parsimony to be statistically incon-sistent. In the (AB)C tree in figure 15 (p. 151), let the root be in state 0 and let transitions from 1-to-0 be impossible. Let P be the probability of a 0-to-1 change on branches 1 and 3 and Q be the probability of such a change on branches 2 and 4. Parsimony will fail to be convergent if $P^2 \gg Q$.

One property of Felsenstein's model that engenders parsimony's incon-sistency is that "parallelism of changes [is] more probable than unique and unreversed changes in an informative part of the tree" (Felsenstein [1978, pp. 407–408/672]). This is one of a set of assumptions that entails statisti-cal inconsistency. The question then arises of whether this result can be generalized to other, more realistic, models. Felsenstein poses this problem without opting for an answer (p. 408/672):

> The models employed here certainly have severe limitations: it will hardly ever be the case that we sample characters independently, with all of the characters following the same probability model of evolutionary change. Extending this analysis to more realistic evo-lutionary models will certainly be difficult. Yet the task must be undertaken: if inconsistency of a parsimony or compatibility technique is suspected, it does little good simply to point out that the evolu-tionary models employed here do not apply to the type of data being encountered in practice. That amounts to a confession of ignorance rather than validation of the inference method in question.

To those who think that Felsenstein's result is an artifact of the simple model he adopts, Felsenstein issues this invitation: Construct a more real-istic model and show that the favored method will be consistent with respect to it. However, in the absence of such a model, we are not entitled to dismiss Felsenstein's result in this way.

What is the significance of this demonstration that cladistic parsimony can fail to be statistically inconsistent? Farris [1983, pp. 14–17/680–682] focuses on the lack of realism in Felsenstein's model. He argues that no practical consequences about the choice of a phylogenetic method flow from Felsenstein's result. The result does not offer any reason to suspect that parsimony will be statistically inconsistent when applied to real data from real taxa. In addition, Farris asserts that any method of phylogenetic inference—overall similarity, compatibility methods, even Felsenstein's own perferred maximum-likelihood approach—can be subjected to Felsenstein's line of argument. For any method you please, you can always construct a model such that the method will fail to be consistent in that model.

It is easy enough to construct an example in which overall similarity will be statistically inconsistent. In the (AB)C phylogeny in figure 15, merely select transition probabilities so that the probability of a character being distributed as either 101 or 010 is greater than the probability of its being distributed as either 110 or 001.[15]

Can maximum-likelihood estimation be inconsistent? If it conforms to the sufficient condition for consistency established by Wald [1949], it cannot. However, Farris's point is simply that maximum-likelihood procedures require that a process model be assumed. If the assumed model is in fact false, there is no guarantee that the method will converge on the truth when applied to the real world. The most that can be said is that such methods will be consistent *if* the model they assume is correct.

The natural reply is to grant that every procedure can fail to be consistent if the model assumed is false. However, Felsenstein's point is simply that parsimony and every other inference method must assume some process model or other. Perhaps, then, the real lesson of Felsenstein's argument is that parsimony and compatibility methods assume that the model stipulated in his paper is false.

It is interesting that Farris [1983, p. 16] appears to endorse this point:

> That is not to say that parsimony requires no assumptions at all; it presumes, one might say, that Felsenstein's models are unrealistic. But as that assumption seems generally agreed upon, that is not much of a criticism of parsimony . . . .

15. Felsenstein [1983b, p. 325], points out that for a simple example like the three-taxon problem just described, the conditions for parsimony to be consistent are less stringent than the conditions under which overall similarity is consistent. It is worth emphasizing that this is not a general result, but one specific to an example.

One might say, of course, that the model illustrates a potential weakness of parsimony: that criterion will fail if the conditions of the model should happen to be met.

These passages show that Farris agrees with a key assumption in Felsenstein's argument—that if a method is statistically inconsistent in the confines of a given process model, then the method implicitly assumes that the process model is false.

Felsenstein and Farris disagree about the significance of this assumption, but not about whether it is true. Felsenstein thinks that if parsimony fails to be consistent in a simple process model, then it may fail in more realistic situations as well. Farris thinks that parsimony's inconsistency in a manifestly unrealistic model has no bearing at all on whether it should be used on real data. Their disagreement, we might say, concerns how one should extrapolate from the failure of consistency in Felsenstein's example. Presumably, this disagreement should not be resolved by declarations of faith: it is open to investigation whether statistical inconsistency can be expected in more realistic evolutionary models.

Rather than pursuing that line of inquiry here, I want to investigate the point of consensus between Farris and Felsenstein: they agree that failure of consistency within a model means that the method assumes that the model is false. Though Farris and Felsenstein agree on little else, they do agree on this. In the next section, I shall argue, to the contrary, that statistical consistency is not necessary. If my argument is sound, then we must conclude that Felsenstein's consistency argument does not identify an assumption about the evolutionary process that parsimony must make.

5.4. Why Consistency?

Statisticians have been of two minds about statistical consistency. Some have held that it is an essential feature of any reasonable estimator or test. Fisher [1950, p. 11] says that inconsistent estimators are "outside the pale of decent usage." Neyman [1952, p. 188] cites this pronouncement and emphatically agrees. Kendall and Stuart [1973, p. 273] say that "it seems perfectly reasonable to require consistency."

This would not make a practical difference for the use of likelihood in estimation and hypothesis evaluation if all uses of likelihood were statistically consistent. But this is not so. Wald's [1949] sufficient condition is quite general, but statisticians have long known that some uses of likelihood fail to be statistically consistent.

How should one view an inconsistent likelihood inference rule or estimator? The tradition just described is clear on this matter. But some statisticians take another approach. In bold contrast to the position of Fisher's just stated is Fisher's [1938] earlier claim that likelihood is a "primitive postulate" that does not stand in need of repeated sampling justifications. Edwards [1972, p. 100] sees the primitive postulate idea as Fisher's mature position; he argues that likelihood measures the degree to which evidence supports some hypotheses better than others quite independently of what may happen to be true of its asymptotic behavior. Hacking [1965, pp. 184–185] also is somewhat skeptical of the importance of consistency; although the maximum-likelihood estimators he considers are consistent, he wonders if consistency might not be a "magical property" of those estimators and not in itself "a criterion of excellence."

My goal in this section is to argue that likelihood without consistency is not "outside the pale of decent usage." To do this, I shall describe an example in which likelihood inference is reasonable, even though there is no guarantee that an infinite data set will lead to the truth. I shall assume without argument that likelihood measures weight of evidence (what I have called support). The example I shall describe involves likelihood considerations alone; no prior probabilities for competing hypotheses will be described. I shall specify an inference rule that correctly describes which of two competing hypotheses is better supported in the light of the data; it will emerge that this inference rule is not statistically consistent. Although no prior probabilities will be given in what follows, it is easy to generalize the argument to take these into account. Merely stipulate that the competing hypotheses have identical priors. In this case, the posterior probabilities are ordered in the same way as the likelihoods. Again, there is nothing specific to the "likelihoodist" position involved in my argument. Supplying prior probabilities does not alter the fact that a rule of inference can correctly judge the plausibility of hypotheses in the light of the evidence (as defined by Bayes's theorem), even though the rule is not statistically consistent.

Suppose a machine producing coins must be in one or another of two states (S_1 and S_2) and that the state influences the probability the resulting coin has of landing heads if it is tossed. The machine is so constructed that state S_1 occurs with probability 0.9 and S_2 occurs with probability 0.1.

The hypotheses we wish to test agree that the machine state influences the coin's bias, but they disagree on the direction of the influence. H_1 asserts that S_1 gives the coin a probability of landing heads of 0.8 and that S_2 gives the coin a probability of landing heads of 0.2. So H_1 says that S_1 biases coins toward heads and S_2 toward tails. The other hypothesis, H_2, makes just the opposite assertion. It says that S_1 gives the coin a probability of landing heads of 0.2 and that S_2 gives the coin a probability of landing heads of 0.8. H_2 thereby says that S_1 biases coins toward tails and S_2 towards heads.

The problem is to toss repeatedly a single coin produced by the machine and use the observed frequency of heads to discriminate between the two hypotheses. We are to do this without knowing what state the machine was in when it produced the coin, knowing only the probabilities of the two machine states.

A likelihood inference, in this case, would take the following form. We compute the expected frequency of heads under the two hypotheses. H_1 says that the expected frequency is $(0.9)(0.8) + (0.1)(0.2) = 0.74$. H_2 says the expected frequency is $(0.9)(0.2) + (0.1)(0.8) = 0.26$. We then adopt the following inference rule:

> If the observed frequency of heads is greater than 50%, infer that H_1 is better supported; if the observed frequency of heads is less than 50%, infer that H_2 is better supported.

This is a likelihood rule of inference, because it implements the idea that hypotheses of higher likelihood are better supported by the evidence.

This rule is not statistically consistent. If H_1 is true, the probability of rejecting H_2 does *not* approach unity as the data set is made large without limit. The probability of rejecting H_2 is 0.9 (asymptotically). Likewise, if H_2 is true, the probability of rejecting H_1 is 0.9 (asymptotically) as well.

Another way to see this point is to begin with the (consequential but unknown) machine states. If the machine was in state S_2, then the frequency of heads will approach 20% if H_1 is true and 80% if H_2 is true. But our likelihood inference rule tells us that a minority of heads differentially supports H_2 and a majority of heads differentially supports H_1. The fact that S_2 has a nonzero probability of being the machine state ensures that there is a finite chance that we shall, even in the limit, prefer a false hypothesis over a true one.

We may generalize this result a little, in terms of the table displayed below. We do not know which conjunctive hypothesis of the form $H_i S_j$ $(i, j = 1, 2)$ is true. Their likelihoods—the probabilities they confer on the coin's landing heads—are the entries in the table. I stipulated above that $w = z$ and $x = y$.

		Machine States	
		S_1	S_2
Hypotheses	H_1	w	x
	H_2	y	z

As the coin is tossed repeatedly, its frequency of heads will converge on either $w = z$ or on $x = y$. If this were all we knew about the chance setup, we would be unable to distinguish between H_1 and H_2. However, we know that the machine was probably in state S_1. This means that if the frequency of heads is quite close to $w = z$ after a very long run of tosses, then H_1 is better supported; similarly, if the frequency is quite close to $x = y$, then we should conclude that H_2 is better supported.

It is crucial to my example that the entries in the above two-by-two table are symmetrical. The asymmetry is introduced by the difference in probability of S_1 and S_2. As long as these two probabilities differ, a likelihood inference can be made, though it will not be statistically consistent.

One reaction to this example is to claim that the likelihood rule of inference is misguided precisely because it fails to be statistically consistent. This strikes me as too extreme. It seems clear that the sample frequency *does* have evidential meaning; given the available information, likelihood correctly reflects which hypothesis is better supported. It would be preferable, of course, if we did not have to proceed in ignorance of the state of the machine. It also would be preferable if we could toss a number of coins drawn at random from the machine. But this hardly shows that the evidence provided by the single coin is totally uninformative when all we know about the machine states is their probabilities of occurrence.

A second reaction might be that my characterization of the example is mistaken. The likelihood rule, so this suggestion runs, *is* consistent, once we see that repeated tossing of this single coin can be thought of as part of a longer experiment involving numerous coins drawn at random from the machine. After all, to see if a rule is convergent, we must formulate some interpretation of what it means to "repeat the experiment." I took this to mean that the coin before us should be tossed repeatedly. But it might be suggested that a repetition of the experiment should be understood in a quite different way. Why not think of our tossing this one coin as part of an experiment in which we toss a coin some large number of times, then return to the machine to obtain another coin that we handle in the same way, and so on, for an indefinitely large mixture of coins? The point is that by embedding what we do with this single coin into this larger context, we describe an experiment in which a consistent likelihood inference can be made.

So in what does a "repetition of the experiment" consist? We have before us a coin whose bias remains unchanged under repeated tossing. We do not have before us a mixture of coins that have different but unknown biases. Just to make this point graphic, imagine that you are handed the single coin by the Keeper of the Machine, who makes it quite clear that no other coins will be forthcoming. I toss this one coin some number of times. I then ask what would happen if the sample size were increased without limit. It is as clear as any counterfactual could be that repeating *this* experiment consists in repeatedly tossing *this* coin (whose probability of heads is presumed to remain constant throughout). It does not mean that I toss this one coin some fixed number of times, then return to the machine for a new coin that I toss that same number of times, and so on.

Whether a method of inference is convergent depends on the model one uses of the process that generates the data. If one knew the machine state or that the experiment will involve tossing a 9:1 mixture of differently biased coins, convergence would be assured. However, if one adopts the process model I have stipulated to be true—that one repeatedly tosses a single coin of constant but unknown bias, where only the probabilities of the machine states are known—then the assurance of convergence disappears.

The interpretation I favor of this example steers a middle course between two extremes. On the one hand, I reject the idea that repeated tossing has no evidential meaning; on the other, I reject the idea that the experiment should be redescribed so that the inference rule comes out convergent after all. The former approach errs in denying that repeated tossing provides any evidence; the latter retains the connection of likelihood and convergence at the price of giving a false picture of the kind of experiment and inference problem one really faces. In this example, likelihood correctly reports which hypothesis is better supported, even though the likelihood rule of inference is not statistically consistent.

In a sense, the requirement of convergence embodies a demand for certainty, albeit of a somewhat denatured and asymptotic sort.[16] Even if the machine state S_2 has a probability of only 10^{-10}, this would not be enough for statistical consistency. The possibility would still remain that the inference rule would point to a falsehood when the data set is made infinitely large. The demand for convergence is the demand that S_2 be *impossible* (more accurately: have zero probability). But surely data can be brought to bear on hypotheses without this absolute guarantee.

In what way is this example parallel to the phylogenetic example that Felsenstein [1978] presents? One point of disanalogy is that Felsenstein's example is such that there is, we might say, a 100% chance that parsimony will converge on a falsehood, whereas in the present case, the chance of this is rather less (being equal to the lesser of the two machine state probabilities). However, I must emphasize that the main point of the coin toss example is not that it parallels Felsenstein's example in all respects; rather, it is intended to show that likelihood inference can go forward even when the inference is not statistically consistent.

Even so, the difference just noted invites the following objection.

16. Farris [1983, pp. 16–17/687] criticizes Felsenstein's consistency argument as implicitly rejecting "all conclusions that cannot be established with certainty." This is false in one sense, but true in another. Statistical inference involves inference in the face of uncertainty. However, the consistency requirement is, in effect, a requirement of *certainty in the limit*.

Although the coin-toss example refutes the requirement that a method must be certain to converge on the truth, it is not a counterexample to the demand that a method must have a greater than even chance of doing so. My reply is that I reject this weaker requirement as well. Consider the following inference problem, in which there are *three* machine states and *three* hypotheses to be tested:

	Machine States			
	$S_1(0.4)$	$S_2(0.4)$	$S_3(0.2)$	
H_1	0.8	0.5	0.2	0.56
H_2	0.5	0.5	0.5	0.5
H_3	0.2	0.5	0.8	0.44

Next to each machine state I have noted its probability of occurring. In the margin, I have written the expected frequency of heads that each hypothesis generates. The problem, as before, is to draw a single coin at random from the machine and toss it repeatedly, using the results to decide which hypothesis is best supported.

Roughly speaking, a likelihood rule of inference would say that H_1 is best supported if the frequency of heads exceeds 0.56, that H_3 is best supported if the frequency of heads is less than 0.44, and that H_2 is best if the frequency of heads is close to 0.5.

With an infinite data set, the frequency of heads is certain to be either 0.8, 0.5, or 0.2. The probability of convergence, if H_1 or H_3 is true, is the probability of S_1, namely, 0.4. This example can be modified so that S_1 is as improbable as you please, as long as it is less probable than S_2 and more probable than S_3. Here, then, is a likelihood inference without even a better than even chance of convergence.

So far I have followed the usage of saying that nonconvergent rules of inference are "misleading." This description *seems* just, since in such cases, the inference rule points to a false hypothesis in the light of an infinite data set. Though this seems an unobjectionable evaluation, I suggest that it is sometimes mistaken. In the coin-tossing case just discussed, it is *the world* that misleads us; the likelihood rule performs its duty as faithfully as it ever does. The rule does not mislead but quite correctly reports what the data (and only the data) say.

Likelihood describes which hypotheses are best supported by the evidence. When the evidence is misleading, the best-supported hypothesis will be a false one. A rule of inference that correctly conveys the evidential meaning of observations *ought* to point to a falsehood when the evidence is misleading. When it does so, it correctly captures what the evidence is saying. When the system generating the evidence is structured so that misleading evidence is overwhelmingly probable, it is hardly surprising that likelihood will point to a false hypothesis when the data set is infinitely large. But this failure to converge in the long run counts against the likelihood rule no more than does its failure to be infallible in the short run.

Likelihood does not provide a "rule of acceptance." It does not say that the best-supported hypothesis ought to be accepted as true. Likelihood has much more modest pretensions; it is a "rule of evaluation," simply indicating which hypotheses are best supported by the data. The idea that likelihood codifies "evidential meaning"[17] brings out the analogy between it and a translator of languages who aims to convey the linguistic meaning of utterances. Likelihood is no more misleading when it fails to be statistically consistent than is an interpreter who correctly reports what an utterance means when *the utterance* is misleading.

Why, then, has convergence been judged, not just desirable, but necessary? I conjecture that there are two reasons that the property has attained this undeserved status. First, statisticians have usually concerned themselves with the design of *optimal* experiments. So, in the example about coin tossing, it is natural to point out that tossing a 9·1 mixture of differently biased coins is a far better experiment than tossing a single coin of unknown bias. To explain why one procedure is better than the other *when both are available,* it is natural to lay down a necessary condition and show that one experiment satisfies it while the other does not. However, even if a consistent estimator were superior to an inconsistent one, it would not follow (i) that the consistent estimator is better *because* it is consistent, or (ii) that we should abstain from making an estimate when consistency is unattainable.

The design of optimal experiments without regard to which experiments can actually be performed is certainly a worthy topic of investigation. But it is important not to forget that we are not always able to carry out optimal experiments. In the coin-tossing example, I hand you a single coin and ensure that no others are available. To insist that no experiment other than an in principle optimal one may be performed means that I cannot use this single coin to gather any evidence at all. Perhaps one reason that statistical consistency has come to seem a necessary property of an estimator or rule of inference is that the problem of "choosing an estimator" has not been constrained very much by limitations on the kinds of data available or on the kinds of experiments that can be performed.

There is another main reason that statistical consistency has seemed important—even necessary—for a rule of inference or estimator. Neyman [1950, 1957] thought of a statistical test as culminating in a practical

<hr/>

17. I take this expression, though perhaps not in the sense in which it was there employed, from Birnbaum [1969].

action. A paradigm case for this behavioral interpretation arises in industrial quality control. For example, suppose we sample light bulbs from a container and have to decide whether the number of defective light bulbs is larger or smaller than some fixed threshold. We draw a sample and, in the light of some chosen statistical rule, decide either to "accept" or "reject" the shipment (Rosenkrantz [1977]).

Acceptance and rejection are possible actions—one either puts the shipment in one's inventory or returns it to the supplier. It is entirely natural for an entrepreneur to take an interest in the long-term properties of the policy adopted. One quite naturally wishes to minimize the number of accepted defectives and rejected nondefective shipments. So different decision policies are naturally judged by their asymptotic properties.

Philosophers like Reichenbach [1938] also placed great stress on asymptotic properties of inference rules, but not because they were interested in deciding how to act. Their interest was in the question of what to believe. Here acceptance and rejection meant regarding as true and regarding as false, where these attitudes often have no particular practical actions associated with them. Reichenbach thought that all nondeductive inference ultimately rests on what he called "the straight rule." This says that if n out of the m observed A's are B, one should infer that the frequency of A's that are B is n/m. This very Humean principle will be convergent under identifiable circumstances, for reasons that statisticians have long recognized.

Reichenbach was working in the context of Hume's problem, in which a "principle of induction" is supposed to tell one what to believe. To defend such a principle, Reichenbach wanted to show that this rule will deliver true beliefs in the limit, if any rule will. If there is such a thing as the true probability that a coin has of landing heads when tosses, then induction will almost certainly lead to the truth, provided one looks at an infinitely large data set.[18]

The application that Reichenbach envisaged for his straight rule was this: We toss a coin some number of times. We then believe that the mean number of observed heads is the coin's true probability. We then toss the coin some more and replace our old belief with one based on the augumented data set. We do this again and again, always updating our beliefs. In the limit, there is virtual certainty that our belief will be true.

Keynes and many others scoffed at the idea that the asymptotic long run has any bearing on the finitude of human life. "In the long run," Keynes said, "we are all dead." What bearing does the behavior of an in-

---

18. Reichenbach wanted to "vindicate" induction, not "justify" it. He wanted to show that induction will provide knowledge if any method of nondeductive inference can. He did not believe that an unconditional claim about the possibility of knowledge could be defended.

ference rule in the face of an infinite data set have on its legitimacy in the face of finite data? I shall not press this question here, but wish to focus on a quite separate part of Reichenbach's picture.

The straight rule tells one what to believe. It is a rule of "acceptance," in the philosopher's sense of that term. But likelihood does not tell one what to believe. It simply says which hypothesis is better supported by the evidence. For precisely the same reason, a Bayesian comparison of posterior probabilities does not tell one what to believe. It says which hypothesis is overall more plausible in the light of the evidence. But the most probable hypothesis may, after all, be quite improbable. And even if it is very probable, this, by itself, is not sufficient to "believe" it.[19]

I am here making the modest point that comparing competing hypotheses for their likelihoods is not a procedure that tells one what to believe. It is worth mentioning a more radical position, which says that there is no such thing as "accepting" hypotheses at all. All that one does in science is assign "degrees of belief"(subjective probabilities). According to this position, the scientific evaluation of hypotheses procedes in accordance with Bayes's theorem; there is not, in addition, a set of rules that tells one what to "accept" (Jeffrey [1956]). My present point is independent of this stronger thesis; I claim only that likelihood, *per se*, provides an "evaluation rule," not a "rule of acceptance."

If so, Reichenbach's reason for emphasizing the importance of convergence is entirely irrelevant to the question of whether a likelihood rule of inference must be statistically consistent. Still less is Neyman's behavioral reason for demanding that an inference rule have specified asymptotic properties relevant to likelihood inference. Reichenbach and Neyman understood inference in terms of a choice between "acceptance" and "rejection." But likelihood, *per se*, involves no such thing. The term "likelihood inference" may perhaps obscure this point. Properly speaking, what one "infers" by using likelihoods is not which competing hypothesis is true, but which is best supported by the evidence.

Reichenbach's project was at a much more foundational level than the ideas presented here. I have assumed without argument that likelihood measures evidential support. Reichenbach thought he had to give an argument to show why the sample mean is the best estimate of the population mean. His argument proposed convergence as a necessary property that an estimator must possess. I take no stand here on whether some non-

---

19. As is shown, I think, by Kyburg's [1961] lottery paradox: Each of the thousand tickets in a fair lottery has a very high probability of not winning. So if your "rule of acceptance" is to believe what is very probable, it seems that you should believe of each ticket that it will not win. But conjoining these implies that no ticket will win, which contradicts the assumption that the lottery is fair.

trivial argument can be given for the interpretation of likelihood I have proposed, or whether it ought to be viewed as a "primitive postulate," which is how Edwards [1972], following Fisher [1938], interprets the idea.

Likelihood evaluations have to do with the data one actually confronts, not with what a hypothetical infinite data set would imply. Suppose a finite data set, regardless of how many observations it contains, will be of one of two types: data of the first type (E_1) favors H_1 over H_2, while data of the second kind (E_2) favors H_2 over H_1. The likelihoods of the hypotheses relative to the two types of evidence are illustrated below:

		Kinds of Data	
		E_1	E_2
Hypotheses	H_1	w	x
	H_2	y	z

The above remarks about the evidential meaning of the two kinds of data merely involve *vertical* comparisons of likelihood: $w > y$ and $z > x$.

If the data we actually confront are of the first type, it is entirely natural to take this for what it is—as evidence favoring H_1. But to invoke the requirement of consistency introduces an entirely hypothetical and contrary to fact consideration. Suppose that if H_1 were true and one made the data large without limit, the resulting data would almost certainly be of type E_2. That is, suppose that $w < x$. This *horizontal* comparison of likelihoods shows that we would most probably *not* confront the data we now see, if H_1 were in fact true.

Does this fact have relevance for how we ought to interpret the data actually before us? I would say not: the vertical inequalities indicate how to interpret each kind of observation. The possibility that a horizontal relationship of the kind just mentioned would make for statistical inconsistency is quite beside the point.

Cladistic parsimony interprets a 110 character as evidence favoring (AB)C over (AC)B, and a 101 character as evidence favoring (AC)B over (AB)C. To investigate whether this thesis has a likelihood rationale, one would consider whether the entries in the following table are constrained by three *vertical* inequalities:

	Kind of Synapomorphy in the Majority		
	110	101	011
(AB)C	x_1	x_2	x_3
(AC)B	y_1	y_2	y_3
A(BC)	z_1	z_2	z_3

If it could be shown that

$$x_1 > y_1, z_1,$$
$$y_2 > x_2, z_2,$$
$$z_3 > x_3, y_3,$$

this would justify the interpretation of synapomorphies that parsimony stipulates. And if circumstances could be described in which these inequalities fail, that would constitute a case in which parsimony and likelihood part ways.

The point to notice is that investigations of statistical consistency focus on a quite different set of comparisons. Statistical consistency involves *horizontal* relations. One would like to know, for example, under what circumstances $x_1 > x_2, x_3$. Felsenstein [1978] constructs an example in which this inequality is violated. The likelihood issue considers how different hypotheses probabilify the same observations; the consistency issue concerns how a single hypothesis probabilifies different observations.[20]

I therefore see a very different significance in the clash between Farris's [1973] likelihood argument and the one constructed by Felsenstein [1973b]. Felsenstein [1978] argues that Farris's procedure is not statistically consistent, but that his is. Felsenstein [1978] holds that he has thereby identified an assumption of parsimony and Farris [1983] apparently agrees: the method assumes that the model in Felsenstein's [1978] paper is false. The hidden premise is that consistency is necessary, not just desirable, if we are to use a method.

Likelihood does not require statistical consistency. It follows that parsimony's failure of consistency in a hypothetical model does not answer the question of whether parsimony and likelihood coincide. For those who think that an inference rule must be statistically consistent, Felsenstein's 1978 article will succeed in identifying a presupposition of parsimony. For those who accept the position I have described here, no such conclusion can be drawn. Parsimony aims at saying which hypothesis is best supported by the evidence. Its function is the same as that possessed by the likelihood concept itself. This does not mean that parsimony has a likelihood rationale, but only that parsimony should not be judged by standards that are alien to the likelihood concept. The demand for consistency embodies just such a standard.

With considerations of likelihood and considerations of consistency now clearly separated, we should see that the question of the connection

---

20. My point is not to deny that consistency is a relevant consideration in experimental design. For example, if the convergence of an estimator is monotonic, this explains why it makes sense to look at larger data sets rather than smaller ones. In Hacking's [1965, 1971] terminology, this issue pertains to *before trial betting*, not to *after trial evaluation*. My argument that consistency is not necessary concerns the latter situation, in which a set of observations has already been obtained.

of likelihood and parsimony is still open. This is not to deny the force of Felsenstein's [1973b] example, in which his best-case approach to likelihood, when applied to a simple data set, provided a case in which the most likely hypothesis was not the most parsimonious one. But this example leaves open what general connections obtain between parsimony and likelihood; it rules out only the most sweeping and unconditional of claims. What is more, it rests on the adoption of Felsenstein's best-case expedient, an approach that should not be confused with a full treatment of the likelihood function.

After considering in the next section some philosophical conequences of the argument presented here against the consistency criterion, I shall proceed in section 5.6 to consider Felsenstein's [1979, 1981, 1982, 1983a,b, 1984] use of likelihood to investigate the question of what parsimony and other phylogenetic methods assume about the evolutionary process.

5.5. Evil Demons and Reliability

It has recently become fashionable in epistemology to propose theories of knowledge and of rationality that lay great stress on the "reliability" of the methods or processes by which beliefs are generated.[21] The age-old problem is to explain why true belief does not suffice for knowledge. People can have correct beliefs by accident or by entirely irrational flights of fancy. What more is needed for true beliefs to count as knowledge?

My interest here is in the related account of rationality. Rational opinions need not be true; they are opinions that are produced by a rational procedure. Reliabilism in epistemology has urged that a rational procedure must be reliable. This is spelled out in different ways, but the minimum notion often seems to be that the method must be convergent in the long run.

No one nowadays would maintain that a method of inference must be infallible if we are to be rational in using it. Rationality does not require one to be completely risk averse. It has seemed to many philosophers that the idea of reliability provides a defensible fallback position. Rationality requires reliability, not infallibility, or so this position maintains. If a method is not required to deliver the truth given the data actually at hand, there is nonetheless the idea that looking at more and more data must bring one closer and closer to the truth.

But, in fact, this demand for convergence in the long run is just as overstated as the demand for truth in the short run. The demand for an infallible method fails to take into account the fact that a rational method

---

21. See Kornblith's [1985] anthology for recent reliability theories of knowledge and justification; also see Goldman [1986].

may nonetheless be faced with misleading evidence. In this circumstance, the method may correctly analyze what the data say and quite reasonably reach a false conclusion. The point of the coin-tossing example discussed in the previous section is to show that precisely the same thing can happen to the demand for convergence. The world may be such that a quite reasonable method for analyzing data may converge on a falsehood as the data set is made large without limit.

The examples discussed thus far about phylogenetic inference and coin tossing may be given a Cartesian reformulation. The presence or absence of an evil demon—of a being who systematically misleads our senses—can be construed as a nuisance parameter that complicates our efforts to make a likelihood assessment of competing hypotheses. To see why this is so, let us consider a very simple model of how we interpret the testimony of our senses.

I glance over at the table next to me and think I see a coffee cup there. Upon reflection, I realize that my belief in the presence of this physical object is supported by the kind of visual experience I now am having. As a first approximation, I might represent this evidential relationship as follows. H_1 is the hypothesis that there is a coffee cup on the nearby table. H_2, let us suppose, is the hypothesis that the table is bare. E_1 is the characteristic visual experience I now am having, which might be described as "seeming to see a coffee cup." E_2 is the visual experience of "seeming to see a table with nothing on it."

If one has an experience in which it looks like there is a coffee cup on the nearby table (E_1), this makes H_1 more likely than H_2. Similarly, if one has an experience in which the table looks bare (E_2), this makes H_2 more likely than H_1. The likelihoods of the two hypotheses, relative to these two possible experiences, might be represented in a two-by-two table:

		Possible Experiences	
		E_1	E_2
Hypotheses	H_1	w_n	x_n
	H_2	y_n	z_n

Vertical comparisons of likelihood seem entirely natural here: $w_n > y_n$ and $z_n > x_n$. This is a rough representation of why we interpret these two possible sorts of experience as we do. E_1 supports H_1 better than H_2; E_2 supports H_2 better than H_1.

The Cartesian problem now intrudes. If we are making our observations in a "normal" situation, then the experiences have the evidential significance just claimed for them (hence the "n" subscripts on the above likelihoods). However, if we make our observations under the influence of a Cartesian evil demon, the evidential meanings are considerably altered. In this case, seeming to see a coffee cup is *not* good evidence that one is present, and seeming to see a table with no objects upon it is *not* good evidence that the table is bare.

Whether we observe in a "normal" context or in the presence of an evil demon is a nuisance parameter. It affects the likelihoods of the hypotheses we wish to consider—whether there is a coffee cup present or not—but we cannot at the outset simply assume that an evil demon is present or not. The following table represents the probability of the experience (E_1) of seeming to see a coffee cup, conditional on the four possible circumstances one might occupy:

	Nuisance Parameters	
	Normal	Evil Demon
H_1	w_n	w_d
H_2	y_n	y_d

We know from before that $w_n > y_n$. If the circumstances of observation are normal, then H_1 makes the experience of seeming to see a coffee cup more probable than H_2 does. But now suppose that if an evil demon is working his magic upon us, $y_d > w_d$. That is, if we have the experience of seeming to see a coffee cup on the table in this context, then the more likely hypothesis is that the table is bare.

In normal conditions, seeming to see a coffee cup makes H_1 more likely than H_2, but this inequality is reversed if an evil demon is present. How, then, are we to assess the *overall* likelihood, which takes account of both possible values of the nuisance parameter? If the nuisance parameter is independent of which hypothesis is true and if the presence of an evil demon is sufficiently improbable, then considering the possibility of an evil demon will not perturb our initial likelihood assessment. We shall conclude that E_1 supports H_1 better than H_2, even though there is a small chance that an evil demon is confounding our perceptions.[22]

Just as in the coin-toss example of the previous section, the likelihood rule of inference at work here is not statistically consistent. If the evil demon hypothesis is improbable enough (e.g., let us suppose its probability is 10^{-10}), we shall say that our seeming to see a coffee cup offers considerable differential support for the hypothesis that one is present. But for those who believe that consistency is a *necessary* property of a reasonable inference rule, this will not do. Their scruples compel them to make the following point: If the evil demon is present, then as you gather more and more evidence (by touching, smelling, trying to look from different angles, etc.), you will converge on H_2 if H_1 is true.

---

22. The assumptions mentioned entail that $\Pr(E_1/H_1) = (1 - e)w_n + ew_d$, while $\Pr(E_1/H_2) = (1 - e)y_n + ey_d$, for some very small e.

All this is quite correct, but surely insisting on there being a *guarantee* of convergence is demanding too much. Reasonable epistemological worries would be allayed if the evil demon hypothesis were shown to be sufficiently improbable. My point here is that this is not enough to establish statistical consistency.

I suspect that one reason reliabilism has become popular in philosophy is the wish to dismiss evil demon problems as frivolous. These and kindred epistemological nightmares (e.g., how do you know that you are not a brain in a vat ...?) have seemed like science fiction examples that ought not to trouble the working scientist. The feeling has been that philosophers should ignore such idle fantasies and restrict themselves to dealing with plausible circumstances in which observational error can occur.

I have no quarrel with the injunction that philosophers should be more realistic about the kinds of epistemological issues they address. But Felsenstein's question about convergence shows that one does not have to imagine an evil demon to conjure up cases in which an inference rule is inconsistent. The question of whether convergence in the long run is a necessary condition on the use of a method arises in the context of Descartes' problem; but the same question can arise in the case of scientific work as well. It is fine to be realistic, as long as one does not assume without argument that traditional philosophical problems have no counterparts in the world of natural science.

There is another reason why we should not sweep Descartes' problem from the field of serious inquiry. If we wish to be realistic about what we do and do not take seriously, we should, if we are Bayesians, represent our attitude toward the evil demon hypothesis and its ilk by assigning them a tiny, but finite, probability. It is not rational, I suggest, to assign the evil demon hypothesis a probability of 0. This is because Bayes's theorem implies that hypotheses assigned probabilities of 0 cannot be made more probable by new data. For those who wish to be undogmatic, no hypothesis ought to be assigned a probability of zero, since this forecloses the possibility that future experience may lead us to see things differently.

If we are realistic in the way we represent our (hopefully rational) attitude to Descartes' fanciful idea, we shall see that convergence is not essential for rational inference. If there is a finite chance that we are in the sway of an evil demon, then there is a finite chance that we shall be misled as the data are made large without limit. But if this small probability is not to deter us in evaluating what the evidence says, we must reject the demand that a rule of inference be statistically consistent.

This is not to say that Descartes' skeptical worries are easily laid to rest. Nothing said here shows that we know that a coffee cup is on the table on the basis of our sensory states. Nor have I shown that we are in any position to say that the evil demon hypothesis has a low probability. My point is simply that *if* one thought the evil demon improbable enough, one could use experience to test hypotheses without this implying the satisfaction of a convergence requirement. Surely scientific rationality demands no more than this.

Reliabilism in epistemology has placed heavy emphasis on considering what is "really possible," as opposed to what is "merely conceivable." If, in fact, the probability that there are evil demons is 0, then conceiving of their distorting influence must be entirely irrelevant. But this sensible-sounding dismissal of fantasies runs amok, it seems to me, if confronting evil demons (or their technological equivalents) is really possible, though extremely improbable. If the probability is low enough that I am deceived by an evil demon, then a likelihood rationale can be provided for the interpretation of sensory experience we all customarily make. If, improbably enough, I actually am under the long-term influence of an evil demon, then my inference processes will be unreliable. In this circumstance, then, rationality and reliability part ways.

5.6. Necessity and Sufficiency

Felsenstein's 1973b paper, recall, uses a best-case expedient solution to the problem of nuisance parameters to discover when the most parsimonious hypothesis is the hypothesis of maximum likelihood (section 5.2). Felsenstein's result there was that parsimony and likelihood will necessarily coincide if the expected amount of change in a character during the entire duration of the tree is much less than unity, but that the two may diverge if this constraint is removed. In two subsequent papers, Felsenstein [1979, 1981] continues this line of investigation: he specifies a model of evolution and investigates the parameter values that affect whether parsimony and likelihood will coincide.

In his 1979 paper, Felsenstein considers an evolutionary model in which there are three character states: 0 and 1, as usual, mean ancestral and derived, while 01 indicates a polymorphism (i.e., both 0 and 1 are present in such populations). Felsenstein stipulates a "clock" model so that a given kind of evolutionary event has a constant probability per unit time. A population can evolve from state 0 to state 01 (and vice versa) and from state 01 to state 1 (and vice versa), but it cannot evolve directly from 0 to 1. The probabilities of these events, during an infinitesimal interval of time dt, are as follows:

$$0 \underset{b/2\,dt}{\overset{a\,dt}{\rightleftarrows}} 01 \underset{c\,dt}{\overset{b/2\,dt}{\rightleftarrows}} 1$$

It is important to see that these probabilities are not *branch* transition probabilities. They are "instantaneous" probabilities—chances of change in an infinitesimal unit of time. We shall eventually need to see how this model of instantaneous change translates into a calculation of branch transition probabilities.

An additional probability is then introduced, one that is psychological, not evolutionary. There is a probability M that a character is "misinterpreted" by the systematist. This does not mean that the character's polarity is misconstrued, or that a character that has, say, a 110 distribution is erroneously thought to be distributed as 101. Felsenstein's model says that misinterpretation, when it occurs, is so serious as to render the character completely informationless. Felsenstein [1979, pp. 50–51] grants that "this is not a very good model of misinterpretation: it is chosen not for its realism but because it is the one which most readily allows us to obtain the compatibility method as a limit of maximum likelihood estimation of the phylogeny."

Felsenstein uses this model to find the most likely phylogeny, relative to a set of characters attaching to taxa that occupy the tips of the tree. To do this, we first must be clear on how this model constrains the likelihood of a single tree. Recall that we are using the term "phylogenetic tree" to indicate the topology of a branching structure only. A tree does not indicate times of interior branching events or the states at interior nodes.

We first must consider how a model of this sort confers a probability on a single character. Then we must consider how the probabilities conferred on each character combine to yield a probability that the tree confers on all the characters taken together. Both these problems pertain to the case in which the characters have not been "misinterpreted," in Felsenstein's sense. Finally, we must say more about how to model the idea of misinterpretation.

As a simple example, let us consider the (AB)C tree in figure 5a (p. 30), relative to a character that has the 110 distribution. Assume that species Zero at the root of this tree has the plesiomorphic (0) form. To compute the probability that this tree will generate a 110 character at its tips, we need to consider the different possible ways this distribution can arise. As we move from the root to Species A, there are two interior nodes in this tree. Call these x and y, in that order. Each of these nodes may have the ancestral or the derived state, so there are four possible assignments of states to the interior nodes ($x = y = 0, x = 0$ and $y = 1, x = 1$ and $y = 0$, and $x = y = 1$). For each such assignment of states, we can compute the probability that the tree will yield a 110 character distribution at its tips. So the probability of a 110 character, given (AB)C, is the sum of the probabilities of obtaining that character distribution, conditional on each possible assignment of states to interior nodes. Notice that to carry out this computation, we need to be able to say what the branch transition probabilities are.

A branch transition probability, recall, is just the chance that a node will exhibit one state, given the state of the node that is immediately ancestral. Felsenstein's model, recall, describes branch transition probabilities as depending on two quantities: the instantaneous transition probabilities mentioned before and time. So his branch transition probabilities are represented as quantities of the form $P_{BkEk}(t_k)$; this is the probability that the kth branch will end in state E_k, given that it begins in state B_k and has a duration t_k.

Suppose we have obtained this summation and therefore know what probability the tree confers on the 110 character. A similar calculation will show how probable it is for the tree to produce a different character, perhaps one distributed as 100. How are we to combine these two probabilities, obtaining a single probability that the tree confers on the two observations together? Felsenstein assumes that the characters are independent and takes this to mean that the probability of obtaining 110 and 100 is just the product of the probabilities of obtaining each.[23]

I turn, finally, to the way Felsenstein models "misinterpretation." For each character i, we must take into account the probability (M) that it has been misinterpreted, and also the probability (K_i) that we would obtain the observed data if character i were misinterpreted. This is assumed to be a constant which may depend on the data, but not on the tree.

Felsenstein then identifies the likelihood L of a tree with the following product:

$$L = \prod [MK_i + (1 - M)\sum \prod P_{BkEk}(t_k)].$$

Here the summation $(\sum)$ is over the probabilities of obtaining the observations conditional on the different possible interior node assignments; each of these "ways of obtaining the observations" is itself a product term $(\prod)$ that multiplies together the different branch transition probabilities that a given assignment of interior nodes requires. The initial product term in the expression ranges over the different characters in the data set.

To use this equation to calculate a number for the likelihood of any tree, we must specify values for K_i, a, b, c, and M. Calculating this value for data sets in which there are more than a few terminal taxa is very complicated, Felsenstein observes, because the number of possible interiors consistent with any given tree is enormous, once one has more than four or five

23. This is not quite right. A tree with the (AB)C topology is consistent with various suites of interior branch durations. But even independent characters must evolve in a single tree interior. This means that if Pr[110 & 100/(AB)C] is a summation over all possible ways of evolving the two characters, where the sum takes account of the different temporal durations the branches may have, then this term is not equal to Pr[110/(AB)C] Pr[100/(AB)C], even if the two characters are independent. This point will recur in the context of the model explored in chapter 6.

taxa.[24] However, Felsenstein [1979, p. 52] notes that a special assumption about the values of the parameters just mentioned drastically reduces the amount of computation: "If the probabilities of the four types of event (origination, reversion, loss of polymorphism, misinterpretation) are very different, then we intuitively expect that of the many possible reconstructions of events, most of the likelihood will be contributed by one reconstruction."

One such case obtains when the instantaneous transition probabilities mentioned before are all assumed to be tiny. Felsenstein [1979, p. 54] then examines four "subcases" of this assumption. He describes his first result as follows:

> I. $c, e^{-b}, M \ll a$. "In this case there is far less contribution to the likelihood [of a tree] from reconstructions [of interior states] involving even one case of reversion, misinterpretation, or retention of polymorphism than there is from reconstructions involving only $0 \to 1$ changes. However, since a is small (though larger than the other three quantities) the likelihood for a given tree will be contributed almost entirely by those reconstructions in which there are fewest $0 \to 1$ changes. Also since a is small, the likelihood of the tree will be smaller, the more such changes it requires. The maximum likelihood estimate of the phylogeny is then easily seen to be that tree which requires the fewest $0 \to 1$ transitions to explain the observed data (with no misinterpretations, reversions, or retention of polymorphisms). This is precisely the Camin-Sokal parsimony criterion."

Felsenstein [1979, pp. 54–55] then argues that three other relationships between the parameters of his model pick out three other phylogenetic methods:

> II. $e^{-b}, M \ll a \ll c$. "When c is by far the largest of these four quantities, the only reconstructions which contribute significantly to the likelihood term for a particular character are those with no misinterpretations assumed, no retentions of polymorphism, at most one $0 \to 1$ change per character, and within those constraints, as few $1 \to 0$ transitions as possible. The likelihood of a tree will be smaller the more $1 \to 0$ changes are required on that tree to explain the ob-

---

24. Actually, the difficulty is not just computational. Even after we fix the values of the parameters Felsenstein mentions, the branch transition probabilities still are not determined. The reason is that the temporal durations of the branches have yet to be constrained. We need in addition a model that describes the probability of different possible branch durations, conditional on tree topology and the parameters that Felsenstein mentions for the instantaneous transition probabilities. This is not provided by Felsenstein's model. The model explored in chapter 6 takes account of the fact that a given tree topology is consistent with many assignments of branch durations.

served character states in the tip species. The tree which will be the maximum likelihood estimate will be the one which requires the fewest $1 \to 0$ changes, given that there are no misinterpretations or instances of retention of polymorphism, and at most one $0 \to 1$ change per character. This is precisely the tree which will be found by the Dollo parsimony method presented by Farris" [1977].

III. $c, M \ll a \ll e^{-b}$. "In this case, the bulk of the likelihood term for a given character will be contributed by reconstructions having no reversion or misinterpretations postulated, at most one origination of character state 1, and as short a stretch of the evolutionary tree as possible containing polymorphism for the character." This picks out a new method that Felsenstein calls "the polymorphism method."

IV. $c, e^{-b} \ll a^2 \ll M \ll a$. "In this case, the reconstruction contributing the bulk of the likelihood for each character will be one having a single $0 \to 1$ transition or, if this is not possible, an assumed misinterpretation of the character. The likelihood will be smaller the more characters must be interpreted as having a misinterpretation. Thus the maximum likelihood estimates of the phylogeny will be the ones on which as many characters as possible require no more than one $0 \to 1$ transition.... This corresponds to the compatibility approach of Estabrook, Johnson, and McMorris" [1976].

Although Felsenstein describes the methods derived in Camin and Sokal [1965] and in Farris [1977] as distinct, I think it is more natural to see them as providing two different derivations of the same method, which I have called cladistic parsimony. In Camin and Sokal's [1965] model, reversions from 1 to 0 are assumed to be impossible although multiple originations of the 0 to 1 variety are permitted. In Farris's [1977] model, 0 to 1 changes are assumed to be far less probable than changes in the opposite direction. My preference is to view this as differences in the models, not in the methods. Both papers sought to provide an evolutionary context in which inference should proceed by minimizing the number of required changes. They differ in the "weights" assigned to the two changes $0 \to 1$ and $1 \to 0$.

Felsenstein [1979, p. 60] describes the significance, and the limitation, of these likelihood derivations as follows:

> We have seen that a common model can be developed, which yields both existing and new phylogenetic inference methods when we allow the parameters of the model to take extreme values. However this cannot be an entirely satisfactory justification for the use of these methods. For if we are willing to assume that (for example) origination of character state 1 is a rare event over the time span of our evolutionary tree, we expect little or no parallelism or convergence

to appear in our data. This is rarely the case. It is not unusual to find that only a minority of characters could have all their changes of state be unique and unreversed.

The first sentence just quoted correctly observes that Felsenstein has derived a *sufficient* condition for each of the four methods described to coincide with maximum likelihood. Felsenstein then notes that this sufficient condition is not plausible. This is the same "fly in the ointment" that Felsenstein [1973b, p. 244] observed to attach to his earlier derivation of a sufficient condition for parsimony and likelihood to coincide.

Notice that this argument does not demonstrate that parsimony or any other method assumes that the probability of change is very small. Rather, this is something that Felsenstein himself assumes; it allows Felsenstein to develop a condition under which parsimony and likelihood will coincide and a condition under which they will part ways. So the logical form of Felsenstein's result is this: *if* the probability of change is very small, then parsimony and likelihood will coincide if inequality I or II is satisfied, whereas if inequality IV is satisfied, compatibility and likelihood will coincide. Thus, Felsenstein's argument shows that the assumption of low rates, *per se*, does *not* suffice for parsimony to be the method of choice. Nor does his argument settle the question of whether the low-rate assumption is necessary.

Felsenstein observes that the sufficient condition he derives is not at all biologically plausible. So not only does the derivation not show that parsimony assumes that change is rare; in addition, according to Felsenstein, it does not supply a plausible sufficient condition under which parsimony would make sense.

The vital difference between conditions that are necessary and those that are sufficient for a phylogenetic method to have a likelihood rationale, present in the passage just quoted, seems to blur in the paper's conclusion. Felsenstein notes that one cannot use a direct maximum likelihood approach to phylogenetic inference unless one knows the numerical values of the parameters in one's model. Alternatively, we could estimate the values from the data itself, presumably using the best-case expedient with which we are by now familiar. But then Felsenstein [1979, p. 61] describes a third alternative:

> One can take the various parsimony and compatibility approaches, which are maximum likelihood methods under various extreme assumptions, as candidate methods for use when these conditions do not hold. *While they would not then be maximum likelihood methods,* they might nevertheless share with the likelihood method certain desirable statistical properties (notably consistency, sufficiency, and efficiency). I have elsewhere ... [Felsenstein 1978] made a small start

in this direction, by examining the statistical consistency of certain parsimony and compatibility methods in simple cases. They seem to have passed the few tests applied so far. However, much more work along these lines remains to be done if we are to have a sound logical basis for our methods of estimating phylogenies [italics mine].

It is curious that Felsenstein here describes his 1978 paper as showing that parsimony and compatibility methods "have passed the few tests applied so far." But the main point I wish to make concerns the italicized phrase: note that Felsenstein slides from viewing the conditions in his derivation as sufficient to viewing them as necessary. He says that if those conditions do not obtain, then parsimony and the other methods considered will not have likelihood rationales.

This is no momentary slip; Felsenstein's subsequent papers contain the same mistake—a condition proven to suffice for a method's legitimacy is then said to be an "assumption" of the method. It will be profitable to trace this transition from proven sufficiency to claimed necessity in some detail.

However, before doing so, I want to note, first, that Felsenstein himself has come to the same conclusion. He now grants that "I have not given a general proof that parsimony requires either low rates of change or equal rates in different lineages to be statistically well-behaved, but that is the pattern found in those cases I could analyze"(Felsenstein and Sober [1986, p. 624]). Second, I also want to say that I intend no disrespect by the objections I register. Felsenstein has contributed a great deal to our present understanding of the problem of phylogenetic inference. Indeed, I have the same high opinion of Farris's contribution, which I also criticized, in chapter 4. I suspect that the current biological debate is so polarized that admiring the work of both may place me in a minority of one. At any rate, the idea that knowledge progresses by a process of conjectures and refutations, to borrow Popper's [1963] phrase, is as true for the study of methodology as it is for other subjects.

Felsenstein's 1981 paper is entitled "A Likelihood Approach to Character Weighting and What It Tells Us about Parsimony and Compatibility." The problem is divided into two parts: "direct weighting" is appropriate when it is known which characters in one's data set have which rates of change, whereas "indirect weighting" involves situations in which one knows that some characters have a high probability of evolution while the rest have low probabilities of change, but one does not know which characters fall into which category. Within the former context, Felsenstein develops a sufficient condition for parsimony; within the latter, he finds a likelihood rationale for compatibility methods.

The model stipulated differs from the one used in Felsenstein [1979]. There are just two character states "0" and "1," each having a probability of 1/2 of being ancestral. A symmetrical clock assumption is invoked, although it is not assumed that all characters evolve at the same rate: the probability of a $0 \to 1$ and a $1 \to 0$ transition in character i in a small interval of time dt is $r_i dt$. As before, characters are assumed to evolve independently of each other, as are different lineages.

As in Felsenstein's 1979 paper, the question immediately arises of how to compute a *branch* transition probability from these *instantaneous* transition probabilities. Felsenstein assumes that all the $r_i t_j$'s are sufficiently small that it is extremely improbable that a character should change more than once on any branch. Assuming further that the r_i's are very small, Felsenstein notes that the branch transition probabilities asymptotically approach

$$\Pr(0 \to 0; t_j) = \Pr(1 \to 1; t_j) = 1 - r_i t_j,$$
$$\Pr(0 \to 1; t_j) = \Pr(1 \to 0; t_j) = r_i t_j.$$

Felsenstein [1981, p. 186] then assumes that the branches are sufficiently similar in duration that it is more probable for a character to change on one branch than it is for it to change on two

$$r_i t_j \gg (r_i t_k)(r_i t_l), \qquad \text{for all } i, j, k, \text{ and } l.$$

"In effect," says Felsenstein [1981, p. 187], this "ensures that if we have a choice between a reconstruction of the character states of hypothetical ancestors which involves two changes in character i in different segments, and a reconstruction involving only one change, the latter will make a much greater contribution to the likelihood." As in his 1979 paper, Felsenstein takes this stipulation to have the effect of simplifying the likelihood calculation: instead of having to sum over all the different interiors that are consistent with a given tree topology, we can simply consider the one that involves the fewest changes—it will contribute "the bulk of the likelihood." The likelihood expression for a tree, relative to all the characters in the data, thereby simplifies to [1981, p. 187]

$$L = \prod_{i=1}^{\text{characters}} \prod_{j=1}^{\text{segments}} (r_i t_j)^{n_{ij}}.$$

Here n_{ij} is the number of changes in segment j that allows one to account for the distribution of character i with the fewest changes. Each of the n_{ij} is either 1 or 0—depending on whether the character changes once or not at all in the segment. Since $r_i t_j$ is so small, we can assume that $1 - r_i t_j$ is well approximated by 1. So the likelihood expression need only take account of the minimum number of changes required by a tree.

Felsenstein then shows that a parsimony method that assigns different characters different weights has a straightforward likelihood interpretation within this model: high weight characters are ones for which change is very improbable. A conservative character i will have a lower value for $r_i t_j$, and so requiring a change in it will lower the likelihood to a greater extent than would requiring a change in a character that is more labile.

An unweighted parsimony calculation, on the other hand, would be correct if the characters had sufficiently equal rates of evolution, so that one change in character i is more probable than two changes—one in character k and one in character m:

$$r_i t_j \gg (r_k t_l)(r_m t_n), \qquad \text{for all } i, j, k, l, m, \text{ and } n.$$

This condition is more stringent than the one cited above in that we now are comparing the chance of change across different characters.

Felsenstein [1981, p. 190] turns next to the subject of "indirect weighting." He assumes that some characters (p of them) have a very high probability of change while the rest, as stipulated earlier, have a low chance of change. In this situation, the likelihood of a phylogeny is a product over the (i) characters:

p × probability of data for character i given r_i is high + (1 − p) × probability of data for character i given $r_i = r$.

How to compute branch transition probabilities if r_i is high? In this case, Felsenstein says, all branch transition probabilities $\Pr(0 \rightarrow 1)$, $\Pr(1 \rightarrow 0)$, $\Pr(0 \rightarrow 0)$, and $\Pr(1 \rightarrow 1)$ are the same, namely, 1/2.

The result of these assumptions is to guarantee "that when we are evaluating the likelihood of a phylogeny, most of that likelihood will be contributed by that reconstruction of events which has one character state change when possible, and places the character in the high-rate category when that is not possible. Since the latter contributes far less likelihood, the overall likelihood will be greater, the more characters require one or fewer changes of character state." In other words, a maximum likelihood rationale for compatibility methods has been derived.

The sufficient condition provided for compatibility methods does not involve a model in which the systematist misinterprets data, which was how compatibility was handled in Felsenstein [1979]. The present model is purely evolutionary, not psychological: compatibility emerges as a maximum likelihood method under certain assumptions about rate inequalities.[25]

25. Recall the example in section 5.1, in which all the branch transition probabilities in figure 15 were assumed to equal 1/2, with the result that P[110/(AB)C] = P[110/A(BC)] = 1/8. This is the intuitive idea behind Felsenstein's argument that with high probabilities of change, a character distribution will be informationless. It is essential to this argument that the instantaneous probabilities of 0 to 1 and of 1 to 0 change are the same, a point that I shall explain in the next chapter. I also shall show that this symmetry assumption implies a branch transition probability of 1/2 *only* asymptotically; for branches of finite duration, synapomorphies are not informationless.

As before, the interest of these constructions must lie in what they reveal about the evolutionary assumptions that parsimony and compatibility methods require. Felsenstein [1981, pp. 194–195] begins by observing that he has identified sufficient conditions for a phylogenetic method to coincide with the dictates of likelihood:

> ... parsimony methods gain credibility the lower is the rate of change of the characters over the time-spans involved in the divergence from a common ancestor. The minimization of the number of changes of state then has a very simple and intuitive justification: we prefer that reconstruction of evolutionary history which strains our credulity least, by requiring the smallest amount of change. Furthermore, parsimony will be a robust method, in that it is specified as the preferred estimate whatever the rate of evolution, provided only that that rate is small. We have seen that as the rates of evolution are made small, the weights of the different characters become more equal, and an unweighted parsimony method is approached in the limit. This tends to lend support to the use of these methods.
>
> Compatibility methods gain credibility from their association with variable rates of evolution in different characters. They are best justified when many characters evolve at low rates but a few may be evolving quickly, and we do not know in advance which characters will evolve at which rates.

These claims are basically correct, provided we do not forget that they are conditional on the model that Felsenstein stipulates at the outset. However, the transition from proven sufficient conditions to asserted necessary ones then makes its appearance: "All three approaches (parsimony, compatibility, and threshold methods)[26] have one major weakness: they implicitly assume very low rates of change of most characters...." (p. 194). As before, Felsenstein observes that there is a fly in the ointment: "Many sets of data I have seen require extra changes of state in almost all characters. This is contradictory to the assumption of low rates of evolution in most characters.... This renders the use of either parsimony or compatibility methods questionable; if we expect a moderate amount of change, should we not prefer a method which attempts a reconstruction involving a moderate amount of change rather than the minimum possible?" Again, it is important to realize that it is Felsenstein who has assumed very low rates of change for most characters. He stipulates this as part of his model, within which the rationale for weighting some characters more heavily than others is explored. This is worlds away from showing that parsimony or compatibility methods assume any such thing.

---

26. This last method is one that Felsenstein derives; I have not described it here.

There is no need to trace this pattern through Felsenstein's [1982, 1983a,b, 1984] subsequent articles; citing the articles I have just canvassed, he consistently claims to have shown that parsimony assumes that rates of evolution are low and then notes that this assumption is rarely plausible.[27] My point here is not that this conclusion is false, but that Felsenstein has not established that it is true. The analytic problem of computing the likelihood of a phylogenetic hypothesis in the light of a given data set led Felsenstein to adopt a simplifying assumption: so as to avoid having to consider *all* the tree interiors that allow a tree topology to generate a probability for the data in question, the assumption of low rates of evolution allows one to focus on the single interior in which the number of changes is minimal; this interior will then contribute "the bulk of the likelihood." Unfortunately, this analytic shortcut makes it impossible to tell whether *parsimony* requires that the number of changes be minimal. Farris's thesis—that parsimony minimizes assumptions without assuming minimality (section 4.4)—has yet to be refuted.

There is a more modest result to which these models can lay claim: Assuming low evolutionary rates is not, *per se*, enough to vindicate parsimony. Felsenstein's goal was to show that low rates are *necessary* for parsimony; but the result he actually achieved was to show that the low rate assumption is not *sufficient*. Within the models explored in Felsenstein [1979] and [1981], methods *other than parsimony* sometimes are justified when the low-rate idea is conjoined with other assumptions.

5.7. Concluding Remarks

If statistical consistency were a necessary condition on a method of inference, Felsenstein's 1978 argument would have shown how parsimony makes assumptions about the rarity of homoplasy. Or more precisely, if consistency were a requirement, then parsimony would have to assume that not all the assumptions in Felsenstein's 1978 model could be true. If the best-case expedient for handling nuisance parameters in likelihood inference were a satisfactory substitute for an evaluation of the full likelihood function, then we could conclude that parsimony and likelihood may sometimes diverge under one way of implementing that expedient (Felsenstein [1973b]), but that they must coincide under another (Farris [1973]). However, if we keep the distinction between likelihood and consistency clearly in mind and if we realize that the best-case expedient is

---

27. In Felsenstein [1983a, pp. 321–322] he conjectures that the assumption of low rates of evolution can be relaxed somewhat if rates of change among contemporaneous branches are sufficiently similar.

not the same as a comparison of the full likelihood functions, then we are still very much in the dark as to what parsimony assumes.

This question is not resolved by Felsenstein's [1979, 1981, 1983a,b, 1984] subsequent treatments of the issue. Having found that extreme improbability of change is part of a sufficient condition under which parsimony and likelihood coincide, Felsenstein concludes that parsimony assumes that change is improbable. My objections have been to the logic of this reasoning; I have not claimed that the conclusion is false. Perhaps parsimony, after all, does assume that rates of evolution are so low that little or no homoplasy can occur. If so, Felsenstein's observation that systematists typically confront data sets in which this is patently untrue should be taken very seriously. This would be a "fly in the ointment," as Felsenstein says: if a method really does *assume* something that is known to be untrue, it is hard to see how one can blithely continue to use the method. But the suspicion may linger that parsimony does not require rarity of homoplasy. In the next chapter, some small steps will be taken toward resolving this question.

Chapter 6
A Model Branching Process

6.1. Desiderata

The purpose of this chapter is to investigate some probabilistic properties of two main approaches to the problem of phylogenetic inference: overall similarity and cladistic parsimony. To do this, we cannot ignore a major conclusion of the previous chapters: No model, no inference. One cannot study the legitimacy of these conflicting claims about the evidential significance of character distributions without assuming, however provisionally, a concrete model of the evolutionary process.

The double dilemma that Felsenstein repeatedly emphasized likewise cannot be avoided. Mathematically tractable models are often biologically unrealistic. And biologically realistic models that have identifiable implications about the interpretation of evidence are frequently unkown. Systematists confronting a group of taxa are often more certain about which process models they hold to be false than about which they take to be true.

Even so, the goal of this chapter is perhaps modest enough that these formidable difficulties will not prove overwhelming. I shall abstain from sweeping pronouncements about the presuppositions of the different methods that are not conditioned on the assumption of a model. Results obtained within one model may extend to others; the opinions I offer about this issue of robustness should be viewed as no more than plausible hunches, pending the supply of a formal argument. In addition, I shall not claim to justify any one method of phylogenetic inference even within the context of the model investigated. Rather, my interest is in some of the leading ideas that distinguish the two approaches. It is these few leading ideas that I shall explore, without pretending that they exhaust all there is to the approaches from which they derive.

One of the main concerns will be to consider the impact of frequency of homoplasy on the legitimacy of parsimony. To see whether abundance of homoplasy undermines cladistic methods, we cannot simply assume that homoplasy is rare and then show that parsimony is a legitimate method. To do so would conflate the sufficiency of an assumption with its necessity. Nor will it do to construct a model in which homoplasy is common, which

is such that parsimony fails whatever criterion of adequacy we have selected. The perhaps more subtle problem here is that it will be unclear
whether frequent homoplasy, or some other property of the model, should
be viewed as the culprit. Rather, we should consider a model in which the
frequency of homoplasy is an *adjustable parameter*. We then want to see
whether setting the homoplasy rate high or low diminishes or enhances the
legitimacy of parsimony.

In this book, I have adopted the assumption that likelihood measures
evidential support. I also have accepted the point of consensus between
Bayesians and likelihoodists: Posterior probability is superior to likelihood
as a measure of the overall plausibility of hypotheses if prior probabilities
are grounded in a specified model of a chance process. In this chapter, I shall
consider a branching process in which the prior probabilities of various
phylogenetic hypotheses are well-defined. This will permit discussion of
the posterior probabilities, not merely the likelihoods, of the hypotheses in
question. The real benefit of this model, however, lies in how it elucidates
the way the likelihood concept applies to phylogenetic hypotheses.

In keeping with the argument of chapters 3 and 5, I shall eschew the use
of best-case expedients in assessing likelihoods. The alternative method for
handling nuisance parameters, noted in section 3.5, is to constrain them,
rather than estimate their values. The idea is to develop a set of assumptions that implies inequalities in the likelihoods of competing phylogenetic
hypotheses, which hold true whatever the true values of the nuisance
parameters happen to be.

Felsenstein [1973b, 1981, 1983a, 1984] formulated a sufficient condition
for cladistic parsimony: If the rate of character change is so low that
homoplasies occur very rarely, then parsimony is an acceptable method.
This sufficient condition, Felsenstein notes, is seldom satisfied by real data.
Real data sets often require the investigator to assume that homoplasies
have occurred in a very high percentage of the characters taken as evidence. It will be a step forward if we can identify a sufficient condition for
at least some of the ideas distinctive of the parsimony approach that does
not involve this very serious "fly in the ointment."

In Felsenstein [1983a] and in Felsenstein and Sober [1986], Felsenstein
also suggested (without proof) that uniformity of evolutionary rates
among branches may constitute a separate sufficient condition. Rate uniformity means that, at any given time, all branches have the same proportion of characters undergoing evolutionary change. This does not require
that rates remain constant through time; uniformity does not imply constancy. It is worth recalling from section 3.1 that Sneath and Sokal [1973]
claimed, in contrast, that uniformity of rates guarantees the legitimacy of
phenetic methods. The model I shall investigate assumes uniform rates; it

is the sort of model that has been viewed by different participants in this biological debate as favorable to different competing phylogenetic methods. It will be especially interesting, therefore, to see which phylogenetic method fares better in this setting.

The competing approaches to phylogenetic inference can be thought of as differing in the way they apportion weights to characters. Phenetic methods accord equal weight to plesiomorphic similarity and apomorphic similarity. Cladistic parsimony accords zero weight to symplesiomorphies. Among the apomorphic characters, cladistic parsimony may apportion different weights, based on the biological judgment of the investigator; the method, per se, does not dictate how these weights are to be assigned. Compatibility or "clique" methods also accord zero weight to symplesiomorphies; but unlike parsimony, they accord zero weight to the smallest number of synapomorphic characters whose removal would result in a fully congruent data set. Within the context of the postulated model, we shall want to see what the biological requirements are for these different strategies of character weighting.

Although "overall similarity" is a method that intreprets characters, I believe that the conclusions reached here bear on the use of "distance measures" as well. Distance measures take overall dissimilarities between pairs of taxa, rather than the character states of each, as data; they have been especially popular because certain kinds of molecular data come in this form. For example, techniques are available that allow one to take strands of DNA obtained from different species and compute the fraction of sites on those strands at which they differ; one can do this without knowing the actual sequence of molecular characters found at any site on either strand. Instead of inferring phylogenies from characters, one infers them from distances. Nevertheless, distance measures share with phenetic treatments of characters the central feature that both ancestral similarity and derived similarity are assumed to be evidentially relevant.[1]

The model to be considered is the simple one illustrated by figure 2 (p. 16), which was introduced to explain cladistic terminology in chapter 1. A single ancestral species (Zero) begins the process. After a certain length of time, it gives birth to two daughter species. After that same length of time, each of those daughters begets two daughters. And so on, so that in the nth generation of the process, 2^n new species make their appearance. I shall model the phylogenetic inference problem as follows: The systematist samples three taxa at random (without replacement) from the tips of the resulting tree and notes their character states for one or more characters. The question, then, is how to use the observed character states to decide

1. See Nei [1987, pp. 293ff] for discussion of distance matrix methods.

which pair of taxa forms a monophyletic group that does not include the third.[2]

The three sampled taxa bear some definite degree of relatedness to each other. For example, it might be that A and B are "sibs" whereas B and C are "fifth cousins." The precise degree of relatedness that obtains between two species is given by the number of generations one needs to go back to find their most recent common ancestor. So "sibs" will be said to be 1-related; the most distantly related species in a process lasting n generations are n-related. The exact degree of relatedness between A and B will be an integer; $R_i(A, B)$ says that A and B are i-related ($1 \leqslant i \leqslant n$).

Systematists wishing to infer monophyletic groups do not care about the exact degree of relatedness of the species they investigate. It does not matter much whether A and B are 4-related or 5-related. What does matter is whether some species are *more closely related* to each other than to others. The paradigmatic phylogenetic hypothesis, recall, is expressed as (AB)C. Within the model branching process, this asserts that there are numbers i and j such that $R_i(A, B)$ and $R_j(B, C)$ and $i < j$.

Note the main simplification in this model of the branching process: Species always produce two daughters and do so at time intervals that are necessarily regular. It would be more realistic to allow that at any time, there are different probabilities that a species will have different numbers of daughters. Greater realism still would be achieved by allowing these probabilities to vary from time to time and from node to node. The degree to which results obtained for the simple branching process can be extended to these more complicated cases will be discussed in section 6.6.

I turn now to assumptions about character evolution. I stipulate that characters evolve independently of each other and that events within one branch are independent of those occurring elsewhere. I also assume uniformity, though not constancy, of rates (unless otherwise noted). Uniformity means that each generation of the branching process has its own branch transition probabilities, which apply to all characters. Different generations may differ from each other, but all contemporaneous branches are assumed to have the same probabilistic properties.

Characters come in two states, 0 and 1, which as usual mean ancestral and derived. The uniformity assumption means that we can assign a single pair of branch transition probabilities to all the characters on all branches within the same generation; for each character, there is the probability that a branch in generation i ends in state 1 if it begins in state 0, and the

2. Edwards and Cavalli-Sforza [1964], Cavalli-Sforza and Edwards [1967], Felsenstein [1973a], and Thompson [1975] investigated branching processes with a constant probability that each line splits in each instant of time. They did not include a sampling step.

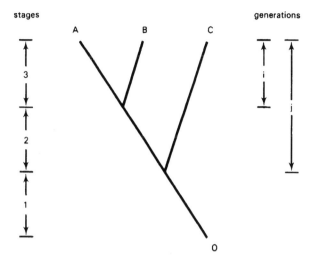

stages   generations

Figure 17.
If A and B are i-related and B and C are j-related (where $i < j$), the probability of a character distribution can be represented by dividing the passage from root to tips into three "stages," with stage k assigned its own pair of transition probabilities e_k and r_k. This assumes that evolutionary rates are uniform, not that they are constant.

probability that a branch in generation i ends in state 0 if it begins in state 1. Note that the opposite of these two sorts of "change" does not mean that the character has remained unchanged; a branch may end in the same state in which it began by undergoing any even number of flip-flops between 0 and 1. I do not assume that the probability of one sort of change (0-to-1) is the same or different from that in the other direction (1-to-0).

Some of the simplifications in this picture of character evolution are harder to dispense with than others. I shall comment in section 6.6 on the effect of relaxing the assumption of independence among characters. I also shall discuss the consequences of allowing characters to come in more than two states. The same holds for the assumption that all characters are assumed to have the same suite of branch transition probabilities. However, the uniformity assumption is more difficult to relax and still obtain general results. More on this later.

It is worth noting that cladistic parsimony is satistically consistent in this model. The three sampled taxa A, B, and C have some specific degree of relatedness among them. Let us suppose that (AB)C is the true cladistic grouping and that A and B are i related and that B and C are j related (with $i < j$), as depicted in figure 17. To demonstrate statistical consistency, we need to show simply that the probability of obtaining a 110 character at the tips exceeds the probability of obtaining 101 and the probability of obtaining 011. The uniformity assumption means that 101 and 011 have the same probabilities of occurring in the tree.

I divide the process from root to tips into three "stages." Let "e_k" denote the probability that stage k ends in state 1 if it begins in state 0; let "r_k" denote the probability that stage k ends in state 0 if it begins in state 1. These letters are chosen to suggest "evolution" and "reversion," respectively. The probability of obtaining a 110 character and a 101 character are, respectively,

$$(110) \quad e_1[r_2(1 - e_3) + (1 - r_2)r_3][r_2e_3^2 + (1 - r_2)(1 - r_3)^2]$$
$$+ (1 - e_1)[e_2r_3 + (1 - e_2)(1 - e_3)][e_2(1 - r_3)^2$$
$$+ (1 - e_2)e_3^2],$$

$$(101) \quad e_1[r_2(e_3) + (1 - r_2)(1 - r_3)][r_2e_3(1 - e_3)$$
$$+ (1 - r_2)r_3(1 - r_3)] + (1 - e_1)[e_2(1 - r_3)$$
$$+ (1 - e_2)e_3][e_2(1 - r_3)r_3 + (1 - e_2)e_3(1 - e_3)].$$

(110) exceeds (101) precisely when

$$e_1 r_2 (1 - r_2)(1 - r_3 - e_3)^2$$
$$+ (1 - e_1)e_2(1 - e_2)(1 - r_3 - e_3)^2 > 0.$$

If all transition probabilities have values between 0 and 1, noninclusive, then this condition is satisfied, provided that $r_3 + e_3 \neq 1$. This is a very general circumstance; in section 6.5, an argument will be provided for a relationship I call "the backward inequality," which asserts that $e_3 < 1 - r_3$. Notice that if $r_3 + e_3 = 1$, then in the limit 110 characters will occur as frequently as 101 characters, and so parsimony will indicate that we should suspend judgment as to which phylogenetic grouping is correct. In no circumstance, therefore, will parsimony converge on a falsehood in the face of infinite data.

A salient difference between this argument and the one developed by Felsenstein [1978] concerns the uniformity assumption. Parsimony is inconsistent in Felsenstein's example when large inequalities of rates obtain among contemporaneous branches. The model investigated here assumes that that cannot occur.

Overall similarity will be statistically consistent in this model as well. An argument parallel to the one just given yields the same general circumstance in which 001 characters have a higher probability than 010 characters.[3] This means that, in the limit, the sum of the frequencies of 110 and 001 characters can be expected to be at least as great as the sum of the

---

3. Simply replace e_3 with $(1 - e_3)$ and r_3 with $(1 - r_3)$ in the above argument; note that the necessary and sufficient condition for consistency remains unchanged under this substitution.

frequencies of 101 and 010 characters. So overall similarity will also converge on the truth in the face of infinite data.[4]

I noted in section 5.3 that statistical consistency is never taken as a condition that *suffices* to justify an estimator. There are always many different estimators that converge on the truth in the limit, though they differ in their evaluations of finite data sets. Here is a case in point. Even if we believed that the model presented here is fairly realistic for some specific problem of phylogenetic inference, the fact that parsimony is consistent is not enough to justify that method of phylogenetic inference. Nor can a phenetic method be adopted just because it is statistically consistent. Even for those who think, contrary to the argument of section 5.4, that statistical consistency is necessary, no choice of one method *as opposed to the other* is mandated by the above result.

In section 3.1, I discussed Sneath and Sokal's [1973] claim that rate uniformity suffices for the use of overall similarity to reconstruct genealogical relationships. Although they present no argument for this conclusion, I considered an argument that appeals to the notion of statistical consistency. That argument, we now see, fails to justify overall similarity as *as opposed to* parsimony as the method of choice.

I argued in earlier chapters that it is often quite difficult to determine what assumptions are necessary for a method to make sense. Here is a symmetrical point about sufficiency. It is often not obvious what assumptions suffice to justify a method. This is surprising; it *seems* clear that overall similarity would be the right method to use if overall similarity were perfectly correlated with propinquity of descent. But this limpid judgment begins to cloud, once an optimality criterion is explicitly stated. Rate uniformity guarantees the statistical consistency of *many* methods, so consistency within a uniform rates model cannot be cited as a sufficient reason for using one of them *as opposed to any other*.[5]

These asymptotic considerations, in my opinion, are beside the point. A finite data set provides information about phylogenetic relationships. A method of inference is better or worse to the degree that it manages to extract as much of that information as possible, and to distort its testimony as little as possible. Even a method that fails to exploit a great deal of the information contained in finite data sets may converge on the truth when supplied with infinite data. Competing methods of phylogenetic inference

4. A third (not very popular) method also is convergent—one that takes ancestral similarity, but not derived similarity, as evidence of propinquity of descent. So is a fourth—a Reichenbachian method of the sort described by Forster [1986] in which positive covariance is taken to indicate propinquity of descent.

5. Notice a parallel result of Felsenstein's [1979, 1981] models, discussed in section 5.6: Assuming low rates of evolution is not, *per se*, sufficient to justify the use of parsimony as opposed to the other methods that Felsenstein enumerates.

should be evaluated by the way they represent or misrepresent the meaning of finite evidence, not by their behavior in the infinite long run.

6.2. Matches Confirm

The assumptions of the model allow us to use Bayes's theorem to pinpoint the evidential significance of different character distributions. We would like to know under what circumstances observed synapomorphies have the evidential meaning that parsimony claims for them. This will lead us to ask whether, in the model, $Pr[(AB)C/110] > Pr[A(BC)/110]$. Parsimony also maintains that observed symplesiomorphies are evidentially meaningless. To see whether this is true, we shall wish to determine if it is ever true, in the model, that $Pr[(AB)C/001] > Pr[A(BC)/001]$.

The first result I shall prove—the theorem referred to in the title of this section—is that *matching confirms*. Synapomorphies (defined to mean derived matchings, not derived homologies) always have the evidential significance claimed for them, regardless of whether character change is probable or improbable. But the same conclusion holds for symplesiomorphies. Although parsimony's view of synapomorphy does not depend on the frequency of homoplasy, its absolute dismissal of symplesiomorphy is found to be an error within the model under investigation.

This does not mean, however, that phenetic methods are vindicated by the model under consideration. The spirit, if not the letter, of cladistic theory would be vindicated in the model if it could be shown that synapomorphies have vastly more evidential meaning than symplesiomorphies. The idea here is that symplesiomorphies are *relatively* uninformative, not that they are *totally* informationless. If 110 favors (AB)C over A(BC) and if 100 tells in the opposite direction, as the first theorem will show, then the question arises of what this combined data set says. That is, we will want to find out when $Pr[(AB)C/110 \& 100] > Pr[A(BC)/110 \& 100]$; this will be the main subject of section 6.3.

A related question concerns incongruence among synapomorphies. When will it be true that $Pr[(AB)C/110 \& 011] > Pr[A(BC)/110 \& 011]$, and when will these quantities be equal? It is worth bearing in mind that equal weighting of synapomorphies ("one synapomorphy, one vote") must involve biological assumptions just as much as an assumption of unequal weighting. We shall want to see what features of the evolutionary process, as described in the model under investigation, bear on this question.

Before any observations are made of the character states in the three taxa, the probability of (AB)C, A(BC), and (AC)B are the same, namely, 0.33. This is not based on some fallacious principle of indifference ("there is no more reason to believe one hypothesis rather than another, so they are equally probable"), but on the sampling scheme for drawing taxa from the

tips of the tree. If the phylogenetic hypotheses are to differ in their posterior probabilities, this means that they must differ in their likelihoods.
However, the likelihood is a somewhat complicated business, owing to the
fact that the hypotheses do not assert a specific degree of relatedness
among the taxa; they merely say that some are more closely related than
others.

What is the probability of a 110 character if (AB)C is true? First, we must
take account of all the ways that (AB)C could be true—that is, of all the
i, j pairs such that $R_i(A, B)$ and $R_j(B, C)$ and $i < j$. Each of these confers its
own probability on the observation. The likelihood will be an average over
these:

$$\Pr[110/(AB)C]$$
$$= \sum_{i<j} \Pr[110/R_i(A, B) \& R_j(B, C)] \Pr[R_i(A, B) \& R_j(B, C)/(AB)C].$$

As stressed throughout this book, the problem of phylogenetic inference
has always involved a minimum of three taxa. But the way forward in the
probabilistic problem before us is to drop from three to two. We shall
consider how the matching or mismatching of a pair of taxa bears on their
expected degree of relatedness. After proving results for the case of two, I
shall address the case of three taxa.

Two taxa drawn at random from the top of the tree can be related in
numerous ways—they may be 1-related, 2-related, and so on, with the
most distant degree of relatedness being n. It is more probable that they are
distantly related than that they are closely related. The exact formula
(Carter Denniston, personal communication) is this:

$$\Pr[R_i(A, B)] = 2^{i-1}/(2^n - 1).$$

For example, in a three-generation process ($n = 3$), the probability of being
a sib ($i = 1$) is 1/7, of being a first cousin ($i = 2$) is 2/7, and of being
maximally unrelated ($i = 3$) is 4/7.

The above expression defines the *a priori* probability (i.e., the probability
before any character states are observed) of each specific degree of relatedness that might obtain between the two sampled taxa. We now can define
the *a priori* expected degree of relatedness. Let $R(A, B) = i$ if and only if
$R_i(A, B)$. The *a priori* expectation is then

$$\text{Exp}[R(A, B)] = \sum_{i \leq n} i \Pr[R_i(A, B)].$$

If we observe that the two taxa are both in the 1 state, how does this
information bear on how we should expect them to be related? We wish to
identify circumstances in which that information leads us to expect that the
taxa are more closely related than we thought before the observation was

made. That is, we wish to discover when $\mathrm{Exp}[R(A, B)/11] < \mathrm{Exp}[R(A, B)]$. Note that the expectation of closer relationship is here represented by a lower expected value for $R(A, B)$.

It is suggestive to think of this by analogy with the case of human family trees. Two people sampled at random have a certain *a priori* expected degree of relatedness. How would discovering that they both are named "Smith" bear on this expectation? The intuitive guess is something I shall now show to hold within the context of the model: *matches confirm*.

I first shall show that

(1) $\mathrm{Pr}[11/R_i(A, B)] > \mathrm{Pr}[11/R_{i+1}(A, B)],$ for all i.

This proposition asserts that there is no more likely guess about a specific degree of relatedness, in the light of an observed apomorphic match, than to suppose that the taxa are *sibs*. This likely guess, as noted before, is *a priori* very improbable.

Let us consult figure 17 here, which shows A and B to be i-related; merely suppose that $j = i + 1$. As before, e_k represents the probability of a 0-to-1 change in stage k and r_k is the probability of a 1-to-0 change in that stage. The two probabilities, then, are as follows ("R_i" is shorthand for $R_i[A, B]$):

$$\mathrm{Pr}[11/R_i] = e_1[r_2e_3^2 - (1 + r_2)(1 - r_3)^2]$$
$$+ (1 - e_1)[e_2(1 - r_3)^2 + (1 - e_2)e_3^2],$$

$$\mathrm{Pr}[11/R_{i+1}] = e_1[r_2e_3 + (1 - r_2)(1 - r_3)]^2$$
$$+ (1 - e_1)[e_2(1 - r_3) + (1 - e_2)e_3]^2.$$

Some algebraic manipulation shows that $\mathrm{Pr}[11/R_i] \geqslant \mathrm{Pr}[11/R_{i+1}]$ precisely when

$$e_1r_2(1 - r_2)[1 - r_3 - e_3]^2 + (1 - e_1)e_2(1 - e_2)[1 - r_3 - e_3]^2 \geqslant 0.$$

This requirement is unconditionally satisfied; if all probabilities are intermediate and $e_3 \neq (1 - r_3)$, then a strict inequality obtains.[6] Both of these *if*s I assume for now; the nonidentity will be justified in section 6.5, by defending the *backward inequality* ($e_3 < 1 - r_3$).

This establishes proposition (1). If we let $a_i = \mathrm{Pr}(11/R_i)$, we may state this result as asserting that $a_1 > a_2 > \cdots > a_n$.

The next stage in the argument is to consider the most distant degree of relationship (R_n). I wish to show that

(2) $\mathrm{Pr}(R_n) > \mathrm{Pr}(R_n/11).$

---

6. The strict inequality displayed above is the same one derived for parsimony's consistency in section 6.1.

Bayes's theorem implies that (2) is true precisely when

(2') $\Pr(11) > \Pr(11/R_n)$.

If we let $p_i = \Pr(R_i)$ (where $\sum p_i = 1$), then (2') can be expressed equivalently as

(2") $\sum_i a_i p_i > a_n$,

which is implied by (1). This establishes (2"), and hence (2).

The third stage in the argument is to consider the most intimate degree of relatedness (R_1) and to show that

(3) $\Pr(R_1) < \Pr(R_1/11)$.

This is true if and only if

(3') $\Pr(11) < \Pr(11/R_1)$,

which is equivalent to

(3") $\sum_i a_i p_i < a_1$,

a result again guaranteed by (1).

The fourth step in the argument is to see that

(4)   There is at most one degree of relatedness i
        such that $\Pr(R_i) = \Pr(R_i/11)$.

First note that the equality cited in (4) holds precisely when $\Pr(11) = \Pr(11/R_i)$. Result (1) (with the assumption that $e_3 \neq 1 - r_3$) guarantees that $\Pr(11/R_i)$ decreases with i. This suffices to establish (4).

If we assemble results (2), (3), and (4), we obtain a picture of the relationship of $\Pr(R_i)$ and $\Pr(R_i/11)$ like that shown in figure 18. For simplicity, I have depicted each as continuous functions of i; however, since i takes only integral values, the functions are really defined just at those values. The important features of this figure are the monotonic increase of $\Pr(R_i)$ with i, the relationship between the conditional and unconditional probabilities at the extreme values—as established in propositions (2) and (3)—and the fact that there is a single crossover point (4).

From this we may conclude that the expected degree of relatedness, given the 11 observation, is less than the a priori expected degree of relatedness:

(5) $\mathrm{Exp}[R(A, B)/11] < \mathrm{Exp}[R(A, B)]$.

This follows because $\mathrm{Exp}[R(A, B)/11]$ places high weight on small values of i and low weight on large values of i, whereas $\mathrm{Exp}[R(A, B)]$ does just the

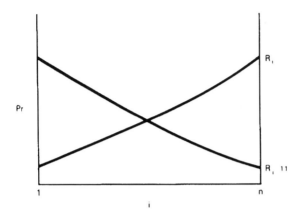

Figure 18.
If two species randomly sampled from the tips of the tree displayed in figure 2 both exhibit the 1 state, then the expectation is that they are more closely related than one would expect a priori.

reverse. So observing that the two taxa are both in state 1 should lead one to think that they are more closely related than would be expected in the absence of such information.

The above argument focused on *apomorphic* matches. But a perfectly symmetrical conclusion can be reached for *plesiomorphic* matches:

(6) $Exp[R(A, B)/00] < Exp[R(A, B)]$.

To construct this argument, merely carry out the algebraic substitutions noted in footnote 2.

I summarize these two results by saying that *matches confirm*, regardless of whether they involve apomorphic or plesiomorphic characters.

It also follows that *mismatches disconfirm*:

(7) $Exp[R(A, B)/10] > Exp[R(A, B)]$.

To see this, note that since $Pr(11/R_1) > Pr(11)$ and $Pr(00/R_1) > Pr(00)$, it follows that $Pr(10/R_1) < Pr(10)$. This implies that $Pr(R_1/10) < Pr(R_1)$. Similarly, since $Pr(11/R_n) < Pr(11)$ and $Pr(00/R_n) < Pr(00)$, it follows that $Pr(10/R_n) > Pr(10)$. This implies that $Pr(R_n/10) > Pr(R_n)$. This permits one to plot $Pr(R_i)$ and $Pr(R_i/10)$ as in figure 18, except that $Pr(R_i/10)$ is less than $Pr(R_i)$ for low values of i, with this inequality reversing for high values of i.

Before considering the relative weights that should be accorded to apomorphic and plesiomorphic matches, I want to indicate how these results, which concern observing taxa two at a time, pertain to phylogenetic hypotheses involving at least three taxa. Suppose we observe that taxa A, B, and C have character states 1, 1, and 0, respectively. I now shall show that

(8) $\text{Exp}[R(A, B)/110] < \text{Exp}[R(B, C)/110]$.

This is equivalent to

$$\sum_i i\,\text{Pr}[R_i(A, B)/110] < \sum_j j\,\text{Pr}[R_j(B, C)/110],$$

which Bayes's theorem allows us to rewrite as

$$\sum_i i\,\text{Pr}[110/R_i(A, B)]\,\text{Pr}[R_i(A, B)] < \sum_j j\,\text{Pr}[110/R_j(B, C)]\,\text{Pr}[R_j(B, C)].$$

With "R_i" as shorthand for $R_i(A, B)$ and "R_j" as shorthand for $R_j(B, C)$, this can be expanded to

$$\sum_{i,j} i\,\text{Pr}[110/R_i\ \&\ R_j]\,\text{Pr}[R_j/R_i]\,\text{Pr}[R_i]$$
$$< \sum_{i,j} j\,\text{Pr}[110/R_i\ \&\ R_j]\,\text{Pr}[R_i/R_j]\,\text{Pr}[R_j],$$

which simplifies to

$$\sum_{i,j} i\,\text{Pr}[110/R_i\ \&\ R_j]\,\text{Pr}[R_i\ \&\ R_j] < \sum_{i,j} j\,\text{Pr}[110/R_i\ \&\ R_j]\,\text{Pr}[R_i\ \&\ R_j].$$

Each side of this inequality requires that we consider all possible values for i and j. Since i and j must be different (a consequence of the fact that the branching process always bifurcates), the set of i, j pairs may be split in two. Let the first set consist of all i, j such that $i < j$; the second will comprise all such pairs such that $i > j$. The inequality may then be rewritten as

$$\sum_{i<j} i\,\text{Pr}[110/R_i\ \&\ R_j]\,\text{Pr}[R_i\ \&\ R_j]$$
$$+ \sum_{i>j} i\,\text{Pr}[110/R_i\ \&\ R_j]\,\text{Pr}[R_i\ \&\ R_j]$$
$$< \sum_{i<j} j\,\text{Pr}[110/R_i\ \&\ R_j]\,\text{Pr}[R_i\ \&\ R_j]$$
$$+ \sum_{i>j} j\,\text{Pr}[110/R_i\ \&\ R_j]\,\text{Pr}[R_i\ \&\ R_j].$$

This becomes

$$\sum_{i>j} (i - j)\,\text{Pr}[110/R_i\ \&\ R_j]\,\text{Pr}[R_i\ \&\ R_j]$$
$$< \sum_{i<j} (j - i)\,\text{Pr}[110/R_i\ \&\ R_j]\,\text{Pr}[R_i\ \&\ R_j].$$

I want to evaluate the above inequality of summations by comparing some addends with others. For example, I want to compare the probability of the 110 observation when $i = 1$ and $j = 2$ with its probability when $i = 2$ and $j = 1$. My general claim is that

$$\Pr[110/R_x(A, B) \& R_y(B, C)] \Pr[R_x(A, B) \& R_y(B, C)]$$
$$> \Pr[110/R_y(A, B) \& R_x(B, C)] \Pr[R_y(A, B) \& R_x(B, C)]$$

if and only if $x < y$.

Note that $\Pr[R_x(A, B) \& R_y(B, C)] = \Pr[R_y(A, B) \& R_x(B, C)]$. Note also that the consistency proof in section 6.1 entails that

$$\Pr[110/R_x(A, B) \& R_y(B, C)] > \Pr[110/R_y(A, B) \& R_x(B, C)]$$

for each x, y such that $x < y$.

From this, the claimed inequality of expectations follows.

An entirely parallel argument would show that symplesiomorphies are evidence of genealogical relationship:

(9) $\text{Exp}[R(A, B)/001] < \text{Exp}[R(B, C)/001]$.

I want to emphasize that these results do not depend on assuming anything about abundance of homoplasy. The branching process depicted in figure 2 may be saturated with originations and reversals; it also may be true that change is exceedingly rare. The strict inequalities stated in (5), (6), (8), and (9) depend only on $e_3 \neq 1 - r_3$; nonstrict inequalities do not depend even on that.

The reader will perhaps now understand more fully why I have wanted to use the term "synapomorphy" to mean derived *matching* rather than derived *homology*. A *matching* confirms, even when one has no idea whether it is a *homology*. In section 4.6 I stressed that homologies are not observed in advance of the genealogies we wish to infer; if only presumed homologies could count as evidence of relationship, this would threaten to make genealogical inference *viciously circular*. The present point is that it is *false* that only presumed homologies can count as evidence. That which is available before genealogical relationships are known—matchings, not homologies—provides evidence pertinent to the inference problem at hand.

6.3. The Smith/Quackdoodle Problem

In the previous section, I argued that matches confirm, whether they are derived or ancestral. But which kind of matching confirms *more*? That is, suppose that three taxa are scored for two characters; the first character has the 110 distribution, whereas the second is distributed as 100. Proposition (8) says that the first character, taken by itself, favors (AB)C over A(BC); proposition (9) says that the second character tells in the opposite direction. The task is to discover how generally it will be true that (AB)C is better supported than A(BC), relative to the two characters taken together.

As before, I shall begin with pairs of observations, since that is simpler. The question is when a derived matching of two taxa indicates a closer degree of relatedness than an ancestral matching. That is, when is it true that $\text{Exp}[R(A, B)/11] < \text{Exp}[R(C, D)/00]$? The condition for this inequality, I shall argue, is a good indication (though not a perfect one) of when $\text{Exp}[R(A, B)/110 \& 100] < \text{Exp}[R(B, C)/110 \& 100]$.

A useful guide to intuitions is provided by the analogy with family names. Suppose you met two individuals (chosen at random) from the U.S. population, and found that both are named Smith. The main result of the previous section implies (within the model there assumed) that you should take this observation to support the hypothesis that the two individuals are more closely related to each other than might be expected *a priori*. But suppose that two other individuals are sampled, and both are found to be named Quackdoodle. This too confirms the hypothesis of relatedness. The question I now want to raise is this: Would you expect the two Smiths or the two Quackdoodles to be more closely related? Intuition suggests that the Quackdoodles are probably more closely related. A hunch as to why this is so is that *rare characters are better evidence of relatedness than common ones*.

The analogy with family names is not an argument, but a source of suggestive guesses. We cannot ignore the possibility that some special feature of the way names are transmitted underlies the above judgments about the evidential meaning of family names, and that no extrapolation from family names to taxonomic characters can be made. However, in this section I shall show that the intuitions just described are fairly accurate guides to the phylogenetic inference problem. I now shall derive the second main theorem: A shared apomorphy is better evidence of relatedness than a shared plesiomorphy precisely when the expected frequency of apomorphies within a character is lower than the expected frequency of plesiomorphies.

We imagine that two individuals (A and B) drawn at random from the tips of the tree in figure 2 exhibit state 1 and that two others (C and D), also drawn at random, exhibit state 0. The two character states, 0 and 1, recall, are states of a single character. Let p be the expected frequency at the tips of the tree of the apomorphic trait ($\text{Pr}[1] = p$) and q be the expected frequency of the plesiomorphic trait ($\text{Pr}[0] = q$), where $p + q = 1$. The Smith/Quackdoodle conjecture may be stated as follows:

(SQ-1) $\text{Exp}[R(A, B)]/11] < \text{Exp}[R(C, D)/00]$ if and only if
$p < q$.

The first step in the proof is to establish a generalization about the probability of any particular degree of relatedness:

(10)   For any i, $\text{Pr}(R_i/11) > \text{Pr}(R_i/00)$ if and only if
$(q - p)[\text{Pr}(10/R_i) - \text{Pr}(10)] < 0$.

By Bayes's theorem,

(11) $\Pr(R_i/11) > \Pr(R_i/00)$ if and only if
$\Pr(11/R_i)/\Pr(00/R_i) > \Pr(11)/\Pr(00)$.

Let us focus first on the likelihood terms in proposition (11), $\Pr(11/R_i)$ and $\Pr(00/R_i)$. The expected frequency (p) of 1's at the tips is also the probability that any branch extending from the root to the tips should terminate in the 1 state. Hence

$p = \Pr(11/R_i) + \Pr(10/R_i)$,
$q = \Pr(00/R_i) + \Pr(10/R_i)$.

This means that the two likelihood terms may be expressed as

(12) $\Pr(11/R_i) = p - \Pr(10/R_i)$, $\Pr(00/R_i) = q - \Pr(10/R_i)$.

I turn next to the unconditional probabilities of the observations in proposition (11). We know from proposition (1) that $\Pr(11/R_i)$ declines as i increases. Its lower bound is at $i = n$ and has the value p^2. Since $\Pr(11) = \sum \Pr(11/R_i)\Pr(R_i)$, it follows that $\Pr(11) > p^2$. Symmetrically, $\Pr(00) > q^2$. And so $\Pr(10) = \Pr(01) < pq$. This may be a little surprising; the idea of sampling without replacement may lead one to expect just the opposite. The reason, however, is that $\Pr(11)$ involves sampling twice from the same realization of the branching process. The branching process induces a correlation between items found at the tips of the same realization.[7]

Not only is it true that $\Pr(11) > p^2$ and $\Pr(00) > q^2$. In fact each exceeds the square of the singleton probability by the same amount:

(13) $\Pr(11) = p^2 + X$,
$\Pr(00) = q^2 + X$,
$\Pr(10) = pq - X$,
$\Pr(01) = pq - X$.

Propositions (12) and (13) allow (11) to be rewritten as

(14) $\Pr(R_i/11) > \Pr(R_i/00)$ if and only if
$[p - \Pr(10/R_i)]/[q - \Pr(10/R_i)] > (p^2 + X)/(q^2 + X)$.

The right side of the biconditional simplifies to

$(q - p)[\Pr(10/R_i) - (pq - X)] < 0$.

From this, proposition (10) follows.

---

7. Population geneticists may see an analogy here with Wahlund's Principle.

Now consider the right-hand side of proposition (10). Recall from the discussion of proposition (7) in the previous section that $Pr(R_i/10)$ − $Pr(R_i)$ is negative for low values of i and positive for high values. By Bayes's theorem, the same holds true of $Pr(10/R_i)$ − $Pr(10)$. Proposition (10) implies that if $q > p$, then $Pr(R_i/11) > Pr(R_i/00)$ for small values of i, but that the reverse is true for large values. This means that if $q > p$, then $Exp(R(A, B)/11) < Exp(R(C, D)/00)$. On the other hand, if $q < p$, then $Pr(R_i/11) < Pr(R_i/00)$ for small values of i, but the reverse is true for large values. So if $q < p$, then $Exp(R(A, B)/11) > Exp(R(C, D)/00)$. This establishes the Smith/Quackdoodle conjecture (SQ-1).

The next task is to establish a Smith/Quackdoodle theorem for three taxa. A natural extension of the result just obtained for two taxa to the case of three would be as follows:

(SQ-2) $Exp[R(A, B)/110 \& 100] < Exp[R(B, C)/110 \& 100]$
          if and only if $p < q$.

In the appendix to this chapter (section 6.8) I show that (SQ-2) is not precisely correct, though it is rather close. What I do establish is that a synapomorphy deserves more weight than a symplesiomorphy if $p \leqslant q$, but that there are circumstances in which a synapomorphy deserves *less* weight than a symplesiomorphy. When this is true, it will be the case that $p > q$. For the duration of this chapter, I shall refer to the upshot of these proofs as "the" Smith/Quackdoodle result: A synapomorphy (110) deserves more weight than a symplesiomorphy (100) precisely when apomorphies have a lower expected frequency than plesiomorphies. Fine-tuning and technical qualifications I consign to the appendix.

In the previous section, I established a point of symmetry between synapomorphy and symplesiomorphy—both confirm hypotheses of relationship. I now have a condition under which a synapomorphy deserves more weight than a symplesiomorphy and a symmetrical condition under which the reverse is true. The matching theorem of section 6.2 makes no mention of the difference between ancestral and derived characters. And even the Smith/Quackdoodle theorem does not reveal how character polarity plays any direct role in affecting the evidential significance of character matching. The Smith/Quackdoodle result states its criterion in terms of the expected frequency of characters at the tips of the tree; it does not explicitly mention the character state found at the root. For this reason, these two theorems may be termed "ahistorical."

This does not mean that character polarity makes no difference, only that I have yet to describe its significance. It now is time to see how character polarity affects when the ahistorical criterion established in the Smith/Quackdoodle theorem is satisfied.

6.4. History Redux

In the model here considered, in which all characters have the same suite of branch transition probabilities, the criterion for a synapomorphy to be more informative about phylogenetic relationships than a symplesiomorphy is that the expected frequency of apomorphies (p) be less than that of plesiomorphies (q). How might one determine whether this criterion is satisfied? Two general strategies are available here: *observation* and *theory*.

Sampling from the tips of the tree will provide evidence as to whether 1 or 0 predominates within a given character. From the sampled taxa we infer what the actual frequency is among all the taxa at the tips. A likelihood inference would indicate that if 1's are in the minority among the sampled taxa, then the best guess is that 1's are in the minority across the whole of the tree.

But this does not state a conclusion as to whether $p < q$. These quantities, recall, are *expected* frequencies, not *actual* frequencies. One and the same tree, with a single suite of transition probabilities, can generate different actual frequencies of 1 s and 0 s at the tips. A systematist examining the distribution of a single character across the tips is examining just one possible result of this branching process. Nevertheless, it seems clear (though I have not proved it) that if 0 predominates in the sampled taxa, then this is evidence that $p < q$.

It is worth noticing that this likelihood inference is not statistically consistent for reasons that exactly parallel those pertaining to the coin toss example in section 5.4. The systematist, trapped in the real world, can only look at a single realization of the branching process. It is possible that repeated sampling (with replacement) from the tips of this single realization will converge on a false estimate of whether 1's or 0's have the higher expected frequency, since those expected frequencies sum over all possible realizations, not just the actual one. However, I do not think this means that the observed frequencies of 1's and 0's in a character are evidentially meaningless. Here, then, is a biological case of likelihood without consistency.

A more "theoretical" approach to the problem of inferring whether $p < q$ might focus on the fact that the expected frequency of 1's at the tips is also the probability that a branch extending from the root to the tips will terminate in the 1 state; $p < q$ means that such a branch will more probably end in state 0 than in state 1.

There is no unconditional guarantee that 0 must remain the majority character (in expectation) at the end of the process just because the process began in state 0. Such a guarantee, in conjunction with the Smith/Quackdoodle theorem, would imply that a synapomorphy *always* provides better evidence than a symplesiomorphy, thus providing an absolute vindication of a fundamental asymmetry posited by cladistic methodology. But this guarantee is simply not available. I now shall investigate the range of parameter values within which a tree beginning in state 0 can be expected to retain a majority of 0's at the tips.

The expected frequency of 1's at the tips is the probability that a branch will end in state 1, given that it begins in state 0, with n generations in between. Figure 17 and the notation used to discuss it would allow this probability to be defined as a function of e_k and r_k ($k = 1, 2, 3$). However, I now shall describe this probability in a quite different way—not in terms of those branch (or "stage") transition probabilities, but in terms of *instantaneous* transition probabilities.

Let us divide this n-generation process into a very large number of very brief temporal intervals. Let there be N of these. The probability of going from 0 to 1 in one of these intervals is u and the probability of going from 1 to 0 is v; I call each of these "instantaneous" probabilities to emphasize the fact that they are not branch (as in figure 2) or stage (as in figure 17) transition probabilities.[8] Since the intervals are short, we can assume that u and v are each less than 0.5 (in fact we could also assume that they are *tiny*, but that will not be necessary). There is no assumption that u and v are equal in value, however. Notice that this formulation assumes not just that transition probabilities are *uniform*, as I have done heretofore, but that they are *constant*.

A branch may end in a state different from the one in which it began by making any odd number of changes; likewise, it may exhibit the same state at the end that it exhibited at the beginning by changing zero or any even number of times. The probabilities of these branch events must take all these possibilities into account. They may be expressed as functions of u, v, and N as follows:

$$(16) \quad Pr_N[0 \to 0] = v/(u + v) + (1 - u - v)^N[u/(u + v)] = q,$$
$$Pr_N[0 \to 1] = u/(u + v) - (1 - u - v)^N[u/(u + v)] = p,$$
$$Pr_N[1 \to 0] = v/(u + v) - (1 - u - v)^N[v/(u + v)],$$
$$Pr_N[1 \to 1] = u/(u + v) + (1 - u - v)^N[v/(u + v)].$$

Here "$Pr_N[x \to y]$" denotes the probability that a branch that is N units long will end in state y, given that it began in state x ($x, y = 0, 1$). Note that though the instantaneous probabilities (u, v) of change are tiny, this by itself leaves open what the probability is that a branch may end in a

---

8. "Instantaneous" is not the precise term, since the instants of time involved, though very small, still have finite duration. "Momentary" would be more accurate, though less graphic.

state different from the one in which it began. The effect of stipulating that u, $v < 0.5$ is that $Pr_N[0 \rightarrow 0]$ and $Pr_N[1 \rightarrow 1]$ monotonically decline as N increases, whereas $Pr_N[0 \rightarrow 1]$ and $Pr_N[1 \rightarrow 0]$ monotonically increase.[9]

To discover the circumstances in which 1 can be expected to be less common than 0 at the tips of the tree (i.e., after N units of time), we must compare $Pr_N[0 \rightarrow 1]$ and $Pr_N[0 \rightarrow 0]$. The relationship of these two quantities is depicted in figure 19. Each of the three graphs shows how a branch's probability of ending with 0 or 1, given that it began in state 0, depends on u, v, and N.

In all three cases, the initial generations of the process can be expected to have a majority of taxa exhibiting the ancestral form, regardless of how u and v are related. However, as the process continues, the relationship of u and v starts to play a more determining role. If $u < v$, then 0 remains more probable than 1 and so the expectation throughout such a process is that 0 will be in the majority ($p < q$). If $u = v$, the two expected frequencies asymptotically approach each other. And with $u > v$, the expectation is that 0 will become a minority character if the process unfolds long enough. In all three cases, the expected frequency of 1's asymptotically approaches $u/(u + v)$ and that of 0's approaches $v/(u + v)$; note that these limits are independent of whether the process began in state 0 or 1.

The following table summarizes these conclusions:

	Little Time	Lots of Time
$u < v$	$p < q$	$p < q$
$u = v$	$p < q$	$p < q$
$u > v$	$p < q$	$p > q$

The entry for the case in which $u = v$ and there is lots of time is $p < q$ because I assume that the time elapsed is finite; it is only in the infinite limit that $p = q$ when $u = v$. Note also that if $u > v$, then the difference between "little time" and "lots of time" depends on the values of u and v. In this case, the expectation is that more time will be required for the system to reach the crossover point where $p = q$ if u and v are small than if they are large.

When conjoined to the Smith/Quackdoodle theorem, these results imply that there are five cases in which a synapomorphy provides better evidence than a symplesiomorphy (because $p < q$) and one case in which a symplesiomorphy deserves more weight than a synapomorphy (because $p > q$).

These results throw light on the idea that parsimony depends on the

9. This model describes character evolution as a two-state Markov chain (Feller [1966, vol. 1, p. 432]); it is formally the same as standard mutation process models in population genetics.

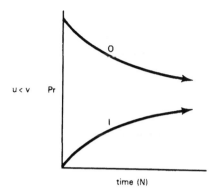

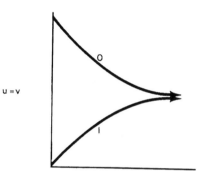

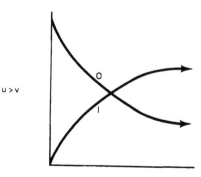

Figure 19.
If the branching process displayed in figure 2 begins in state 0, is it to be expected that 0 will remain the majority character? The answer to this question depends on the relationship of u and v and on the amount of time (N) that the process is allowed to unfold.

assumption that homoplasy is rare. The superiority of synapomorphy over symplesiomorphy, which is central to the idea of parsimony, depends on whether $p < q$. The abundance of homoplasy, I take it, may be measured by the expected number of changes that a trait experiences in the entire branching structure from which the systematist samples. Roughly speaking, this quantity increases as N increases and as u and v increase. How is the inequality $p < q$ related to the question of whether N, u, and v are large or small?

Figure 19 permits the following conclusions: If $u \leqslant v$, then $p < q$ regardless of whether N, u, and v are large or small. However, where $u > v$, $p < q$ does depend on N, u, and v being small.

These conclusions concern the direction of an inequality, not its magnitude. The Smith/Quackdoodle theorem says *when* a synapomorphy provides more evidence than a symplesiomorphy; it does not provide a measure of *how much* they differ in evidential value. A not implausible conjecture, though, is that a synapomorphy matters more than a symplesiomorphy to the degree that p is less than q.

If this is right, then making N, u, and v small does have an effect on the *degree to which* a synapomorphy deserves more weight than a symplesiomorphy. Notice that in all three cases displayed in figure 19, Pr(0) exceeds Pr(1) most when N is small. But making N small for given values of u and v has the same effect on p and q as making u and v small, while holding N fixed. So abundance of homoplasy does diminish the degree to which a synapomorphy should be valued over a symplesiomorphy.

Parsimony's absolute dismissal of symplesiomorphies as evidentially meaningless is not sustained within the model investigated here. Yet the idea that a synapomorphy provides more evidence than a symplesiomorphy turns out to be true within a wide range of parameter values. In addition, for a synapomorphy to provide more evidence than a symplesiomorphy, it is not essential that homoplasies be rare.

6.5. Character Polarity

To use cladistic parsimony to infer phylogenetic relationships, the investigator must know whether an observed matching between the characters of two taxa is ancestral or derived. The latter sort of matching, but not the former, is taken by that method as evidence of relatedness. In this section, I shall examine one of the main tools (some would say: *the* main tool) that cladistic theory provides for determining which state is ancestral and which derived. This technique for polarizing characters is the method of outgroup comparison. At the end of this section, other methods for polarizing characters will be considered briefly.

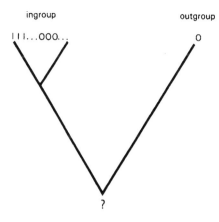

ingroup   outgroup

I I I...OOO...   O

?

Figure 20.
If there is just one outgroup, then the outgroup comparison method for polarizing characters asserts that the state of the outgroup is the best estimate of the ancestral condition.

Figure 20 depicts the main features of the outgroup method. The taxa whose phylogenetic relationships we wish to reconstruct are said to belong to the ingroup. We score these taxa and find that two states are present. I shall call these states 1 and 0, but with no assumption as yet that 1 means derived and 0 ancestral.

The biologist infers which state is ancestral by consulting the character state found in a taxon that is not a member of the ingroup, but is closely related to it. If that outgroup taxon is in state 0, one infers that the species at the root of the tree shown in figure 20 was in state 0 as well. The procedure becomes more complicated if several outgroups are known, whose character states differ. But one simple and central part of the method of outgroup comparison can be stated for the case in which there is just one outgroup to consider (or when all the outgroups exhibit the same character state): *The state of the outgroup is the best estimate of the state of the ancestor.*

It is sometimes argued that the method of outgroup comparison is circular (Bock [1981], Cartmill [1981], Patterson [1982], Sneath [1982]). A systematist wishing to use parsimony coupled with the method of outgroup comparison to infer phylogenetic relationships must already know something about phylogeny—after all, to say that O is an outgroup, relative to the ingroup taxa $I_1, I_2, \ldots, I_n$, is to say that the I's are more closely related to each other than any of them is to O. So to infer phylogenies, one must already know them.

The reply to this criticism is to grant that the outgroup method makes phylogenetic assumptions, but to deny that it is circular as a result. One wishes to infer the relationships that obtain *among* the members of the ingroup; one assumes that the ingroup forms a monophyletic group apart from the outgroup. This is not a case of assuming the very proposition one wishes to infer.[10]

If we restrict our attention to the single character under consideration, it is quite clear that this method is very much in the spirit of parsimony as a method of phylogenetic inference. When polarity is already known, parsimony says to prefer the phylogenetic hypothesis that minimizes the number of required changes in state. This preference for minimizing requirements of change, when applied to the problem of polarizing characters, yields the method of outgroup comparison. Whether one takes 0 or 1 as the ancestral form in figure 20, at least one change in state will be required to explain the character states found in the ingroup. Therefore, the only difference hypotheses of polarity make to the number of required changes concerns the branch leading from the root to the outgroup. By following the method of outgroup comparison, one ensures that no origination events are required on that branch.

I say that the method of outgroup comparison is "in the spirit" of cladistic parsimony, because I do not want to beg the question of whether the two differ in their presuppositions. Cladistic parsimony is a method for inferring phylogenetic relationships, given assumptions about character polarity. The method of outgroup comparison estimates character polarity, given the phylogenetic assumption (shown in figure 20) that the outgroup is an outgroup. These are, *prima facie*, quite different inference problems.[11] It may be that the two methods have identical presuppositions, but this is something that needs to be shown by an argument, not assumed at the outset.[12]

In the previous section, I examined the conditions under which a probabilistic inequality—$Pr_N(0 \rightarrow 0) > Pr_N(0 \rightarrow 1)$—holds true. This inequality might be termed a *forward inequality*: a branch begins in state 0 and the question is whether it will more probably end in state 0 or in state 1. The method of outgroup comparison requires us to consider a quite different relationship, which I term the *backward inequality*. We need to discover when $Pr_N(0 \rightarrow 0) > Pr_N(1 \rightarrow 0)$, a relationship that is logically in-

10. Recall the parallel point argued in section 4.6 about the distinction between observation and hypothesis: it is not essential that observation statements be *absolutely* theory neutral. But if an observation statement is to provide evidence for or against a hypothesis, it must be possible to reach a verdict on the truth or falsehood of the observation statement without already assuming that the hypothesis in question is true.

11. See Sober [1989] for discussion of the difference between inferring the existence of a common cause and inferring the state of that common cause, given the assumption that it exists.

12. See Watrous and Wheeler [1981], Farris [1983], and Maddison, Donoghue, and Maddison [1984] for discussion of the relationship of parsimony and the method of outgroup comparison.

dependent of the forward inequality. Given that a branch of length N ends in the 0 state, is this result made more probable by the supposition that it began in state 0 or by the supposition that it began in state 1? The backward inequality compares the *likelihoods* of competing hypotheses about the state in which a branch began, given the observation of the state in which it ends. Its pertinence to the problem of inferring character polarity by observing the state of the outgroup is patent.

The model of character change given in the previous section in terms of the instantaneous probabilities u and v entails this backward inequality. From (16), it follows that $Pr_N[0 \rightarrow 0] > Pr_N[1 \rightarrow 0]$ if and only if

$$v/(u + v) + (1 - u - v)^N[u/(u + v] \\ > v/(u + v) - (1 - u - v)^N[v/(u + v)].$$

This inequality holds, for any value of N, if u, $v < 0.5$. This latter assumption, recall, is entirely reasonable; the probability of change in a tiny interval of time must be less than 0.5. The two expressions in the above inequality approach each other as N approaches infinity; but for finite N, the inequality is strict. The same holds true, of course, for $Pr_N[1 \rightarrow 1] > Pr_N[0 \rightarrow 1]$. Note that the backward inequality entails the nonidentity $e_3 \neq 1 - r_3$, which was assumed in the consistency proof and the matching theorems of sections 6.1 and 6.2, respectively.[13]

The difference between the highly contingent forward inequality and the extremely robust backward inequality might be put this way: Given that 0 is the state at the root, it may or may not be probable that 0 will be the majority character at the tips. This depends on the relationship of u and v and on the amount of time (figure 19). However, given that 0 is the majority character at the tips, it is likely that 0 was the state at the root. This fact about likelihood is independent of the values of u, v, and N.

So if polarizing characters only required one to attend to the state of a single outgroup, then a perfectly general likelihood rationale would be available for the method of outgroup comparison. This rationale is even more general than the one provided by the Smith/Quackdoodle theorems for thinking that a synapomorphy provides better evidence than a symplesiomorphy. Within the model explored here, a synapomorphy is worth more than a symplesiomorphy precisely when $p < q$. But no such assumption is needed to guarantee the truth of the backward inequality.

The present model provides no prior probabilities for different hypotheses about polarity. Because of this, I have considered the likelihoods of hypotheses about polarity, not their probabilities. Naturally, if priors

13. The backward inequality also holds for a branch that has one pair of values for u and v initially and switches to a second pair of values subsequently. No assumption of rate constancy is required here.

could be placed on hypotheses about polarity, they, in conjunction with the backward inequality, would yield conclusions about the posterior probabilities.

I should stress that this argument for how the initial state of a branch is to be reconstructed from its end state is entirely independent of how much change is expected to occur in between. It is true that postulating a 0 beginning for a branch ending in the 0 state requires no intervening changes. *If* change were extremely improbable, that would suffice to justify the hypothesis that the branch began in state 0, given the observation that it ended in state 0. But sufficiency is not necessity. The parameters u, v, and N may be as high as you please (as long as u, $v < 0.5$), so that the expected number of changes[14] on a branch is also as high as you please; even then, the backward inequality remains correct. Here is a clear case in which minimizing assumptions is not the same as assuming minimality (section 4.4).

Another feature of the outgroup method is also illuminated by the backward inequality. If only one outgroup is considered, it is best to choose one that is very closely related to the ingroup. Note that this preference minimizes the duration of the outgroup branch. In so doing the ratio $\Pr_N(0 \to 0)/\Pr_N(1 \to 0)$ is maximized. Reducing the size of N increases the weight of evidence favoring the hypothesis that the state of the outgroup is the ancestral form; if the size of N is increased, the likelihood ratio asymptotically approaches unity.

These remarks about the backward inequality should not be taken to vindicate totally the method of outgroup comparison, even for the simplified problem investigated here, in which there is a single outgroup. The likelihoods of the different possible states of the root must be considered relative to the states found in the *ingroup*, not just relative to the state of the outgroup. In figure 20, we must consider how assigning 0 or 1 as the state of the root affects the probability that the tips of the tree will exhibit the mixture of 1's and 0's found there, not just how that assignment affects the probability that the outgroup will exhibit character state 0.

To see why this larger consideration can make a difference, let us suppose that $u \ll v$, so that any branch of length i will be such that $\Pr_i(0 \to 1)$ is not only very small, but is much smaller than $\Pr_i(1 \to 0)$. I assume here that the values of u and v attaching to the outgroup branch also attach to branches in the ingroup. In this circumstance, the likelihood that the root is in state 1 can exceed the likelihood that it is in state 0, even though the outgroup is in state 0. For if the root were in state 1, no 0-to-1 transitions

---

14. The formula for the expected number of changes is $2Nuv/(u + v) + [1 - (1 - u - v)^n](u^2 - uv)/(u + v)^2$. Note that if $u = v$, the expected number of changes is Nu. I owe this formula to Carter Denniston (personal communication).

would ever have to occur; however, if it were in state 0, there would have to be at least one of these very improbable events.

This suggests that the method of outgroup comparison depends on more than the unproblematic backwards inequality just discussed. By treating a 0-to-1 and a 1-to-0 transition required on an ingroup branch as equally unproblematic, the method assumes that u and v are roughly comparable in value. Note that this assumption is not required for a synapomorphy to deserve more weight than a symplesiomorphy, according to the Smith/Quackdoodle theorem. Here is a respect in which the method of outgroup comparison and a fact about the use of parsimony to reconstruct phylogenetic hypotheses differ in their presuppositions.

In the previous section, I identified a single circumstance in which parsimony errs in thinking that a synapomorphy is worth more than a symplesiomorphy. A tree that begins in state 0 and goes through the branching process for sufficiently many generations will be such that $p > q$ at the tips if $u > v$. In this case, a 110 character will be worth *less* than a character distributed as 100. So if you *knew* the characters' polarity and let parsimony be your guide, you would err in valuing a synapomorphy more than a symplesiomorphy.

However, suppose polarity is not known in advance, but is to be inferred by the outgroup method. Since $p > q$, chances are that the outgroup will be in state 1, not in state 0. If this more probable event turns out to be true, then the outgroup method will lead one to infer (erroneously) that 1 is the state of the root. And from this, parsimony will conclude (erroneously) that 110 is a symplesiomorphy and 100 a synapomorphy. These two errors then engender the conclusion that 100 deserves more weight—which is correct, since $p > q$.

The condition for a synapomorphy to matter more than a symplesiomorphy is $p < q$. In the model branching process assumed here, this inequality applies to the branches leading to the outgroup, as well as to those leading to the ingroup. So if an outgroup taxon is sampled at random, it will probably display the majority character state. The method of outgroup comparison therefore makes it probable that the state assumed to be ancestral is the one that is a majority character at the tip of the tree.

There is no guarantee that the majority character is ancestral. But if one is going to use parsimony, it is a good thing (in the present model) to assume that majority characters are ancestral, whether they are or not. For the Smith/Quackdoodle theorem asserts that it is $p < q$, not the ancestral/derived distinction, that is fundamental.

This suggests that cladistic methodology is more than the sum of its parts. Under some parameter values, the outgroup method has good likelihood credentials for recovering polarity; and under some parameter values, parsimony is right in treating a synapomorphy as worth more than a symplesiomorphy. But the two components of cladistic methodology may be better when taken together than either is when taken alone. Within the model explored here, *it is probable that a match judged by cladistic principles to be apomorphic will provide more evidence than one judged to be plesiomorphic.* The irony is that this will be true whether the judgment about polarity is right or not. This result, it should be noted, is independent of whether $p < q$.

I noted at the beginning of this section that methods besides outgroup comparison have been used to polarize characters. The main ones are the *ontogenetic criterion*, the *paleontological criterion*, and, to a lesser extent, the *functional criterion.*[15]

The ontogenetic criterion explicitly relies on a process assumption— the first of Von Baer's laws: "The general features of a large group of animals appear earlier in the embryo than the special features" (translation due to Gould [1977, p. 56]). So, for example, the law says that in the development of a primate, traits common to all animals will be found earlier in the embryo than ones common just to mammals, and these in turn will occur before traits common only to primates (Ridley [1986, pp. 66–68]). Let us denote these ontogenetic stages as $a \rightarrow a' \rightarrow a''$. A cladistic interpretation of this law provides a rule for polarizing characters: more general means relatively ancestral and more specific means relatively derived.

Von Baer's law is taken to depend on the assumption that ontogenetic patterns evolve according to the rule of *terminal addition*: new characters appear by being added to the end of ontogenetic development, rather than by insertions, deletions, or rearrangements occurring in midstream (Gould [1977]).

So, for example, the law implies that there are characters in the ontogenies of a trout, a bear, and a chimp that exhibit the following form:

Trout $a \rightarrow a$
Bear $a \rightarrow a'$
Chimp $a \rightarrow a'$

By polarizing characters in accordance with the ontogenetic criterion and applying parsimony to the result, one obtains the conclusion that the bear and the chimp belong to a monophyletic group that does not include the trout. The idea here is that a' in the adult stage is derived and a is ancestral because it is a, not a', that is found universally in the embryo.

One class of counterexamples to the rule of terminal addition involves *neotony*. This occurs when the ontogenetic trajectory is modified so that the adult stage of the new organism retains the juvenile form found in the

15. Crisci and Stuessy [1980] and Stevens [1980] provide useful reviews of the main methods.

ancestral organism. For example, the ancestral pattern is $a \rightarrow a'$, whereas the derived pattern is $a \rightarrow a$. Here the ontogenetic criterion will reach a mistaken conclusion about character polarity.[16]

Although numerous violations of Von Baer's law are well documented,[17] biologists usually agree that the law is reliable enough to provide some guidance about character polarity (Gould [1977], Fink [1982], Kluge [1985], Ridley [1986]). This is not to deny that there is need for both more theory and more systematic observation to substantiate this conclusion. A general theory of development, if such could be had, might explain when and how often Von Baer's law should be true. In addition, intensive comparative work should offer a more fully developed picture of how often counterexamples to the ontogenetic criterion actually occur.

I now turn to another method for polarizing characters, which also involves an obvious process assumption. This is the paleontological criterion. It is a matter of definition that the ancestral form of a character was present before the derived form made its appearance. The paleontological criterion says that the dates of fossils correspond to the order of evolution: If the earliest fossil instance of the 1 form is more recent than the earliest instance of the 0 form, then 1 should be judged derived and 0 ancestral. If the fossil record were complete, the paleontological criterion would be umproblematic. And even with incompleteness, the criterion would be reasonable if fossilization occurred at random. If the probability of leaving a fossil trace were independent of the organism's character state and the time at which it lived, then fossils might provide a reasonably representative sample of the groups to which they belong. However, both these *ifs* have been thought by many biologists to be too big to swallow (Schaeffer, Hecht, and Eldredge [1972], Patterson [1981], Janvier [1984]). They conclude that the paleontological criterion is extremely weak, if not entirely useless. On the other hand, some biologists hold that the paleontological criterion is reliable enough so that totally writing it off would be to reject a useful source of data (Paul [1982], Ridley [1986]).

The *functional criterion* for polarizing characters has also been controversial. Suppose that natural selection is assumed to be the major force governing the way a given character changes in the taxa under study, and that one takes seriously a model of natural selection that says that evolving from 0-to-1 is much more probable than evolving from 1-to-0. For example, Ridley [1986, pp. 131–137] suggests that vestigial organs should be judged derived by this criterion. He argues that it is very hard for a vestigial eye to evolve into a functioning eye, but much easier for a working eye to lose its function. Cracraft [1981], on the other hand, argues that

16. My thanks to Ted Garland (personal communication) for clarification on this point.
17. See Gould [1977] and Kluge and Strauss [1985] for a taxonomy of such violations.

appealing to adaptive scenarios of this kind is to build a house on sand. He holds that the ideas about selection on which they rely are not well confirmed, and so the conclusions about polarity they imply should not be given much weight.

The reader may recognize that the functional criterion involves an asymmetry in transition probabilities that I discussed earlier in this section. I pointed out that an extreme asymmetry in the values of u and v can undermine the implications of the outgroup method. Even though the outgroup is in state 0, likelihood will favor assuming that the root was in state 1, if 0-to-1 transitions are much harder to achieve than transitions in the opposite direction. The conclusion I reached was that the outgroup method assumes that u and v are approximately equal in value.

The functional criterion depends on a biological argument for thinking that 0-to-1 transitions differ dramatically in probability from changes in the opposite direction. The outgroup criterion rejects this asymmetry and the biological assumptions on which it rests. But this does not mean that the outgroup method assumes nothing at all. To assume that u and v are roughly the same in value is just as much an assumption as assuming that u and v are grossly different.[18] All methods for polarizing characters depend on biological assumptions.

When two methods for polarizing characters conflict, which should be used? I venture no universal and timeless conclusion. It may be true that no conclusion about the comparable worth of these methods can be reached *in general*; different methods may deserve different weights in different circumstances. In addition, as theories are developed about underlying evolutionary processes, the evidential status of these different considerations may change. What is at one time a weak line of evidence may later become stronger if it is bolstered by a well-confirmed process theory.

But beyond these points, I see a theoretical difficulty facing the task of comparing different methods for polarizing characters. It is not difficult to see how *a single method* may vary in the weight it should be accorded from application to application and from time to time. But how should one compare the merits of *different methods* when they conflict? It does not resolve this difficulty to point out that *one* of the methods is fallible, since *both* in fact have this property.

The difficulty here goes beyond the problems detailed in this book for comparing parsimony and overall similarity. Although comparing these two approaches is hardly a simple problem, it is fairly clear that their rela-

---

18. In probability theory, it is standardly recognized that the principle of indifference is incoherent: one cannot assign two events equal probability just because one sees no reason to assign them different probabilities. The systematics literature would benefit from seeing this principle for the fallacy that it is.

tive merits depend on the same set of facts about the evolutionary process. This is not to say that they are equally (or unequally) adequate, only that an evolutionary model that has implications about the adequacy of one method will probably have implications about the adequacy of the other. But the adequacy of the outgroup method, the paleontological criterion, and the ontogenetic criterion all seem to turn on *different* evolutionary issues. We seem to confront here an apples-and-oranges problem.

This problem may not be insurmountable. Perhaps there are evolutionary variables that affect the adequacy of all three criteria at once. And perhaps detailed, though separate, theories about the processes pertinent to each can be developed that will settle this comparative problem. But the present situation in biology strikes me as one in which we know very little about the theoretical basis for comparing methods for polarizing characters.

This is not to say that all comparisons are groundless. There may be local biological arguments concerning specific taxa and specific characters that are now quite compelling. But the goal of formulating a *general* assessment of the relative strengths and limitations of these methods has yet to be fully achieved.

6.6. Robustness

The results of this chapter do not constitute a general justification of cladistic techniques of phylogenetic reconstruction. Indeed, they do not even provide a full justification of those techniques within the context of the model under investigation. Rather, I have shown that certain central ideas in cladistic philosophy have a fairly general probabilistic rationale within the model branching process considered.

In section 4.4, I considered an argument developed by Farris [1983] that attempts to show that parsimony does not assume that homoplasies are rare. Farris considered a data set made of eleven characters; the first ten have the 110 distribution, whereas the eleventh is distributed as 011 (where "0" means ancestral and "1" derived). Farris argued that this data set favors (AB)C over A(BC), regardless of whether homoplasies are common or rare. Although I criticized Farris's argument for this conclusion, we now can see that something like his conclusion is available within the context of the present process model.

A synapomorphy (110) is evidence of phylogenetic relationship regardless of the expected number of changes that occur in the tree. This is the matching theorem of section 6.2. Furthermore, since the model assumes that the characters evolve independently and have the same transition probabilities, a principle of equal weighting of synapomorphies is correct. This means that the eleven-character data set that Farris considered has precisely the significance he claimed, and that this significance is independent of the issue of whether homoplasies are common or rare.

Farris also argued that increasing the number of homoplasies affects the magnitude, but not the direction, of inequalities in evidential support. If homoplasies are rare, then (AB)C is far better supported than A(BC), relative to the eleven character data set; as homoplasies become more common, the difference in support declines. But in no case does A(BC) become better supported than A(BC). This conclusion, also, receives a justification within the model here explored. The backward inequality ($e < 1 - r$), which suffices to justify the matching theorem, does not require rarity of change. Yet, the magnitude of this inequality is greatest when the expected number of changes is small.

Details aside, the difference in strategy between Farris's argument and my own concerns the role of a process model. Farris's argument was pretty much unconditional on a model. Mine relies on a model to obtain the relevant probabilities. It is worth bearing in mind that the model I have used is highly idealized: I assumed that branching is regular and bifurcating and that characters evolve independently and at uniform rates.

One cannot conclude from this that *parsimony* assumes any of these constraints on the evolutionary process. These were assumptions that *I* made; no argument has been given to show that they are essential to obtain the conclusion reached.[19] Still, the question of robustness looms large: can it be shown that the eleven characters favor (AB)C over A(BC) in the context of other models?

I want to emphasize that the independence assumption and the assumption that the characters have the same transition probabilities play a critical role in justifying the rule "one synapomorphy, one vote." If characters 1–10 were constrained to evolve in tandem, then they would not count as ten separate and independent sources of evidence. Rather, in the extreme case, they would count as a single character, observed ten different times. If so, the eleventh character might deserve ten times the weight assigned to any of the first ten, in which case (AB)C and A(BC) would be equally well supported.

Likewise, if the eleven characters evolved independently, but differed in their transition probabilities, it might turn out that the eleventh character deserves more weight than the first ten combined. The Smith/Quackdoodle theorems of section 6.3 show that one matching deserves more weight than another precisely when the first involves a character

---

19. Recall the distinction drawn in section 5.6 between *the investigator's* making an assumption in an argument, and the argument's establishing that *a method of inference* makes a given assumption.

that is expected to be rarer than the second. What does this imply about the eleven-character example?

My conjecture is that the main drift of the Smith/Quackdoodle theorems applies to the present problem. If p_1 is the frequency of an apomorphy within each of the first ten characters, then the probability that a taxon will have 1's on all of the first ten characters is $(p_1)^{10}$. If two taxa *both* have 1's on all ten characters, this is a *rare* matching indeed. Let p_2 be the expected frequency of apomorphies in character eleven. My conjecture is that the first ten characters deserve more weight than the eleventh if $(p_1)^{10} < p_2$.

Biologists have long held that conservative characters are better indices of phylogenetic relationship than highly labile ones. Evolutionists who believe that natural selection is a very powerful modifier of organisms often conclude from this that adaptive characters are less reliable guides to genealogy than nonadaptive ones. An adaptive similarity may be a convergence effected by natural selection, but a nonadaptive similarity is less easily explained away.[20]

The model explored here helps show what is right and wrong about these intuitions. According to the Smith/Quackdoodle results, it is not the magnitudes of u and v that determine the degree to which a similarity reflects phylogenetic relationship. Rather, the criterion is the expected frequency of the character in question. These issues are related, but they are not the same.

Suppose, for example, that u and v are equal in value. Given enough time, the expected frequencies of apomorphies and plesiomorphies will be about the same, regardless of whether u and v are both large or both small. For in the limit, the expected frequency goes to 0.5, regardless of the magnitudes of the two transition probabilities. On the other hand, for a fixed amount of time (N), a way to get $p \ll q$ is to have u and v both be small. In this case, we expect the apomorphic form of a highly conservative character to be rare.

As another example, compare two characters. The first has high values for u and v, but small N; the second has low u and v, and large N. The first character is the more labile. Yet, the two characters may have precisely the same expected frequency of apomorphies at the tips, and so, from the point of view of the Smith/Quackdoodle theorems, precisely the same evidential significance. Also worth considering are two characters that evolve for the same number of generations. The first has small u and large v, whereas the latter has small values for both u and v. The former, I sup-

---

20. The pleiotropic correlates of an adaptive character have the same lability as the adaptive character itself. So the contrast should not be between adaptive and nonadaptive characters, but between adaptive characters and their pleiotropic correlates on the one hand, and independent neutral characters on the other.

pose, is more labile. Yet its apomorphies are expected to be rarer than those of the second character.

As a third example, consider a tree that has evolved for so large an amount of time that the characters are probably close to their expected equilibrium frequencies. This means that a character with $u = 0.001$ and $v = 0.009$ will have virtually the same expected frequency of 1's and 0's as a character[21] with $u = 0.0001$ and $v = 0.0009$. The former character is less conservative, but that difference makes no difference if the system evolves for a sufficiently long time.

The model here considered is highly favorable to the cladistic idea that parsimony correctly identifies the best phylogenetic hypothesis, given a data set (like the one in Farris's example) made of conflicting synapomorphies, where those characters are assumed to evolve independently and to deserve equal weight. However, I must emphasize that the assignment of equal weights involves biological assumptions just as much as the assignment of unequal weights. The idea of "one synapomorphy, one vote" is not presupposition free; the point is that its use to evaluate conflicting synapomorphies is free of the assumption that homoplasies are rare.

Matters are rather less straightforward when we focus on another central element in cladistic theory—that symplesiomorphies are evidentially meaningless. Taken at its word, this is simply false within the model considered; the matching theorem of section 6.2 pertains to ancestral matches just as much as to derived ones. The idea then arises that cladistic practice would make sense if symplesiomorphies, though not totally informationless, were much less informative than synapomorphies. This led me to consider the Smith/Quackdoodle problem in section 6.3.

I argued that under a wide (though not universal) range of parameter values, a 110 synapomorphy provides more evidence than a 100 symplesiomorphy. This asymmetry reverses only when $u > v$ and there is lots of time. If polarity is established by the outgroup criterion (when only a single outgroup is examined), the case for according greater weight to a matching judged to be synapomorphic than to one judged to be symplesiomorphic is stronger still. I argued in section 6.5 that this is probably correct if $u, v < 0.5$—a highly general circumstance.

But even this result is a far cry from assigning zero weight to any and all symplesiomorphies. In particular, the Smith/Quackdoodle theorem compares *one* synapomorphy (110) and *one* symplesiomorphy (100). What result should we expect if the problem is to evaluate a data set in which one synapomorphy (110) conflicts with *two* identically distributed symplesiomorphies (100 & 100)?

21. Recall that the expected frequency of apomorphies at equilibrium is $u/(u + v)$.

If a taxon's probablility of having a plesiomorphy on a character is q, then its chance of being plesiomorphic for two independent characters sharing the same suite of transition probabilities is q^2. When comparing the testimony of 110 and 100, the criterion for assigning the former a determining role is $p < q$. When comparing 110 and *two* 100 characters, the criterion for preferring (AB)C over A(BC) will be more stringent. I conjecture that it will be $p < q^2$, at least approximately. When a synapomorphy (110) conflicts with a set of symplesiomorphies all of the form 100, preferring (AB)C to A(BC) requires more and more restrictive assumptions as the number of symplesiomorphies increases. This may be defensible; if lots of plesiomorphies are observed, this may be evidence that the expected frequency of the apomorphic form is quite low. Nevertheless, the zero weight that parsimony assigns to symplesiomorphies must involve a nontrivial constraint on the biological process, if the model explored here is any guide.

Overall similarity assigns equal weight to synapomorphies and symplesiomorphies; parsimony assigns unequal weight to them, because it assigns zero weight to ancestral similarities. Equal weighting is by no means a consequence of the process model here assumed, but neither is the kind of unequal weighting that parsimony recommends. It seems safe to say that *heavier* weight should be placed on synapomorphies, but rather more difficult to say whether overall similarity or parsimony is closer to the mark. It is not impossible that data should be brought to bear on this question. Observation should indicate whether p and q are close together or far apart. Within the model, $p \ll q$ would favor parsimony, whereas approximately equal values would point towards overall similarity.

I noted in section 6.1 that both parsimony and overall similarity will be statistically consistent in the present model if three taxa are drawn at random from the tips and then scored for more and more characters. This means that in the limit, parsimony and overall similarity should not disagree. It follows that the Smith/Quackdoodle problem can arise in the model considered only because not enough characters have been sampled. If overall similarity and parsimony disagree in their evaluations of a finite data set drawn from real taxa, this may be due to sampling error. Or it may indicate that the model here assumed is unrealistic.

It may be wondered why it has been worth pursuing the Smith/Quackdoodle problem in a model that suggests that that problem should disappear for a sufficiently large data set. The reason is that it is of theoretical interest to see under what circumstances a synapomorphy deserves more weight than a symplesiomorphy. The hope is that the result obtained within this simple model will hold for other models, or will at least suggest an avenue of inquiry into that question in the context of different models.

The conclusions reached within the confines of the assumed model may be summarized as follows: Synapomorphies are evidence of phylogenetic relationship, whether or not homoplasies are rare. The same holds for symplesiomorphies. If polarity is decided by the outgroup method applied to a single outgroup, then a match judged to be synapomorphic deserves greater weight than one judged to be symplesiomorphic, again with no assumption required that homoplasies are rare. On the other hand, if one knew at the outset how to polarize characters, then a synapomorphy deserves more weight than a symplesiomorphy within a wide, though not universal, range of parameter values. What is more, a process falling within that range of values need not be such that homoplasies are rare.

This suffices, I think, to cast at least some doubt on the idea that cladistic parsimony assumes that homoplasies are rare. The method proceeds by preferring phylogenetic hypotheses that minimize assumptions of homoplasy, but this is not the same as assuming that homoplasies have been minimal.

It is a separate and more tenuous thesis that parsimony is "justified" within the model here considered. I do not claim this. Rather, what I have done is to examine some special features of the parsimony idea within this model branching process. I do not pretend that these few special features exhaust what there is to parsimony. Even if these parts of the parsimony idea were justified, we should not mistake the part for the whole.

For the remainder of this section, I want to speculate on how relaxing this or that assumption in the model would affect the results obtained within it.

What would one expect if the model were the same, but characters came in more than two states? My hunch is that increasing the number of character states makes it easier for the ancestral form to be more common than any other character. This should expand the range of values within which a synapomorphy deserves greater weight than a symplesiomorphy, a conclusion favorable to parsimony.

I suspect that the same holds true if we view the systematist as sampling from the tree's interior as well as from its tips. If the Smith/Quackdoodle criterion for giving heavier weight to synapomorphies holds true under this new sampling scheme, then there will be an even larger range of parameter values under which the derived form has a lower expected frequency than the ancestral form. The reason is that even if $u > v$, the early generations of the process will be such that the ancestral form is still expected to be the majority character. Sampling from the tree's interior brings such generations of the process into the population whose expected frequency of 1's and 0's is relevant. If so, it will take even longer for 1 to become the majority character.

What of the assumption that the branching process involves bifurcation at regular temporal intervals? An alternative would be the idea that a node's going extinct, persisting, bifurcating, trifurcating, etc., obeys some single probabilistic rule. Or one might imagine that different nodes have different chances for these branching events. My guess is that these variations will make no difference, as long as a node's probability of branching, going extinct, etc., is independent of its character state.

If they are not independent, then the branching process and the rules of character evolution will both affect the expected frequency of traits at the tips, which I conjecture will still be roughly criterial in this new process. For example, suppose that branching obeys a form of *species selection*; nodes in state 0 are apt to produce more daughter species than nodes in state 1.[22] This branching rule will serve to increase the frequency of trait 0 at the tips of the tree. The rules of character evolution may push in the same or the opposite direction, depending on the relationship of u and v.

Another simplification in the present treatment, whose significance I shall not venture to assess, is the fact I have focused on the problem of inferring the genealogical relationships of *three* taxa. Although three taxon statements are standardly regarded as the building blocks out of which multitaxon cladistic structures are built (Gaffney [1979], Eldredge and Cracraft [1980]), the question still arises of how properties of the inference problem for three taxa carry over to problems involving more species.

I turn, finally, to the idea of rate uniformity, which has two parts. First, there is the idea that all characters obey the same probabilistic rules of evolution. Second, there is the assumption that the rules governing a character's evolution in one part of the tree are the same as those applying elsewhere. Relaxing the first of these requirements is not terribly problematic. My remarks above about conservative versus labile characters concerned this issue. It is fairly straightforward to envisage how two characters may differ in frequency at the tips of the tree because they differ in their respective values of u and v. If the Smith/Quackdoodle idea remains criterial for this case, the same qualitative results should follow.

The other half of the rate uniformity assumption is more difficult to abandon. What can be said about parsimony and overall similarity if branches vary in their associated transition probabilities? One can invent examples in which matches *disconfirm*; 110 and 001 both favor A(BC) as opposed to (AB)C. For example, consider the two-generation bifurcating tree shown in figure 21. The length of each branch represents the probability of a 0-to-1 transition; evolution in the opposite direction is assumed

22. See Sober [1984c, section 9.4] for discussion of the concept of species selection.

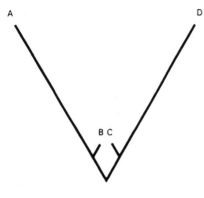

Figure 21.
Let branch lengths represent the probability of a 0-to-1 transition, assume 1-to-0 changes
are impossible, and let the root be in state 0. In this case, synapomorphies and symplesiomorphies both disconfirm hypotheses of relatedness.

to be impossible and 0 is assumed to be the ancestral state.[23] Sampling
three taxa from the tips, one may reason as follows. If you obtain two 1's
and a 0, it is probable that the two 1's are A and D and that the 0 came
from either B or C. On the other hand, if you obtain two 0's and a 1, it is
probable that the 0's came from B and C and the 1 came from A or D. This
is an epistemological nightmare for both parsimony and overall similarity.
I also suspect that it is possible to construct examples in which one sort of
matching reverses its evidential significance, but the other does not.

The way forward, however, is not to accumulate bizarre examples, but
to impose order on them in the context of a model. What is needed is a
model of how transition probabilities will be distributed on a tree. We
have explored the simple case in which all contemporaneous branches
have the same transition probabilities. A random model will, I suspect,
not affect the qualitative conclusions obtained before. If each branch is
assigned its transition probabilities by a random process, with all assignments being drawn from the same underlying distribution, then the previous results should remain in force.

The thing to construct is a nonrandom model—one that uses a biologically plausible reason for assigning different transition probabilities to
different branches. It is to be hoped that general patterns will emerge from
such models, and so the robustness of parsimony and overall similarity
may be compared.

23. This example is inspired by the one Felsenstein [1978] used to show that parsimony
can be statistically inconsistent. The issue here, however, is not consistency, but an inference as to which genealogical hypothesis is more probable in the light of the data.

In chapter 3 and 5 I contrasted two ways of addressing the problem of nuisance parameters. I criticized the best-case strategy and praised the procedure of constraining the nuisance parameters so that the full likelihood function can be evaluated. It is the latter sort of strategy that has been used in the present chapter; no values for u, v, and N, or for i and j, are estimated from the data. Rather, the model induces relationships among these parameters that allow certain inequalities in likelihoods to be derived. Althought this practice is superior to the best-case strategy as a device for treating the likelihoods of the hypotheses under test, it must be admitted that the model described in this chapter fails to take account of a relevant source of information. The data of character distributions provide evidence about the different branch transition probabilities that might obtain under the different cladistic hypotheses. For example, a set of characters that all show the 110 pattern suggests that rates of evolution on branches leading to A and B exceed those on branches leading to C. Yet, the model of the present chapter assumes, without attending to the observed character states of the three taxa, that rates are uniform across branches leading to the three taxa. It would be useful to investigate a model that exploits such information while avoiding the oversimplifications of the best-case strategy.

6.7. Models and Reality

It is hardly unprecedented in science that the intuitions of practitioners should not always coincide with the formalisms of theoreticians. An example of this conflict is provided by the disagreement between ecologists and population geneticists over the efficacy of group selection during the 1930s, 1940s, and 1950s. Although numerous ecologists thought they observed characters in populations that were advantageous to the group but deleterious to the individuals possessing them, population geneticists were largely skeptical of the existence of altruistic characters. Their reason, though, was theoretical, not observational. The models they considered indicated that altruism can evolve and be maintained only in very special circumstances.[24] Such a conflict between naturalists and theoreticians is not a sign that science has gone wrong, but is an inevitable and potentially fruitful consequence of science's division of intellectual labor.

Theoreticians inevitably work with simplified models. Natural phenomena typically are consequences of many effects, but a tractable model usually requires that all but a few of these be ignored. It is hoped that results for simple models extrapolate smoothly to more complex cases; but

---

24. A brief history of this debate, as well as a discussion of its conceptual ramifications, is provided in Sober [1984c].

this is not inevitable and is itself a subject for theoretical investigation. When theoretical results obtained for simple models clash with the intuitions of practitioners, two diagnoses are possible. The first is that the theoretical results for simple models really do carry over to more realistic cases, and so the intuitions of practitioners must be reschooled. The other possibility is that the results for the simple model do not extrapolate and are merely artifacts of the simplifications. Here it is the practitioners who should be taken seriously; they have a better intuitive feel for the phenomena than the grossly imperfect models provide.

The contemporary systematist may find it strange that I do not advocate dismissing all appeals to intuition with total contempt. The two revolutions in modern taxonomy both began with the idea that "intuition" is simply an excuse for substituting authoritarianism for rigor. Pheneticism pressed this idea with respect to the task of classification, cladism in the domain of phylogenetic reconstruction. In both instances, the overriding imperative was to formulate methods explicitly so that the consequences of applying them to data could be entirely unambiguous.

The task of clearly stating one's methods has been carried out with admirable success. But the problem of justification has lagged behind. We now have only the most preliminary picture of the scope and limits of the different methods of phylogenetic inference. All have occasionally been defended with arguments that are defective; and all have been attacked with arguments that are less than totally devastating. But neither sort of error either undermines or establishes the methods in question.

Parsimony has been criticized for assuming that homoplasies are rare. I very much doubt that this charge is true. Overall similarity has been criticized for according evidential significance to ancestral similarities. Yet it is by no means clear that symplesiomorphies are evidentially meaningless. However, to refute these criticisms does not suffice to justify the methods criticized.

Philosophy—empiricist philosophy, especially—has been misled by a mistaken picture of the relationship of the methods of science to its substance. How could science get off the ground, it has been thought, if the methods of science depend for their adequacy on empirical results? Method must be prior to theory if the scientific method is to issue in theories that are defensible.

In philosophy this idea has led epistemologists to formulations like the principle of induction and the principle of the common cause. Methodological principles are stated that purport to bring data to bear on hypotheses without the intervention of an empirical background theory. In systematics, the idea that method must be prior to theory has encouraged scientists to think that a method of phylogenetic inference should be justifiable without assuming anything much about evolution, save perhaps that observed diversity is the result of descent with modification.

It has been a principal theme of this book that no method of inference can bring data to bear on hypotheses without empirical presuppositions. Although this thesis may strike some methodologists as a discouraging one, it need not be. True, there can be no hope of establishing a method of phylogenetic inference that is legitimate no matter what the details of the evolutionary process happen to be. But the obverse point is that if methods have theoretical presuppositions, then methods can be improved as theory improves.

The idea of a presuppositionless "scientific method" implies that methodology is static and insensitive to what we learn about the world. But with theory and method linked by a subtle nexus of interdependence, progress on theories can be expected to improve our methods of inquiry.

Theories and methods may be explicitly connected by constructing and investigating theoretical models. Practicing systematists often feel in their bones that a given method of inference is correct and that others are mere houses of cards. Those of fainter heart often retreat to a position of "eclecticism," taking the compromise position that the different methods have their separate strengths and weaknesses. However, the latter position is no safer than the former, until a satisfactory argument is produced that identifies the scope and limits of the methods in question.

In the face of so much conviction about how methodology should be practiced, it is striking how insecure the theoretical foundations of phylogenetic inference continue to be. This is not for want of trying, of course. Nor does this book pretend to put the theoretical issues on a satisfactory basis. The positive theses I have advanced are both partial and preliminary. However, it is not too much to hope that the intuitions of practitioners and the formalisms of theoreticians can be brought into fruitful interaction. As theory and method grow together, so will our understanding of both the phylogenetic process and the methods appropriate for inferring its pattern.

6.8. Appendix: The Smith/Quackdoodle Theorem for Three Taxa

Three taxa (A, B, and C), sampled at random from the tips of the tree illustrated in figure 2 (p. 16), are scored for two characters. These characters are assumed to have the same suite of branch transition probabilities (so that the expected frequencies of 1's and 0's at the tree's tips for one character are the same for the other character). They are found to be distributed as 110 and 100, respectively. The first character favors the (AB)C grouping, while the second favors A(BC), by the matching theorems already established (section 6.2). What do the characters say, when taken together?

In section 6.3, I proved that the criterion for a derived matching to indicate closer relatedness than an ancestral matching, for the case of two taxa, is that the derived character be less common in expectation than the ancestral one. That is, where the expected frequencies of 1's and 0's at the tree's tips are p and q, respectively ($p + q = 1$), the first Smith/Quackdoodle theorem was that

(SQ-1) $\text{Exp}[R(A, B)/11] < \text{Exp}[R(C, D)/00]$ iff $p < q$

("iff" is shorthand for "if and only if"). Smooth extrapolation from the case of two taxa to the case of three would suggest that 110 deserves more weight than 100 precisely if a 1 is expected to be rarer at the top of the tree than a 0. That is, a natural guess would be that

(SQ-2) $\text{Exp}[R(A, B)/110 \,\&\, 100] < \text{Exp}[R(B, C)/110 \,\&\, 100]$
        iff $p < q$.

I will show that this conjecture is incorrect, though it is very close to the truth. What I shall prove is that

(SQ-3) $\text{Exp}[R(A, B)/110 \,\&\, 100] < \text{Exp}[R(B, C)/110 \,\&\, 100]$
        if $p \leqslant q$. If $p > q$ at the tip of the tree and the branching
        process is near equilibrium one generation after the root,
        then $\text{Exp}[R(A, B)/110 \,\&\, 100] > \text{Exp}[R(B, C)/110 \,\&\, 100]$.

I shall explain later precisely what I mean by "near equilibrium" in (SQ-3). For the moment, note that (SQ-3) does not cover all the cases that might arise; it does not say what will be true when $p > q$ at the tips, but the system is not near equilibrium in any generation. In establishing the first proposition in (SQ-3), I shall show one reason why (SQ-2) is not strictly correct; the case that shows this arises when $p = q$. Since (SQ-2) is simpler to state than (SQ-3), I shall initially formulate the conjectures to be investigated in terms of (SQ-2). By the end of the proof, however, what I shall establish is (SQ-3).

Let "R_i" express the proposition that A and B are i-related; let "R_j" express the proposition that B and C are j-related; let "R_k" express the proposition that A and C are k-related ($1 \leqslant i, j, k \leqslant n$). Note that if the true cladistic grouping is (AB)C, then $i < j = k$; if the relationship is A(BC), then $j < i = k$; and if the truth is (AC)B, then $k < i = j$. Bayes's theorem allows (SQ-2) to be rewritten as

$$\sum_{ijk} i \Pr[110 \,\&\, 100/R_i] \Pr[R_i]$$

$$< \sum_{ijk} j \Pr[110 \,\&\, 100/R_j] \Pr[R_j] \qquad \text{iff } p < q,$$

which is equivalent to

(1) $\displaystyle\sum_{ijk} i\,\Pr[110\ \&\ 100/R_i\ \&\ R_j\ \&\ R_k]\,\Pr[R_i\ \&\ R_j\ \&\ R_k]$

$$< \sum_{ijk} j\,\Pr[110\ \&\ 100/R_i\ \&\ R_j\ \&\ R_k]\,\Pr[R_i\ \&\ R_j\ \&\ R_k]$$

iff $p < q$.

Note that the two summations in (1) sum over *all* ijk triplets; in fact, each summation can be broken down into three subsummations, where one subsummation covers all ijk triplets such that (AB)C, another all triplets such that A(BC), and the third all triplets such that (AC)B.

I now introduce some notation. When $i < j = k$, let

$$\Pr[111/R_i\ \&\ R_j] = r_{ij}, \qquad \Pr[110/R_i\ \&\ R_j] = x_{ij},$$
$$\Pr[101/R_i\ \&\ R_j] = s_{ij}, \qquad \Pr[100/R_i\ \&\ R_j] = y_{ij},$$
$$\Pr[001/R_i\ \&\ R_j] = t_{ij}, \qquad \Pr[000/R_i\ \&\ R_j] = z_{ij}.$$

When $j < i = k$, let

$$\Pr[110/R_i\ \&\ R_j] = g_{ij}, \qquad \Pr[100/R_i\ \&\ R_j] = h_{ij}.$$

When $k < i = j$, let

$$\Pr[110/R_i\ \&\ R_k] = m_{ki}, \qquad \Pr[100/R_i\ \&\ R_k] = n_{ki}.$$

The ten probabilities just defined are illustrated in figure 22.

We now may express (1) equivalently as

(2) $\displaystyle\sum_{i<j=k} i x_{ij} y_{ij} \Pr(R_i\ \&\ R_j\ \&\ R_k)$

$$+ \sum_{j<i=k} i g_{ij} h_{ij} \Pr(R_i\ \&\ R_j\ \&\ R_k)$$

$$+ \sum_{k<i=j} i m_{ki} n_{ki} \Pr(R_i\ \&\ R_j\ \&\ R_k)$$

$$< \sum_{i<j=k} j x_{ij} y_{ij} \Pr(R_i\ \&\ R_j\ \&\ R_k)$$

$$+ \sum_{j<i=k} j g_{ij} h_{ij} \Pr(R_i\ \&\ R_j\ \&\ R_k)$$

$$+ \sum_{k<i=j} j m_{ki} n_{ki} \Pr(R_i\ \&\ R_j\ \&\ R_k) \qquad \text{iff } p < q.$$

This expansion of (1) expresses the idea that the two characters are independent of each other, conditional on each ijk triplet considered. Characters are *not* independent conditional on the cladistic grouping (AB)C, a point that arose in my discussion of Felsenstein [1979] in section 5.6.

Notice that there is a symmetry between g_{ij} and h_{ij} on the one hand and s_{ij} and t_{ij} on the other. In particular, for any a, b such that $a > b$,

$$g_{ab} = s_{ba}, \qquad h_{ab} = t_{ba}.$$

Also note that $i m_{ki} n_{ki} = j m_{ki} n_{ki}$, since m_{ki} and n_{ki} are defined only when $i = j$.

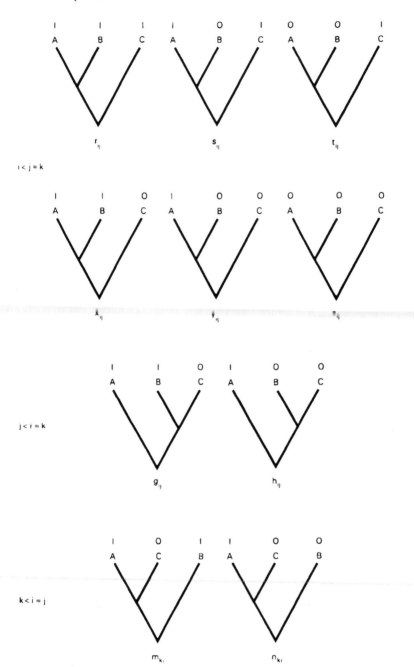

Figure 22.
Ten probabilities, each describing the chance of obtaining an observation at the tips, given the degree of relatedness (denoted by i, j, k) of the three taxa.

It follows that (2) may be rewritten as

(3) $\sum_{i<j} i x_{ij} y_{ij} \Pr(R_i \,\&\, R_j \,\&\, R_k)$

$+ \sum_{i<j} i s_{ij} t_{ij} \Pr(R_i \,\&\, R_j \,\&\, R_k)$

$< \sum_{i<j} j x_{ij} y_{ij} \Pr(R_i \,\&\, R_j \,\&\, R_k)$

$+ \sum_{i<j} j s_{ij} t_{ij} \Pr(R_i \,\&\, R_j \,\&\, R_k)$ iff $p < q$,

which simplifies to

(4) $\sum_{i<j} (j - i)(x_{ij} y_{ij} - s_{ij} t_{ij}) \Pr(R_i \,\&\, R_j) > 0$ iff $p < q$.

Note that the $(j - i)$ term is always positive.[25]
    I now shall prove that

(5)   For any i, j, $x_{ij} y_{ij} > s_{ij} t_{ij}$ iff $y_{ij} > s_{ij}$.

To begin, note that the trees defined in figure 22 imply that

(6)   For any i, j, $r_{ij} + 2s_{ij} + t_{ij} = p$.
       For any i, j, $x_{ij} + 2y_{ij} + z_{ij} = q$.

and that

(7)   For any i, j, $r_{ij} + s_{ij} + x_{ij} + y_{ij} = p$.
       For any i, j, $s_{ij} + t_{ij} + y_{ij} + z_{ij} = q$.

(6) and (7) immediately imply that

(8)   For any i, j, $s_{ij} + t_{ij} = x_{ij} + y_{ij}$.

I now shall use (8) to prove (5). I drop the ij subscripts for convenience:

$(s + t)^2 = (x + y)^2$,   (8)

$2st + s^2 - x^2 = 2xy + y^2 - t^2$,

$2st + (s - x)(s + x) - (y - t)(y + t) = 2xy$,

$2st + (s - x)[(s + x) - (y + t)] = 2xy$,   (8)

$xy - st = (s - x)(s - y)$.   (8)

The consistency proof of section 6.1 guarantees that $(s - x) < 0$. This means that $xy > st$ iff $y > s$. This establishes (5).
    We now know that for each value of i and j, $(y - s)$ has the same sign as

25. There is a conjecture that differs slightly from (SQ-2), which also reduces to proposition (4), namely, one in which the expected degree of relatedness conditional on one character is compared with the expected degree of relatedness conditional on the other: $\text{Exp}[R_i/110] < \text{Exp}[R_j/100]$ iff $p < q$.

($xy - st$). We now need to investigate the general relationship between y and s. The pattern of comparison we will pursue is this: we shall see how changing j while keeping i fixed affects the values of y and s.

I begin with a simple fact:

(9)   If $j = n$, then $y_{ij} > s_{ij}$ iff $p < q$.

To see why this is so, notice that

$$\text{If } j = n, \text{ then } \Pr[A = 1 \ \& \ B = 0 \ \& \ C = k/R_i \ \& \ R_j]$$
$$= \Pr[A = 1 \ \& \ B = 0/R_i \ \& \ R_j]\Pr[C = k/R_i \ \& \ R_j],$$

for $k = 0, 1$. This means that, when $j = n$, $y_{ij} > s_{ij}$ iff

$$q\Pr[A = 1 \ \& \ B = 0/R_i \ \& \ R_j] > p\Pr[A = 1 \ \& \ B = 0/R_i \ \& \ R_j].$$

We now need to obtain a picture of how s_{ij} and y_{ij} each change as j is increased while i is held fixed. Notice that $s_{ij} + y_{ij}$ is constant ($= \Pr[10—/R_i]$) as j increases while i is held fixed. This means that s increases if and only if y declines.

Consider figure 23. I want to investigate when $s_{i,j} < s_{i,j+1}$ for arbitrary i, j. As usual, I divide the process from root to tips into three stages, with e_k representing the probability of a 0-to-1 transition in stage k and r_k representing the probability of a 1-to-0 transition in that stage.

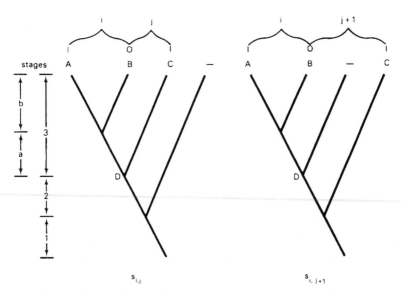

Figure 23.
The probability of obtaining a 101 observation, given the exact degree of relatedness of the three taxa, changes monotonically as j is increased while i is held fixed.

One new piece of notation will help simplify the proof. Let D, as shown in figure 23, be the ancestor of A and B that existed at the beginning of the 3rd stage of the process. Now let

$$f_0 = \Pr(A = 1 \,\&\, B = 0/D = 0),$$
$$f_1 = \Pr(A = 1 \,\&\, B = 0/D = 1).$$

The probability of 101, given the relationship (i, j), now may be expressed as

$$(s_{i,j}) \qquad [e_1 r_2 + (1 - e_1)(1 - e_2)]e_3 f_0$$
$$+ [e_1(1 - r_2) + (1 - e_1)e_2](1 - r_3)f_1.$$

The probability of 101, given the relationship $(i, j + 1)$, takes the form

$$(s_{i,j+1}) \qquad e_1[(1 - r_2)(1 - r_3) + r_2 e_3][(1 - r_2)f_1 + r_2 f_0]$$
$$+ (1 - e_1)[e_2(1 - r_3) + (1 - e_2)e_3][e_2 f_1$$
$$+ (1 - e_2)f_0].$$

Algebraic manipulation yields the result that $s_{i,j} > s_{i,j+1}$ iff

$$e_1 r_2(1 - r_2)(1 - r_3 - e_3)[f_1 - f_0]$$
$$+ (1 - e_1)e_2(1 - e_2)(1 - r_3 - e_3)[f_1 - f_0] > 0.$$

The backward inequality guarantees that $(1 - r_3 - e_3) > 0$. To see whether $f_1 > f_0$, I divide stage 3 in figure 23 into two "substages"—a and b, respectively. Using the usual notation of e's and r's, we can say that $f_1 > f_0$ precisely when

$$r_a e_b(1 - e_b) + (1 - r_a)(1 - r_b)r_b$$
$$> (1 - e_a)e_b(1 - e_b) + e_a(1 - r_b)r_b.$$

This is true iff

$$(1 - e_a - r_a)(1 - e_b - r_b)(r_b - e_b) > 0.$$

The backward inequality guarantees that the two $(1 - e - r)$ terms are positive. So $f_1 > f_0$ iff $r_b > e_b$, which is the circumstance under which s_{ij} declines as j is increased and i held fixed.

A parallel calculation for the relationship of $y_{i,j}$ to $y_{i,j+1}$ reveals that y_{ij} increases precisely when $r_b > e_b$. So s_{ij} and y_{ij} have opposite slopes.

The thing to notice now is that the relationship of r_b and e_b—of the probability of a 1-to-0 and a 0-to-1 transition in the second half of stage 3—is invariant as j is increased but i is held fixed. In fact, the relationship of these two sorts of changes on a branch of any length is settled by the relationship of u and v. This means that s declines monotonically and y increases monotonically iff $u < v$.

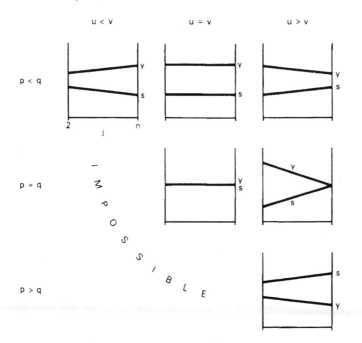

Figure 24.
The relationship of y_{ij} and s_{ij}. Each changes monotonically if j is increased while i is held fixed. The relation of y and s is determined at $j = n$ by the relationship of p and q. The slopes of y and s are determined by the relationship of u and v.

Proposition (9) describes how the relationship of y and s at $j = n$ is determined by whether $p < q$. We have just seen how the slopes of y and s depend on whether $u < v$. So there are several possibilities to consider, displayed in figure 24.

Some items in this figure fall immediately into place. If $u < v$, then p must be lower than q. No matter how many generations the process proceeds, 1 must remain a minority character (in expectation) if the root begins in state 0 and $u < v$. Likewise, if $u = v$, then no matter how many generations the process proceeds, p will never achieve a value greater than q. This is why three of the items in the table are labeled "impossible."

The center entry—the case in which $u = v$ and $p = q$—is also, in a certain sense, impossible, but I have drawn the graph anyway. When $u = v$ the expected frequency of 1's and 0's at equilibrium is $1/2$. Yet, for any finite number of generations, $p < q$. The equilibrium is approached as a limit.

Nevertheless, the graph for the case of $u = v$ and $p = q$ illustrates what the inference problem looks like in this case when the evolving system achieves equilibrium. Note that it is consistent with the (SQ-2) conjecture.

The slopes of y and s are flat, since $u = v$. And y and s have the same value at $j = n$. So the areas under the y and s curves are the same.

I turn now to the top row—the cases in which $p < q$. The cases here in which $u = v$ and $u > v$ fall easily into place. From the result obtained before about the relationship of y and s when $j = n$ and the result describing how the slopes of y and s are determined by the relationship of u and v, we see that in both these cases, $y_{ij} > s_{ij}$, for each $i < j$. Since $(y - s)$ is always positive, so too is $(xy - st)$. So the summation represented in proposition (4) is positive and, in this case, $p < q$.

The case in which $p < q$ and $u < v$ requires more analysis. Since $u < v$, y has a positive slope and s a negative one; since $p < q$, $y > s$ at $j = n$. The question now is, Will y and s ever intersect if j is made small?

The limit of the process of making j small while i is held fixed is a trifurcation: that is, the case in which $i = j$. Although a trifurcation cannot actually occur in the context of our bifurcating model, a trifurcation plays the role of a mathematical limit of the functions y_{ij} and s_{ij}. In particular, when $u < v$ and $p < q$, the trifurcation y_{ii} is a lower bound on y_{ij} and the trifurcation s_{ii} is an upper bound[26] on s_{ij}. We now shall see that $y_{ii} > s_{ii}$ if $u < v$ and $p < q$.

Consider the two trifurcations displayed in figure 25. Note that $s_{ii} < y_{ii}$ iff

$$(1 - e_1)e_2^2(1 - e_2) + e_1(1 - r_2)^2 r_2$$
$$< (1 - e_1)e_2(1 - e_2)^2 + e_1(1 - r_2)r_2^2,$$

which simplifies to

$$e_1(1 - r_2)r_2[1 - 2r_2] < (1 - e_1)e_2(1 - e_2)[1 - 2e_2],$$

and then to

$$(10) \qquad (1 - e_1)/e_1 > \frac{(1 - r_2)r_2(1 - 2r_2)}{e_2(1 - e_2)(1 - 2e_2)}.$$

I now shall express (10) in terms of the "instantaneous" transition probabilities u and v, using the connections between u and v and branch transition probabilities stated on p. 217. Note first that the left-hand side of (10) takes the form

$$(1 - e_1)/e_1 = (v + k^N u)/(u - k^N u),$$

where $k = (1 - u - v)$ and N is the number of temporal intervals in stage 1 of figure 25. In the case before us, in which $u < v$, note that $(1 - e_1)/e_1$

---

26. Note that the argument concerning the relationship of $s_{i,j}$ and $s_{i,j+1}$ in figure 23 is entirely consistent with e_a and r_a both being zero, which is what the trifurcation $s_{i,i}$ would involve.

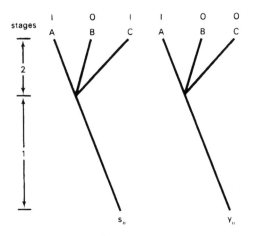

Figure 25.
The trifurcations s_{ii} and y_{ii} are mathematical limits approached by s_{ij} and y_{ij} if j is reduced while i is held fixed.

cannot be less than v/u. Hence, we may establish (10) by showing that v/u is greater than the right-hand side of (10). That is, to establish (10) it will suffice to show that

$$(11) \qquad v/u > \frac{(u + k^M v)(v - k^M v)(1 - 2v + 2k^M v)}{(u - k^M u)(v + k^M u)(1 - 2u + 2k^M u)}.$$

Here M is the number of temporal intervals in stage 2 of figure 25. Proposition (11) simplifies to

$$(v + k^M u)[1 - 2u(1 - k^M)] > (u + k^M v)[1 - 2v(1 - k^M)],$$

which becomes

$$(v - u)[1 - k^M + 2(u + v)k^M(1 - k^M)] > 0,$$

which is true if $v > u$.

This shows that the upper-left-hand case in figure 24 falls into place in accordance with (SQ-2): even when j is made small as i is held fixed, it is still true that $y_{ij} > s_{ij}$.

I turn next to the case in which $p = q$ and $u > v$. Since $p = q$, the y and s curves must take on the same value at $j = n$. Since $u > v$, y must have a negative slope and s a positive one. So the area under the y curve must exceed that under the s curve. So in this case the $(xy - st)$ summation in proposition (4) must come out positive.

The interesting point about this case is that it refutes (SQ-2). According to that conjecture, the expected degree of relatedness of species A and

B and that of species B and C, given the observations 110 and 100, must be the same if apomorphies and plesiomorphies have the same expected frequency at the tips. But the case of $p = q$ and $u > v$ illustrates that an apomorphic matching can deserve more weight, even when $p = q$. Evidently, there is something about an apomorphy, above and beyond its expected frequency, that gives it a special evidential significance.

The conclusion, however, is not that a synapomorphy *always* (in this model) deserves more weight than a symplesiomorphy. The lower-right-hand entry in figure 24 is the case we need to analyze to show this. We know at the outset that at $j = n$, $s > y$ and that s has a positive slope and y a negative one. The question is: when, if it all, will the two curves intersect?

To investigate this, I consider once again the trifurcations shown in figure 25. When $u > v$ and $p > q$, s_{ii} is a lower bound on s_{ij} and y_{ii} is an upper bound on y_{ij}. We need to discover when $s_{ii} > y_{ii}$. Proposition (10) describes the precise conditions under which $s_{ii} < y_{ii}$. Rearranging this a little, we can say that $s_{ii} > y_{ii}$ iff

$$(12) \quad e_1/(1 - e_1) > \frac{e_2(1 - e_2)(1 - 2e_2)}{r_2(1 - r_2)(1 - 2r_2)}.$$

Note that the left side of (12) describes events that occur in the first stage of the trifurcations depicted in figure 25, whereas the right side of (12) concerns events that occur in the second stage. Let T be the ratio $e_1/(1 - e_1)$. I now want to show that (12) will be true if T exceeds a certain quantity that is a function of u, v, e_2, and r_2.

Translating (12) into a representation in terms of instantaneous transition probabilities, we obtain

$$(13) \quad T > \frac{(u - k^M u)(v + k^M u)(1 - 2u + 2k^M u)}{(v - k^M v)(u + k^M v)(1 - 2v + 2k^M v)}.$$

Algebraic manipulation allows this to be rewritten as

$$(14) \quad uv(T - 1) + 2uv(u - vT)(1 - k^M) - k^M(u^2 - v^2 T) \\ + 2(u^3 - v^3 T)k^M(1 - k^M) > 0.$$

Note that T must be less than u/v. This means that the second and fourth addends in (14) must be positive (since $u > v$). I now shall derive a condition that guarantees that the sum of the first and third addends is positive as well. This condition suffices to verify (14).

So the question is what suffices to show that

$$uv(T - 1) - k^M(u^2 - v^2 T) > 0.$$

This simplifies to

$$T > \frac{uv + u^2 k^M}{uv + v^2 k^M},$$

which is to say

$$(15) \qquad T > \frac{u(1 - e_2)}{v(1 - r_2)}.$$

Recall that u/v is the equilibrium value of T. It also is the upper bound on T. In addition, since $u > v$, we know that $(1 - e_2) < (1 - r_2)$. This means that condition (15) describes how close T—i.e., $e_1/(1 - e_1)$—must be to its equilibrium value for the trifurcation s_{ii} to exceed the trifurcation y_{ii}.

The value of the quantity $(1 - e_2)/(1 - r_2)$ depends on how much time there is in stage 2 of the processes described in figure 25. This quantity is largest when there are few temporal intervals in this stage and smallest when there are many. An upper bound on $(1 - e_2)/(1 - r_2)$ is 1 (when $k = 0$). The lower bound is v/u (when k is infinite). This means that T must have achieved its equilibrium value if there is no time in stage 2. On the other hand, if there is an infinite amount of time in stage 2, then T need only have a value of 1.

The equilibrium value of p/q at the tips of the tree is u/v. However, a branching process of finite duration in which p/q exceeds 1.0 will not have reached that larger equilibrium value. The sufficient condition for $s_{ii} > y_{ii}$ just obtained is that one generation after the root, the ratio $e_1/(1 - e_1)$ be "close" to the equilibrium value u/v, how close depending on how much time there is in the second and final stage. At a minimum $e_1/(1 - e_1)$ must exceed 1.0.

I hasten to emphasize that the condition just derived is sufficient but not necessary for a symplesiomorphy to deserve more weight than a synapomorphy. The condition—that $p > q$ and that the system be near equilibrium one generation after the root—suffices for the quantity $(xy - st)$ in proposition (4) to be negative for all ij pairs ($i < j$). But the weighted summation could be negative without this "unanimity" condition being satisfied.

A word of comment is needed to explain what distinguishes (SQ-3) from the simpler conjecture (SQ-2), which we have seen is not strictly correct. Consider the $u > v$ column in figure 24. As we move down this column, we consider what an evolving branching process will look like at three stages in its development.

When $u > v$ but little time is allowed for 1 to displace 0 as the majority character, 0 will remain a majority character (in expectation) at the tips and so apomorphic matches will deserve more weight than plesiomorphic ones. However, if the system is allowed to evolve for more time, a crossover point will be reached—namely, one at which $p = q$. If the process is arrested precisely here, we shall be looking at a branching process that offers a counterexample to (SQ-2). In this case, apomorphies and plesiomorphies have identical expected frequencies, but still the derived matching deserves more weight than the ancestral one.

Suppose, finally, that u is sufficiently greater than v and there are enough small intervals of time between branching events that $p > q$ even after a single generation. Let the process unfold for numerous generations. In this case, an ancestral similarity deserves more weight than a derived one. Here, apomorphies will be common and plesiomorphies rare (in expectation).

Although we have seen that the simple formulation (SQ-2) is not exactly true, it seems to be pretty close. The only counterexample established here to the rule that evidential significance goes by expected rarity will arise naturally at most for a moment and then disappear. This is the case in which $u > v$ and $p = q$. As a theoretical matter, the failure of (SQ-2) and the truth of (SQ-3) shows that a perfectly general condition for $\text{Exp}[R_i/110 \,\&\, 100] < \text{Exp}[R_j/110 \,\&\, 100]$ will be a function of u, v, and N—one that I think is well approximated, though not perfectly, by the condition $p < q$.

References

Ackermann, R. [1976]: *The Philosophy of Karl Popper.* Amherst, Mass.: University of Massachusetts Press.

Ashlock, P. [1971]: Monophyly and associated terms. *Systematic Zoology* 20: 63–69.

Ashlock, P. [1972]: Monophyly again. *Systematic Zoology* 21: 430–437.

Beatty, J. [1982]: Classes and cladists. *Systematic Zoology* 31: 25–34.

Beauchamp, T., and Rosenberg, A. [1981]: *Hume and the Problem of Causation.* Oxford: Oxford University Press.

Bell, J. [1965]: On the Einstein Podolsky Rosen Paradox. *Physics* 1: 196–200.

Birnbaum, A. [1969]: Concepts of statistical evidence. In S. Morgenbesser et al. (eds.), *Philosophy, Science, and Method.* New York: St. Martin's, pp. 112–143.

Bock, W. [1981]: Functional-adaptive analysis in evolutionary classification. *American Zoologist* 21: 5–20.

Burtt, E. [1932]: *The Metaphysical Foundations of Modern Physical Science.* London: Routledge and Kegan Paul.

Camin, J., and Sokal, R. [1965]: A method for deducing branching sequences in phylogeny. *Evolution* 19: 311–326.

Cartmill, M. [1981]: Hypothesis testing and phylogenetic reconstruction. *Zeitschrift für Zoologische Systematik und Evolutionforschung* 19: 73–96.

Cavalli-Sforza, L., and Edwards, A. [1967]: Phylogenetic analysis: models and estimation procedures. *Evolution* 32: 550–570.

Clauser, J., and Horne, M. [1974]: Experimental consequences of objective local theories. *Physical Review* D10: 526-535.

Cohen, M., and Nagel, E. [1934]: *Introduction to Logic and Scientific Method.* New York: Harcourt, Brace.

Colless, D. [1970]: The phenogram as an estimate of phylogeny. *Systematic Zoology* 19: 352–362.

Cracraft, J. [1974]: Phylogenetic models and classification. *Systematic Zoology* 23: 71–90.

Cracraft, J. [1981]: The use of functional and adaptive criteria in phylogenetic systematics. *American Zoologist* 21: 21–36.

Crick, F. [1968]: The origin of the genetic code. *Journal of Molecular Biology* 38: 367–379.

Crisci, J., and Stuessy, T. [1980]: Determining primitive character states for phylogenetic reconstruction. *Systematic Botany* 6: 112–135.

Darwin, C. [1859]: *On the Origin of Species.* Cambridge, Mass.: Harvard University Press, 1964.

Dawkins, R. [1976]: *The Selfish Gene.* Oxford: Oxford University Press.

Dobzhansky, T., Ayala, F., Stebbins, G., and Valentine, J. [1977]: *Evolution.* San Francisco: W. H. Freeman.

Duhem, P. [1914]: *The Aim and Structure of Physical Theory.* Princeton: Princeton University Press, 1954.

Earman, J. [1986]: *A Primer on Determinism*. Dordrecht: Reidel.

Edidin, A. [1984]: Inductive reasoning and the uniformity of nature. *Journal of Philosophical Logic* 13: 285–302.

Edwards, A. [1970]: Estimation of the branch-points of a branching-diffusion process. *J. R. Stat. Soc.* B32: 155–174.

Edwards, A. [1972]: *Likelihood*. Cambridge: Cambridge Univerity Press.

Edwards, A., and Cavalli-Sforza, L. [1963]: The reconstruction of evolution. *Ann. Hum. Genet.* 27: 105.

Edwards, A., and Cavalli-Sforza, L. [1964]: Reconstruction of evolutionary trees. In V. Heywood and J. McNeill (eds.), *Phenetic and Phylogenetic Classification*. New York: Systematics Association Publication No. 6, pp. 67–76.

Eells, E. [1982]: *Rational Decision and Causality*. Oxford: Oxford University Press.

Eells, E., and Sober, E. [1983]: Probabilistic causality and the question of transitivity. *Philosophy of Science* 50: 35–57.

Einstein, A. [1905]: The electrodynamics of moving bodies. In H. Lorentz et al., *The Principle of Relativity*. New York: Dover, 1952, pp. 35–65.

Einstein, A., Podolsky, B., and Rosen, N. [1936]: Can quantum-mechanical description of reality be considered complete? *Physical Review* 47: 777–780.

Eldredge, N., and Cracraft, J. [1980]: *Phylogenetic Patterns and the Evolutionary Process*. New York: Columbia University Press.

Eldredge, N., and Tattersall, I. [1982]: *The Myths of Human Evolution*. New York: Columbia University Press.

Ereshefsky, M. [1988]: Where's the species? *Biology and Philosophy*, forthcoming.

Estabrook, G. [1972]: Cladistic methodology: a discussion of the theoretical basis for the induction of evolutionary history. *Annual Review of Ecology and Systematics* 3: 427–456.

Estabrook, G., Johnson, C., and McMorris, F. [1975]: An idealized concept of the true cladistic character. *Mathematical Biosciences* 23: 263–272.

Estabrook, G., Johnson, C., and McMorris, F. [1976]: A mathematical foundation for the analysis of cladistic character compatibility. *Mathematical Biosciences* 21: 181–187.

Farris, J. [1973]: On the use of the parsimony criterion for inferring evolutionary trees. *Systematic Zoology* 22: 250–256.

Farris, J. [1976]: Phylogenetic classification of fossils with recent species. *Systematic Zoology* 25: 271–282.

Farris, J. [1977]: Phylogenetic analysis under Dollo's law. *Systematic Zoology* 26: 77–88.

Farris, J. [1978]: Inferring phylogenetic trees from chromosome inversion data. *Systematic Zoology* 27: 275–284.

Farris, J. [1979]: The information content of the phylogenetic system. *Systematic Zoology* 28: 483–519.

Farris, J. [1983]: The logical basis of phylogenetic analysis. In N. Platnick and V. Funk (eds.), *Advances in Cladistics*, vol. 2. New York: Columbia University Press, pp. 7–36. (Reprinted in Sober [1984b].)

Feller, W. [1966]: *An Introduction to Probability Theory and Its Applications*. New York: John Wiley.

Felsenstein, J. [1973a]: Maximum likelihood estimation of evolutionary trees from continuous characters. *Amer. J. Hum. Genet.* 25: 471–492.

Felsenstein, J. [1973b]: Maximum likelihood and minimum-step methods for estimating evolutionary trees from data on discrete characters. *Systematic Zoology* 22: 240–249.

Felsenstein, J. [1978]: Cases in which parsimony or compatibility methods will be positively misleading. *Systematic Zoology* 27: 401–410. (Reprinted in Sober [1984b].)

Felsenstein, J. [1979]: Alternative methods of phylogenetic inference and their interrelationships. *Systematic Zoology* 28: 49–62.

Felsenstein, J. [1981]: A likelihood approach to character weighting and what it tells us about parsimony and compatibility. *Biological Journal of the Linnaean Society* 16: 183–196.

Felsenstein, J. [1982]: Numerical methods for inferring evolutionary trees. *Quarterly Review of Biology* 57: 379–404.

Felsenstein, J. [1983a]: Methods for inferring phylogenies: a statistical view. In J. Felsenstein (ed.), *Numerical Taxonomy*. Heidelberg: Springer Verlag.

Felsenstein, J. [1983b]: Parsimony in systematics: biological and statistical issues. *Annual Review of Ecology and Systematics* 14: 313–333.

Felsenstein, J. [1984]: The statistical approach to inferring evolutionary trees and what it tells us about parsimony and compatibility. In T. Duncan and T. Stuessy (eds.), *Cladistics: Perspectives on the Reconstruction of Evolutionary History*. New York: Columbia University Press, pp. 169–191.

Felsenstein, J., and Sober, E. [1986]: Parsimony and likelihood: an exchange. *Systematic Zoology* 35: 617–626.

Fink, W. [1982]: The conceptual relation between ontogeny and phylogeny. *Paleobiology* 8: 254–264.

Fisher, R. [1938]: Comments on H. Jeffrey's 'Maximum Likelihood, Inverse Probability, and the Method of Moments.' *Annals of Eugenics* 8: 146–151.

Fisher, R. [1950]: *Statistical Methods for Research Workers*. London: Oliver and Boyd, 11th edition.

Fisher, R. [1956]: *Statistical Methods and Scientific Inference*. Edinburgh: Oliver and Boyd.

Forster, M. [1986]: Statistical covariance as a measure of phylogenetic relationship. *Cladistics* 2: 297–319.

Friedman, K. [1972]: Empirical simplicity as testability. *British Journal for the Philosophy of Science* 23: 25–33.

Gaffney, E. [1979]: An introduction to the logic of phylogeny reconstruction. In J. Cracraft and N. Eldredge (eds.), *Phylogenetic Analysis and Paleontology*. New York: Columbia University Press, pp. 79–112.

Ghiselin, M. [1969]: *The Triumph of the Darwinian Method*. Berkeley: University of California Press.

Ghiselin, M. [1974]: A radical solution to the species problem. *Systematic Zoology* 23: 536–544.

Glymour, C. [1980]: Theory and Evidence. Princeton: Princeton University Press.

Goldman, A. [1986]: *Epistemology and Cognition*. Cambridge, Mass.: Harvard University Press.

Good, I. J. [1967]: The white shoe is a red herring. *British Journal for the Philosophy of Science* 17: 322.

Good, I. J. [1968]: The white shoe qua herring is pink. *British Journal for the Philosophy of Science* 19: 156–157.

Goodman, N. [1952]: Sense and certainty. *Philosophical Review* 61: 160–167. (Reprinted in Goodman [1972, pp. 60–68].)

Goodman, N. [1958]: The test of simplicity. *Science* 128: 1064–1069. (Reprinted in Goodman [1972, pp. 279–294].)

Goodman, N. [1965]: *Fact, Fiction, Forecast*. Indianapolis: Bobbs Merrill.

Goodman, N. [1967]: Uniformity and simplicity. *Geological Society of America*. Special Paper 89: 93–99. (Reprinted in Goodman [1972, pp. 347–354].)

Goodman, N. [1970]: Seven strictures on similarity. In L. Foster and J. Swanson (eds.), *Experience and Theory*. Boston: University of Massachusetts Press. (Reprinted in Goodman [1972, pp. 437–446].)

Goodman, N. [1972]: *Problems and Projects*. Indianapolis: Bobbs Merrill.

Gould, S. [1977]: *Ontogeny and Phylogeny*. Cambridge, Mass.: Harvard University Press.

Gould, S. [1985]: False premise, good science. In *The Flamingo's Smile*. New York: Norton, pp. 126–138.

Hacking, I. [1965]: *The Logic of Statistical Inference*. Cambridge: Cambridge University Press.

Hacking, I. [1971]: Jacques Bernouilli's art of conjecturing. *British Journal for the Philosophy of Science* 22: 209–229.

Hanson, N. [1958]: *Patterns of Discovery*. Cambridge: Cambridge University Press.

Hempel, C. [1965a]: *Philosophy of Natural Science*. Englewood Cliffs, NJ: Prentice-Hall.

Hempel, C. [1965b]: Studies in the logic of confirmation. In *Aspects of Scientific Explanation and Other Essays*. New York: Free Press.

Hempel, C. [1967]: The white shoe: no red herring. *British Journal for the Philosophy of Science* 18: 239–240.

Hennig, W. [1965]: Phylogenetic systematics. *Annual Review of Entomology* 10: 97–116. (Reprinted in Sober [1984b].)

Hennig, W. [1966]: *Phylogenetic Systematics*. Urbana: University of Illinois Press.

Hesse, M. [1967]: Simplicity. In P. Edwards (ed.), *The Encyclopedia of Philosophy*, vol. 7. New York: Macmillan, pp. 445–448.

Hoenigswald, H. [1960]: *Language Change and Linguistic Reconstruction*. Chicago: University of Chicago Press.

Hooykaas, R. [1959]: *Natural Law and Divine Miracle: A Historico-Critical Study of the Principle of Uniformity in Geology, Biology, and Theology*. Leiden: E. J. Brill.

Hull, D. [1970]: Contemporary systematic philosophies. *Annual Review of Ecology and Systematics*. 1: 19–53. (Reprinted in Sober [1984b].)

Hull, D. [1978]: A matter of individuality. *Philosophy of Science* 45: 335–360. (Reprinted in Sober [1984b].)

Hull, D. [1979]: The limits of cladism. *Systematic Zoology* 28: 416–440.

Hull, D. [1988]: *Science as a Process: An Evolutionary Account of the Social and Conceptual Development of Science*. Chicago: University of Chicago Press.

Hume, D. [1939]: *A Treatise of Human Nature*. L. A. Selby-Bigge (ed.). Oxford: Clarendon Press, 1968.

Hume, D. [1948]: *An Inquiry Concerning Human Understanding*. Indianapolis: Bobbs Merrill, 1955.

Janvier, P. [1984]: Cladistics: theory, purpose, and evolutionary implications. In J. Pollard (ed.), *Evolutionary Theory: Paths into the Future*. Chichester: Wiley, pp. 39–75.

Jeffrey, R. [1956]: Valuation and acceptance of scientific hypotheses. *Philosophy of Science* 23: 237–246.

Jeffrey, R. [1975]: Probability and falsification: critique of the Popperian program. *Synthese* 30: 95–117.

Jeffreys, H. [1957]: *Scientific Inference*. Cambridge: Cambridge University Press, 2nd edition.

Kalbfleisch, J., and Sprott, D. [1970]: Applications of likelihood methods to models involving large numbers of parameters. *Journal of the Royal Statistical Society* B32: 175–208.

Kemeny, J. [1953]: The use of simplicity in induction. *Philosophical Review* 62: 391–408.

Kendall, M., and Stuart, A. [1973]: *The Advanced Theory of Statistics*, vol. 2. New York: Haffner, 3rd edition.

King, M., and Wilson, A. [1975]: Evolution at two levels: molecular similarities and biological differences between humans and chimpanzees. *Science* 188: 107–116.

Kitcher, P. [1982]: *Abusing Science: The Case Against Creationism*. Cambridge, Mass.: The MIT Press. A Bradford book.

Kitcher, P. [1985]: Darwin's achievement. In N. Rescher (ed.), *Reason and Rationality in Science*. Washington, D.C.: University Press of America.

Kitcher, P. [ms]: Species. unpublished.

Kluge, A. [1984]: The relevance to parsimony to phylogenetic inference. In T. Duncan and T. Stuessy (eds.), *Cladistics: Perspectives on the Reconstruction of Evolutionary History*. New York: Columbia University Press, pp. 24–38.

Kluge, A. [1985]: Ontogeny and phylogenetic systematics. *Cladistics* 1: 13–28.

Kluge, A., and Farris, J. [1969]: Quantitative phyletics and the evolution of anurans. *Systematic Zoology* 18: 1–32.

Kluge, A., and Strauss, R. [1985]: Ontogeny and systematics. *Annual Review of Ecology and Systematics* 16: 247–268.

Kornblith, H. [1985]: *Naturalizing Epistemology*. Cambridge, Mass.: The MIT Press. A Bradford book.

Kuhn, T. [1970]: *Structure of Scientific Revolutions*. Chicage: University of Chicage Press.

Kyburg, H. [1961]: *Probability and the Logic of Rational Belief*. Middletown: Wesleyan University Press.

Lakatos, I. [1978]: *Philosophical Papers*. vol. I: *The Methodology of Scientific Research Programmes*. J. Worrall and G. Currie (eds.). Cambridge: Cambridge University Press.

Lane, C., Marbaix, G., and Gurdon, J. [1971]: Rabbit haemoglobin synthesis in frog cells: the translation of reticulocyte 9S RNA in frog oocytes. *Journal of Molecular Biology* 61: 73–91.

Lequesne, W. [1969]: A method of selection of characters in numerical taxonomy. *Systematic Zoology* 18: 201–205.

Maddison, W., Donoghue, M., and Maddision, D. [1984]: Outgroup analysis and parsimony. *Systematic Zoology* 33: 83–103.

Maxwell, G. [1962]: The ontological status of theoretical entities. In H. Feigl and G. Maxwell (eds.), *Minnesota Studies in the Philosophy of Science*, vol. iii. Minneapolis: University of Minnesota Press.

Mayr, E. [1963]: *Animal Species and Evolution*. Cambridge, Mass.: Harvard University Press.

Mayr, E. [1969]: *Principles of Systematic Zoology*. New York: McGraw Hill.

Meacham, C., and Estabrook, G. [1985]: Compatibility methods in systematics. *Annual Review of Ecology and Systematics* 16: 431–446.

Mickevich, M. [1978]: Taxonomic congruence. *Systematic Zoology* 27: 143–158.

Mill, J. [1859]: *A system of Logic, Ratiocinative and Inductive*. New York: Harper and Brothers.

Nei, M. [1987]: *Molecular Evolutionary Genetics*. New York: Columbia University Press.

Nelson, G. [ms]: Cladograms and trees. unpublished.

Nelson, G. [1972]: Comments on Hennig's 'Phylogenetic Systematics' and its influence on ichthyology. *Systematic Zoology* 21: 364–371.

Nelson, G. [1973]: 'Monophyly Again?': a reply to P. Ashlock. *Systematic Zoology* 22: 310–312.

Nelson, G. [1979]: Cladistic analysis and synthesis: principles and definitions with a historical note on Adanson's *Familles des Plantes* (1763–1764). *Systematic Zoology* 28: 1–21.

Nelson, G., and Platnick, N. [1981]: *Systematics and Biogeography: Cladistics and Vicariance*. New York: Columbia University Press.

Newton, I. [1953]: *Newton's Philosophy of Nature: Selections from His Writings*. New York: Haffner.

Neyman, J. [1950]: *First Course in Probability and Statistics*. New York: Henry Holt.

Neyman, J. [1952]: *Lectures and Conferences on Mathematical Statistics and Probability*. Washington, D.C.: Washington Graduate School, U.S. Department of Agriculture, 2nd edition.

Neyman, J. [1957]: "Inductive behavior" as a basic concept of philosophy of science. *Rev. Inst. de Stat.* 25: 7–22.

Patterson, C. [1981]: Significance of fossils in determining evolutionary relationships. *Annual Review of Ecology and Systematics* 12: 195–223.

Patterson, C. [1982]: Morphological characters and homology. In K. Joysey and A. Friday (eds.), *Problems of Phylogenetic Reconstruction*. London: Academic Press, pp. 21–74.

Paul, C. [1982]: The adequacy of the fossil record. In K. Joysey and A. Friday (eds.), *Problems of Phylogenetic Reconstruction*. London: Academic Press, pp. 75–117.

Platnick, N. [1977]: Cladograms, phylogenetic trees, and hypothesis testing. *Systematic Zoology* 26: 438–442.

Platnick, N., and Cameron, D. [1977]: Cladistic methods in textual, linguistic, and phylogenetic analysis. *Systematic Zoology* 26: 380–385.

Poincaré, H. [1952]: *Science and Hypothesis*. New York: Dover.

Popper, K. [1959]: *The Logic of Scientific Discovery*. London: Hutchinson.

Popper, K. [1963]: *Conjectures and Refutations*. London: Routledge and Kegan Paul.

Putnam, H. [1974]: The "corroboration" of theories. In P. Schilpp (ed.), *The Philosophy of Karl Popper*, vol. II. La Salle, Ill.: Open Court. (Reprinted in H. Putnam, *Mathematics, Matter, and Method*. Cambridge: Cambridge University Press, 1975, pp. 250–269.)

Quine, W. [1952]: Two dogmas of empiricism. In *From a Logical Point of View*. Cambridge, Mass.: Harvard University Press, 2nd edition, pp. 20–46.

Quine, W. [1960]: *Word and Object*. Cambridge, Mass.: The MIT Press.

Quine, W. [1966]: Simple theories of a complex world. In *The Ways of Paradox and Other Essays* New York: Random House. pp. 242–246.

Reichenbach, H. [1938]: *Experience and Prediction*. Chicago: University of Chicago Press.

Reichenbach, H. [1949]: The philosophical significance of the theory of relativity. In P. A. Schilpp (ed.), *Albert Einstein: Philosopher-Scientist*. La Salle, Ill.: Open Court, pp. 307–312.

Reichenbach, H. [1951]: *The Rise of Scientific Philosophy*. Chicage: University of Chicago Press.

Reichenbach, H. [1956]: *The Direction of Time*. Berkeley: University of California Press.

Reichenbach, H. [1958]: *The Philosophy of Space and Time*. New York: Dover.

Ridley, M. [1986]: *Evolution and Classification*. London: Longman's.

Rosen, D. [1978]: Vicariant patterns and historical explanations in biogeography. *Systematic Zoology* 27: 159–188.

Rosenkrantz, R. [1977]: *Inference, Method, and Decision*. Dordrecht: Reidel.

Rudwick, M. [1970]: The strategy of Lyell's *Principles of Geology*. *Isis* 61: 5–55.

Ruse, M. [1979]: *The Darwinian Revolution*. Chicago: University of Chicago Press.

Russell, B. [1948]: *Human Knowledge, Its Scope and Limits*. London: George Allen and Unwin.

Salmon, W. [1953]: The uniformity of nature. *Philosophy and Phenomenological Research* 14: 39–48.

Salmon, W. [1967]: *The Foundations of Scientific Inference*. Pittsburgh: University of Pittsburgh Press.

Salmon, W. [1971]: Statistical explanation. In W. Salmon (ed.) *Explanation and Statistical Relevance*. Pittsburgh: University of Pittsburgh Press.

Salmon, W. [1975]: Theoretical explanation. In S. Korner (ed.), *Explanation*. Oxford: Blackwell, pp. 118–145.

Salmon, W. [1978]: Why ask "why?" *Proceedings and Addresses of the American Philosophical Association* 51: 683–705.

Salmon, W. [1984]: *Scientific Explanation and the Causal Structure of the World*. Princeton: Princeton University Press.

Schaeffer, B., Hecht, M., and Eldredge, N. [1972]: Phylogeny and paleontology. *Evolutionary Biology* 6: 31–46.

Sellars, W. [1963]: *Science Perception, and Reality*. London: Routledge and Kegan Paul.

Shapiro, R. [1986]: *Origins: A Skeptic's Guide to the Creation of Life on Earth*. New York: Bantam Books.

Simpson, G. [1961]: *Principles of Animal Taxonomy.* New York: Columbia University Press.

Smart, J. [1963]: *Philosophy and Scientific Realism.* London: Routledge and Kegan Paul.

Sneath, P. [1982]: Review of G. Nelson and N. Platnick's *Systematics and Biogeography. Systematic Zoology* 31: 208–217.

Sneath, P., and Sokal, R. [1973]: *Numerical Taxonomy.* San Francisco: W. H. Freeman.

Sober, E. [1975]: *Simplicity.* Oxford: Oxford University Press.

Sober, E. [1983]: Parsimony in systematics: philosophical issues. *Annual Review of Ecology and Systematics* 14: 335–358.

Sober, E. [1984a]: Common cause explanation. *Philosophy of Science* 51: 212–241.

Sober, E. [1984b]: *Conceptual Issues in Evolutionary Biology.* Cambridge, Mass.: The MIT Press. A Bradford book.

Sober, E. [1984c]: *The Nature of Selection: Evolutionary Theory in Philosophical Focus.* Cambridge, Mass.: The MIT Press. A Bradford book.

Sober, E. [1987]: Explanation and causation: a review of Wesley Salmon's *Scientific Explanation and the Causal Structure of the World. British Journal for the Philosophy of Science* 38: 243–257.

Sober, E. [1988]: Likelihood and convergence. *Philosophy of Science* 55: 228–237.

Sober, E. [1989]: Independent evidence about a common cause. *Philosophy of Science,* forthcoming.

Sokal, R. [1985]: The continuing search for order. *American Naturalist* 126: 729–749.

Sokal, R., and Sneath, P. [1963]: *Numerical Taxonomy.* San Francisco: W. H. Freeman.

Splitter, L. [1988]: Species and identity. *Philosophy of Science,* forthcoming.

Stevens, P. [1980]: Evolutionary polarity of character states. *Annual Review of Ecology and Systematics* 11: 333–358.

Stove, D. [1973]: *Probability and Hume's Inductive Skepticism.* Oxford: Oxford University Press.

Strawson, P. [1952]: *Introduction to Logical Theory.* London: Methuen.

Stroud, B. [1977]: *Hume.* London: Routledge and Kegan Paul.

Suppes, P., and Zinotti, M. [1976]: On the determinism of hidden variable theories with strict correlation and conditional statistical independence of observables. In P. Suppes, *Logic and Probability in Quantum Mechanics.* Dordrecht: Reidel.

Thompson, E. [1975]: *Human Evolutionary Trees.* Cambridge: Cambridge University Press.

Van Fraassen, B. [1980]: *The Scientific Image.* Oxford: Oxford University Press.

Van Fraassen, B. [1982]: The Charybdis of realism: epistemological implications of Bell's inequality. *Synthese* 52: 25–38.

Wald, A. [1949]: Note on the consistency of the maximum likelihood estimate. *Annals of Mathematical Statistics* 20: 595–601.

Watrous, L., and Wheeler, Q. [1981]: The out-group comparison method of character analysis. *Systematic Zoology* 30: 1–11.

Wiley, E. [1975]: Karl R. Popper, systematics, and classification: a reply to Walter Bock and other evolutionary taxonomists. *Systematic Zoology* 24: 233–242.

Wiley, E. [1979a]: Ancestors, species, and cladograms—remarks on the symposium. In J. Cracraft and N. Eldredge (eds.), *Phylogenetic Analysis and Paleontology.* New York: Columbia University Press, pp. 211–226.

Wiley, E. [1979b]: Cladograms and phylogenetic trees. *Systematic Zoology* 28: 88–92.

Wiley, E. [1981]: *Phylogenetics: The Theory and Practice of Phylogenetic Systematics.* New York: John Wiley.

Wiley, E. [ms]: Process and pattern: cladograms and trees. unpublished.

Index

67066666R00160

Made in the USA
Lexington, KY
31 August 2017

Reconstructing the Past